Dobbs Ferry Public Library
55 Main Street
Dobbs Ferry, NY 10522

W9-BMN-575

MARVEL

IRON MAN 3

PRELUDE

MARVEL'S IRON MAN 2 ADAPTATION #1-2
BASED ON THE MARVEL STUDIOS FILM IRON MAN 2
SCREENPLAY: **JUSTIN THEROUX**
ADAPTATION: **CHRISTOS GAGE**
WITH **WILL CORONA PILGRIM**
ARTIST: **RAMON ROSANAS**
COLORS: **CHRIS SOTOMAYOR**
LETTERS: **VC'S CLAYTON COWLES**
EDITOR: **SANA AMANAT**

IRON MAN 3 PRELUDE #1-2
WRITER: **CHRISTOS GAGE** WITH **WILL CORONA PILGRIM**
PENCILS: **STEVE KURTH**
INKS: **DREW GERACI**
COLORS: **SOTOCOLOR**
LETTERS: **VC'S JOE SABINO**
EDITOR: **SANA AMANAT**

MARVEL STUDIOS
CREATIVE EXECUTIVE: **TRENTON WATERSON** • CREATIVE MANAGER: **WILL CORONA PILGRIM**
VP PRODUCTION & DEVELOPMENT: **BRAD WINDERBAUM** • SVP PRODUCTION & DEVELOPMENT: **JEREMY LATCHAM**
SVP PRODUCTION & DEVELOPMENT: **STEPHAN BROUSSARD** • PRESIDENT: **KEVIN FEIGE**

IRON MAN (2005) #1
WRITER: **WARREN ELLIS**
ARTIST: **ADI GRANOV**
LETTERS: **VC'S RANDY GENTILE**
ASSISTANT EDITORS: **ANDY SCHMIDT, NICOLE BOOSE & MOLLY LAZER**
EDITOR: **TOM BREVOORT**

COLLECTION EDITOR: **JENNIFER GRÜNWALD** • ASSISTANT EDITORS: **ALEX STARBUCK & NELSON RIBEIRO** • EDITOR, SPECIAL PROJECTS: **MARK D. BEAZLEY**
SENIOR EDITOR, SPECIAL PROJECTS: **JEFF YOUNGQUIST** • SVP PRINT & DIGITAL PUBLISHING SALES: **DAVID GABRIEL**
EDITOR IN CHIEF: **AXEL ALONSO** • CHIEF CREATIVE OFFICER: **JOE QUESADA** • PUBLISHER: **DAN BUCKLEY** • EXECUTIVE PRODUCER: **ALAN FINE**

MARVEL'S IRON MAN 3 PRELUDE. Contains material originally published in magazine form as MARVEL'S IRON MAN 2 ADAPTATION #1-2 and MARVEL'S IRON MAN 3 PRELUDE #1-2. First printing 2013. ISBN# 978-0-7851-6551-4. Published by MARVEL WORLDWIDE, INC., a subsidiary of MARVEL ENTERTAINMENT, LLC. OFFICE OF PUBLICATION: 135 West 50th Street, New York, NY 10020. Copyright © 2012 and 2013 Marvel Characters, Inc. All rights reserved. All characters featured in this issue and the distinctive names and likenesses thereof, and all related indicia are trademarks of Marvel Characters, Inc. No similarity between any of the names, characters, persons, and/or institutions in this magazine with those of any living or dead person or institution is intended, and any such similarity which may exist is purely coincidental. Printed in the U.S.A. ALAN FINE, EVP - Office of the President, Marvel Worldwide, Inc. and EVP & CMO Marvel Characters B.V.; DAN BUCKLEY, Publisher & President - Print, Animation & Digital Divisions; JOE QUESADA, Chief Creative Officer; TOM BREVOORT, SVP of Publishing; DAVID BOGART, SVP of Operations & Procurement, Publishing; RUWAN JAYATILLEKE, SVP & Associate Publisher, Publishing; C.B. CEBULSKI, SVP of Creator & Content Development; DAVID GABRIEL, SVP of Print & Digital Publishing Sales; JIM O'KEEFE, VP of Operations & Logistics; DAN CARR, Executive Director of Publishing Technology; SUSAN CRESPI, Editorial Operations Manager; ALEX MORALES, Publishing Operations Manager; STAN LEE, Chairman Emeritus. For information regarding advertising in Marvel Comics or on Marvel.com, please contact Niza Disla, Director of Marvel Partnerships, at ndisla@marvel.com. For Marvel subscription inquiries, please call 800-217-9158. Manufactured between 2/14/2013 and 3/9/2013 by QUAD/GRAPHICS, VERSAILLES, KY, USA.

10 9 8 7 6 5 4 3 2 1

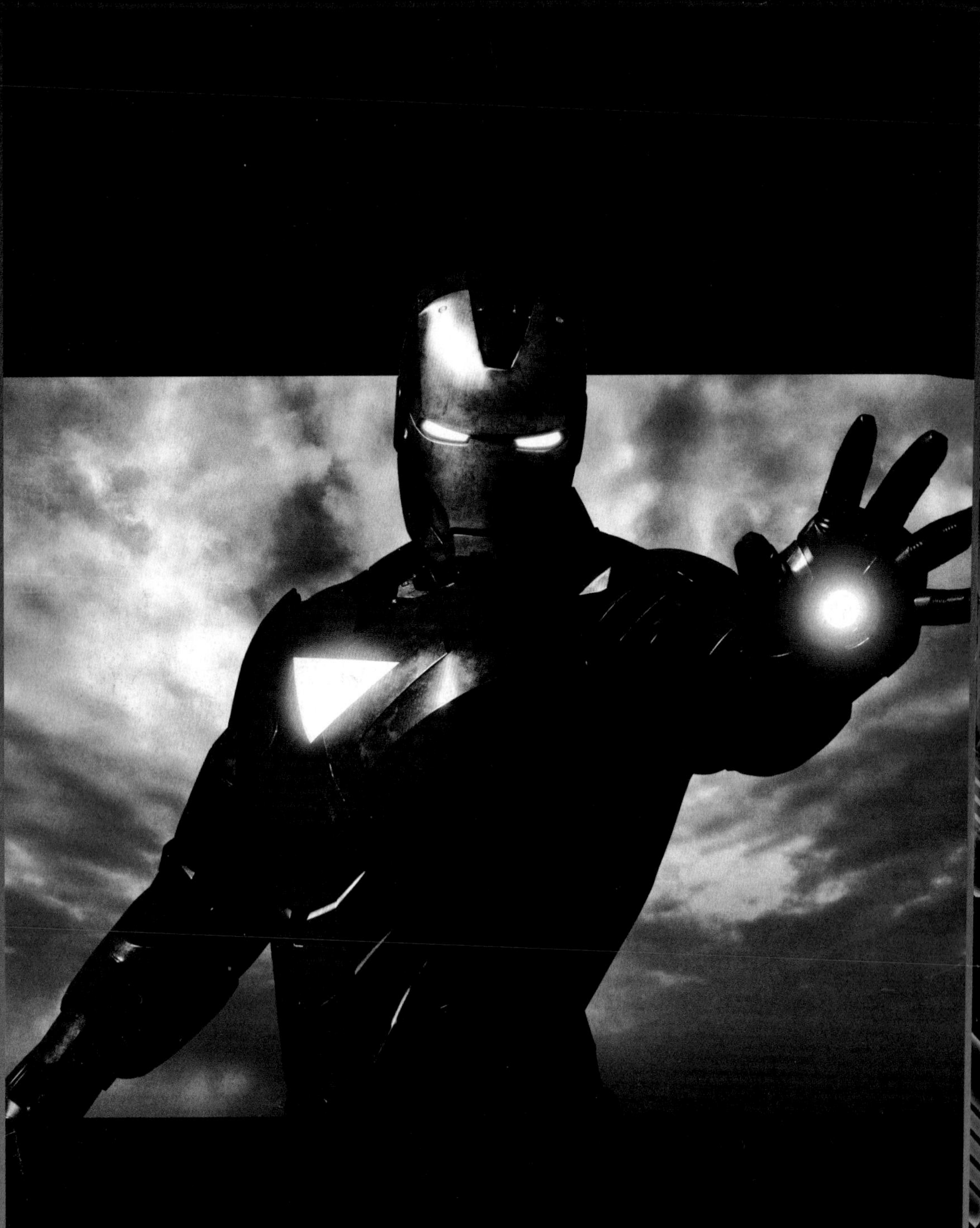

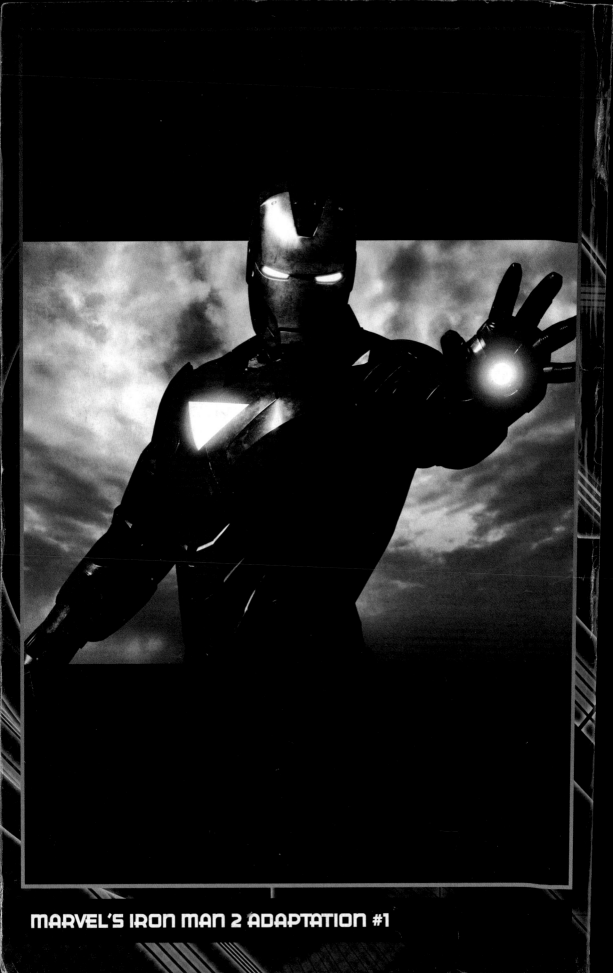

MARVEL'S IRON MAN 2 ADAPTATION #1

MARVEL

IRON MAN 2

BASED ON THE MARVEL STUDIOS FILM IRON MAN 2
SCREENPLAY BY JUSTIN THEROUX

Genius playboy philanthropist Tony Stark ran Stark Industries, the biggest weapons manufacturer in the country. Nearly killed by a terrorist group who was after Stark's weapons arsenal, Tony was saved by a small arc reactor in his chest to keep shrapnel from reaching his heart. Using its untested power, he created the ultimate weapon, the Iron Man suit, to escape.

After defeating those who sought to weaponize the Iron Man tech on a mass scale, Tony eliminated the Stark Industries' weapons division, vowing to protect the world from those who would terrorize it.

Still the genius, still the playboy, Tony Stark is now IRON MAN.

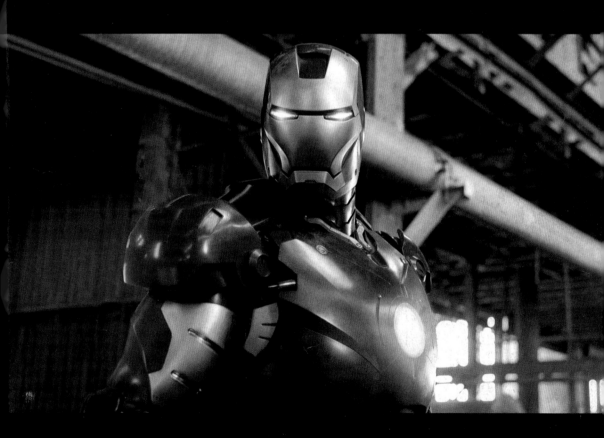

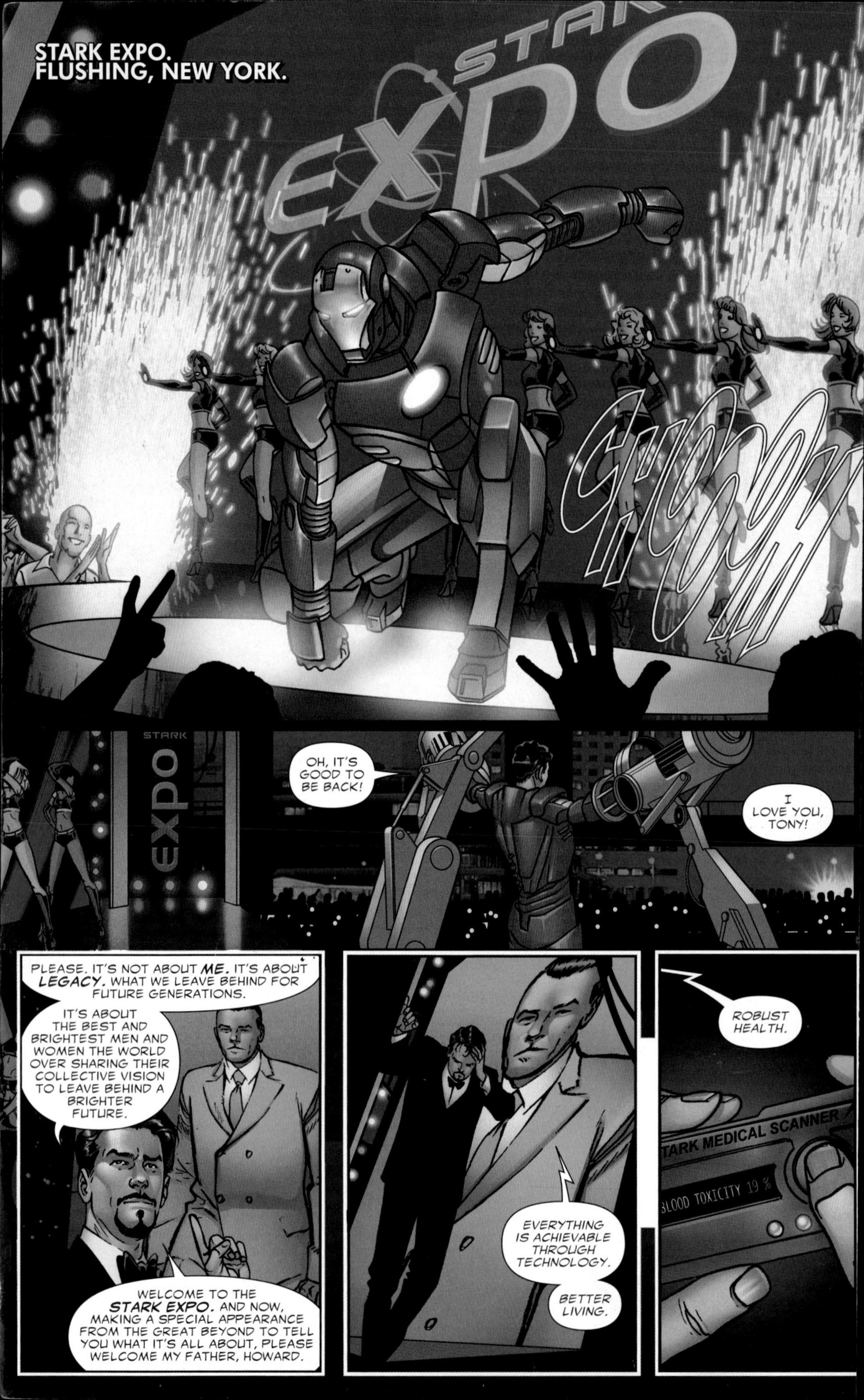
STARK EXPO.
FLUSHING, NEW YORK.
STARK EXPO
CHOOM
STARK EXPO
OH, IT'S GOOD TO BE BACK!
I LOVE YOU, TONY!
PLEASE. IT'S NOT ABOUT ME. IT'S ABOUT LEGACY. WHAT WE LEAVE BEHIND FOR FUTURE GENERATIONS.
IT'S ABOUT THE BEST AND BRIGHTEST MEN AND WOMEN THE WORLD OVER SHARING THEIR COLLECTIVE VISION TO LEAVE BEHIND A BRIGHTER FUTURE.
WELCOME TO THE STARK EXPO. AND NOW, MAKING A SPECIAL APPEARANCE FROM THE GREAT BEYOND TO TELL YOU WHAT IT'S ALL ABOUT, PLEASE WELCOME MY FATHER, HOWARD.
EVERYTHING IS ACHIEVABLE THROUGH TECHNOLOGY.
BETTER LIVING.
ROBUST HEALTH.
STARK MEDICAL SCANNER
BLOOD TOXICITY 19 %

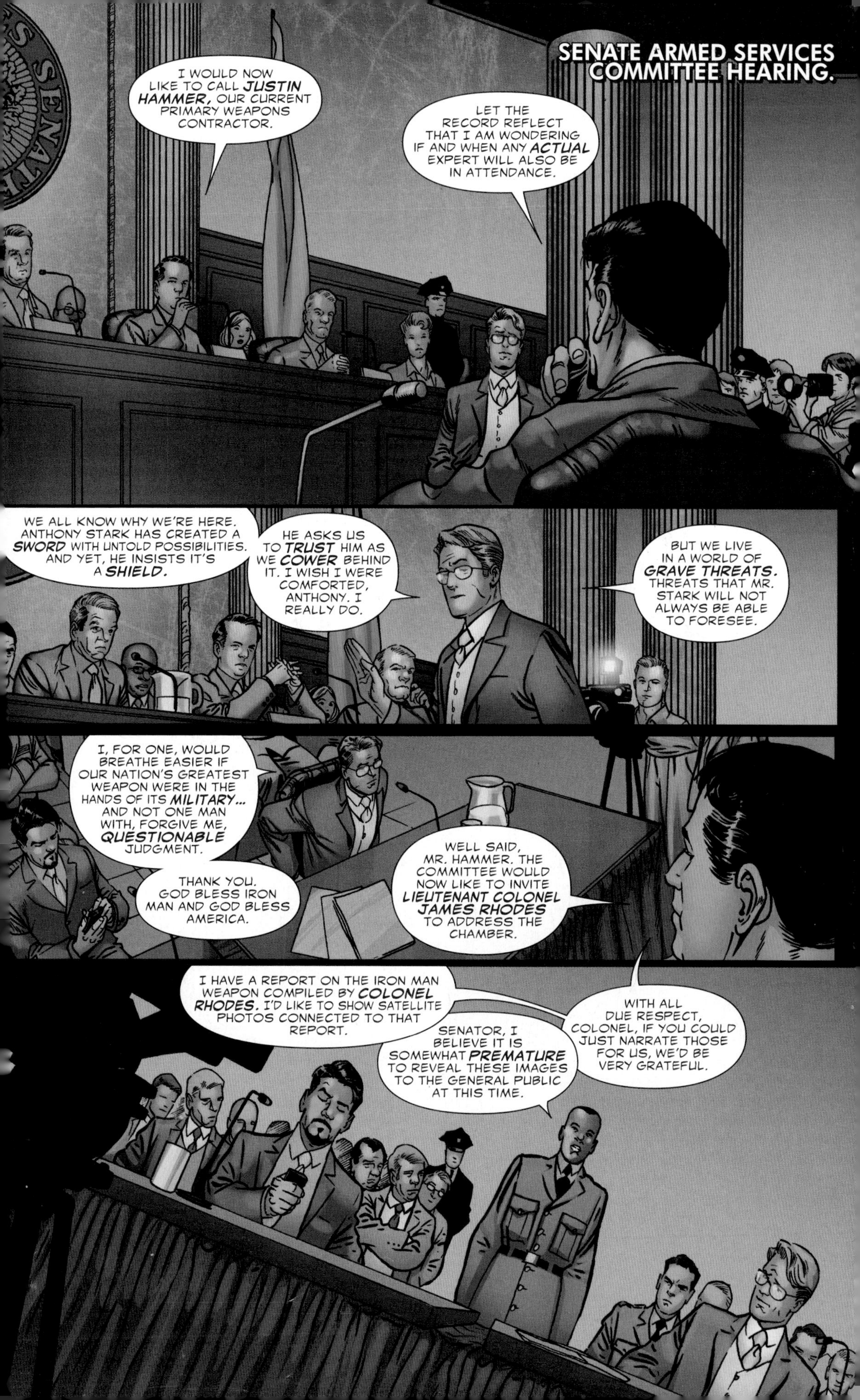
SENATE ARMED SERVICES COMMITTEE HEARING.
I WOULD NOW LIKE TO CALL JUSTIN HAMMER, OUR CURRENT PRIMARY WEAPONS CONTRACTOR.
LET THE RECORD REFLECT THAT I AM WONDERING IF AND WHEN ANY ACTUAL EXPERT WILL ALSO BE IN ATTENDANCE.
WE ALL KNOW WHY WE'RE HERE. ANTHONY STARK HAS CREATED A SWORD WITH UNTOLD POSSIBILITIES. AND YET, HE INSISTS IT'S A SHIELD.
HE ASKS US TO TRUST HIM AS WE COWER BEHIND IT. I WISH I WERE COMFORTED, ANTHONY. I REALLY DO.
BUT WE LIVE IN A WORLD OF GRAVE THREATS. THREATS THAT MR. STARK WILL NOT ALWAYS BE ABLE TO FORESEE.
I, FOR ONE, WOULD BREATHE EASIER IF OUR NATION'S GREATEST WEAPON WERE IN THE HANDS OF ITS MILITARY... AND NOT ONE MAN WITH, FORGIVE ME, QUESTIONABLE JUDGMENT.
THANK YOU. GOD BLESS IRON MAN AND GOD BLESS AMERICA.
WELL SAID, MR. HAMMER. THE COMMITTEE WOULD NOW LIKE TO INVITE LIEUTENANT COLONEL JAMES RHODES TO ADDRESS THE CHAMBER.
I HAVE A REPORT ON THE IRON MAN WEAPON COMPILED BY COLONEL RHODES. I'D LIKE TO SHOW SATELLITE PHOTOS CONNECTED TO THAT REPORT.
SENATOR, I BELIEVE IT IS SOMEWHAT PREMATURE TO REVEAL THESE IMAGES TO THE GENERAL PUBLIC AT THIS TIME.
WITH ALL DUE RESPECT, COLONEL, IF YOU COULD JUST NARRATE THOSE FOR US, WE'D BE VERY GRATEFUL.

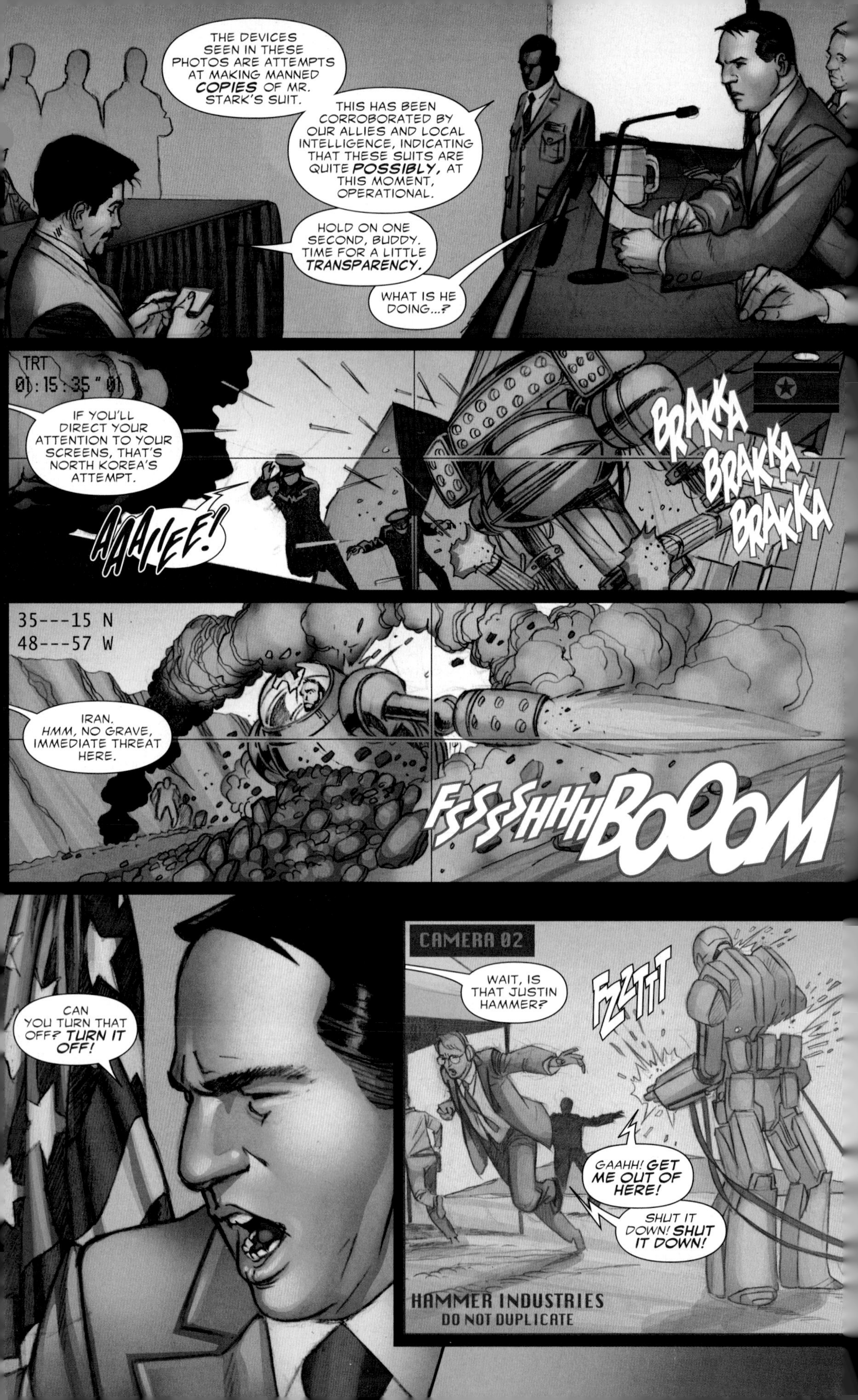
THE DEVICES SEEN IN THESE PHOTOS ARE ATTEMPTS AT MAKING MANNED COPIES OF MR. STARK'S SUIT.
THIS HAS BEEN CORROBORATED BY OUR ALLIES AND LOCAL INTELLIGENCE, INDICATING THAT THESE SUITS ARE QUITE POSSIBLY, AT THIS MOMENT, OPERATIONAL.
HOLD ON ONE SECOND, BUDDY. TIME FOR A LITTLE TRANSPARENCY.
WHAT IS HE DOING...?
TRT
01:15:35"01
IF YOU'LL DIRECT YOUR ATTENTION TO YOUR SCREENS, THAT'S NORTH KOREA'S ATTEMPT.
BRAKKA BRAKKA BRAKKA
AAAIEEE!
35---15 N
48---57 W
IRAN. HMM, NO GRAVE, IMMEDIATE THREAT HERE.
FSSSHHHBOOOOM
CAN YOU TURN THAT OFF? TURN IT OFF!
CAMERA 02
WAIT, IS THAT JUSTIN HAMMER?
FZZTTT
GAAHH! GET ME OUT OF HERE!
SHUT IT DOWN! SHUT IT DOWN!
HAMMER INDUSTRIES
DO NOT DUPLICATE

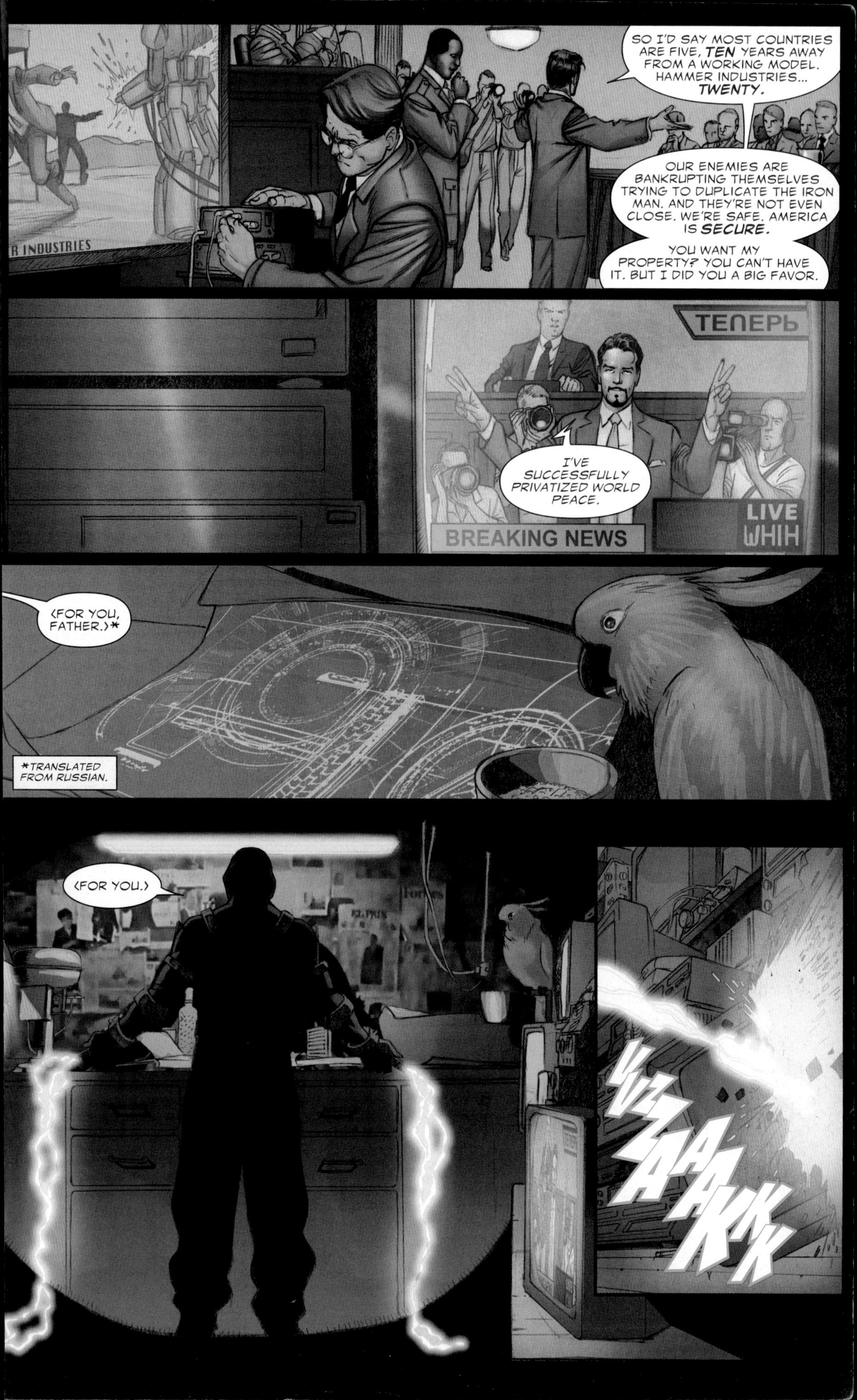

R INDUSTRIES
SO I'D SAY MOST COUNTRIES ARE FIVE, TEN YEARS AWAY FROM A WORKING MODEL. HAMMER INDUSTRIES... TWENTY.
OUR ENEMIES ARE BANKRUPTING THEMSELVES TRYING TO DUPLICATE THE IRON MAN. AND THEY'RE NOT EVEN CLOSE. WE'RE SAFE. AMERICA IS SECURE.
YOU WANT MY PROPERTY? YOU CAN'T HAVE IT. BUT I DID YOU A BIG FAVOR.
ТЕПЕРЬ
I'VE SUCCESSFULLY PRIVATIZED WORLD PEACE.
BREAKING NEWS
LIVE WHIH
‹FOR YOU, FATHER.›*
*TRANSLATED FROM RUSSIAN.
‹FOR YOU.›
VVZZAAAKKK

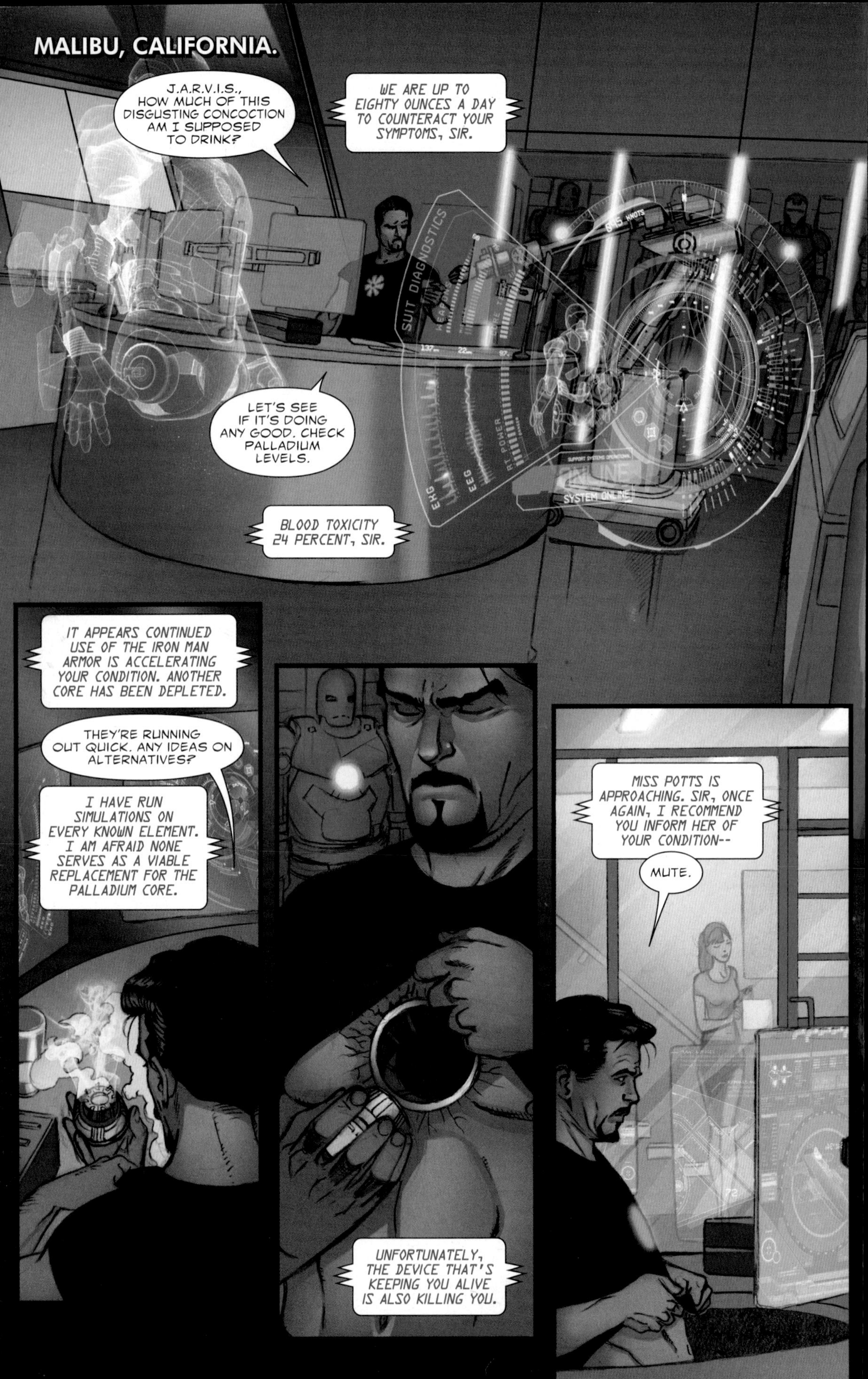

MALIBU, CALIFORNIA.
J.A.R.V.I.S., HOW MUCH OF THIS DISGUSTING CONCOCTION AM I SUPPOSED TO DRINK?
WE ARE UP TO EIGHTY OUNCES A DAY TO COUNTERACT YOUR SYMPTOMS, SIR.
SUIT DIAGNOSTICS
LET'S SEE IF IT'S DOING ANY GOOD. CHECK PALLADIUM LEVELS.
EKG
EEG
RT. POWER
SYSTEM ONLINE
BLOOD TOXICITY 24 PERCENT, SIR.
IT APPEARS CONTINUED USE OF THE IRON MAN ARMOR IS ACCELERATING YOUR CONDITION. ANOTHER CORE HAS BEEN DEPLETED.
THEY'RE RUNNING OUT QUICK. ANY IDEAS ON ALTERNATIVES?
I HAVE RUN SIMULATIONS ON EVERY KNOWN ELEMENT. I AM AFRAID NONE SERVES AS A VIABLE REPLACEMENT FOR THE PALLADIUM CORE.
UNFORTUNATELY, THE DEVICE THAT'S KEEPING YOU ALIVE IS ALSO KILLING YOU.
MISS POTTS IS APPROACHING. SIR, ONCE AGAIN, I RECOMMEND YOU INFORM HER OF YOUR CONDITION--
MUTE.

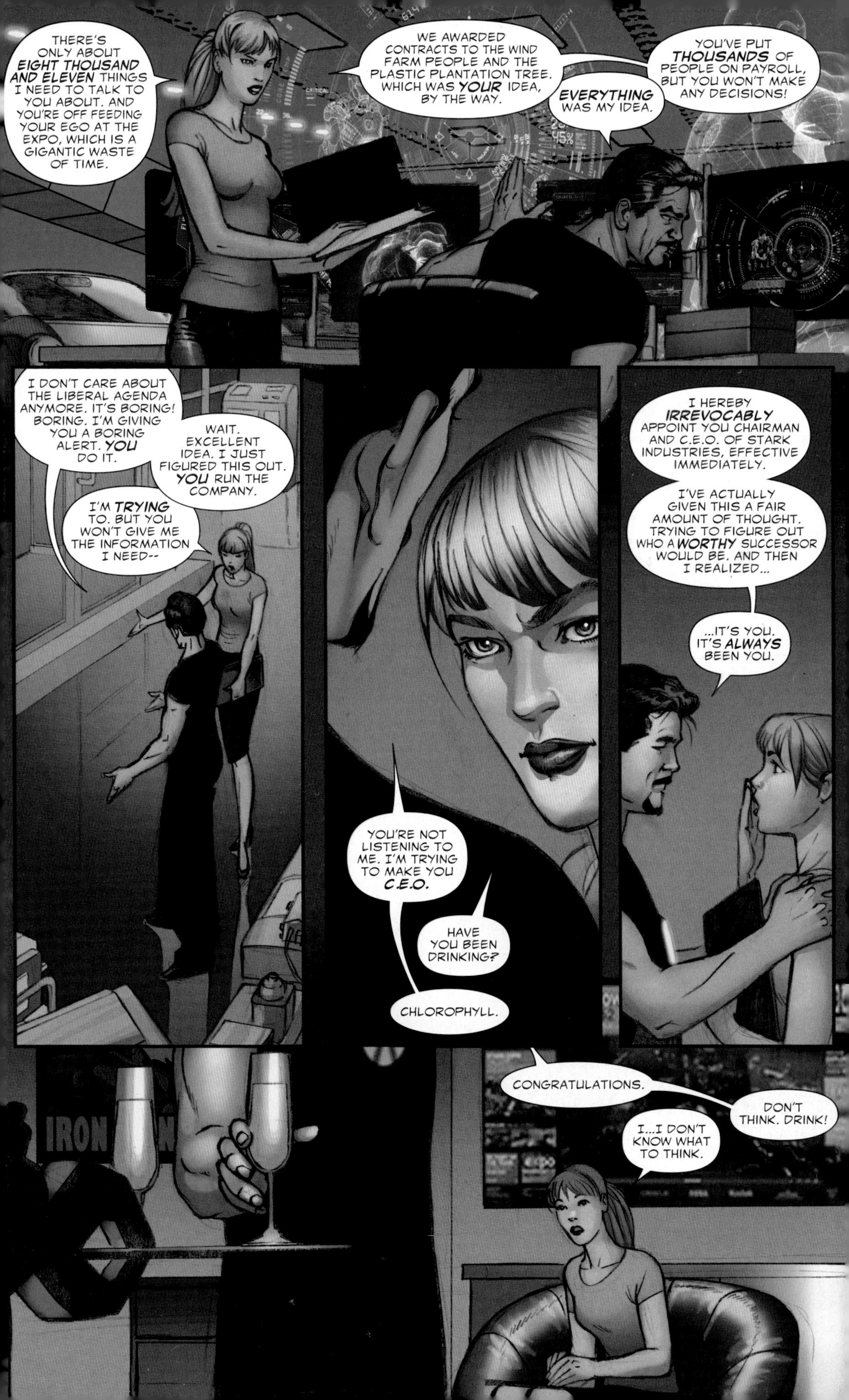
THERE'S ONLY ABOUT EIGHT THOUSAND AND ELEVEN THINGS I NEED TO TALK TO YOU ABOUT. AND YOU'RE OFF FEEDING YOUR EGO AT THE EXPO, WHICH IS A GIGANTIC WASTE OF TIME.
WE AWARDED CONTRACTS TO THE WIND FARM PEOPLE AND THE PLASTIC PLANTATION TREE. WHICH WAS YOUR IDEA, BY THE WAY.
EVERYTHING WAS MY IDEA.
YOU'VE PUT THOUSANDS OF PEOPLE ON PAYROLL, BUT YOU WON'T MAKE ANY DECISIONS!
I DON'T CARE ABOUT THE LIBERAL AGENDA ANYMORE. IT'S BORING! BORING. I'M GIVING YOU A BORING ALERT. YOU DO IT.
WAIT. EXCELLENT IDEA. I JUST FIGURED THIS OUT. YOU RUN THE COMPANY.
I'M TRYING TO. BUT YOU WON'T GIVE ME THE INFORMATION I NEED--
YOU'RE NOT LISTENING TO ME. I'M TRYING TO MAKE YOU C.E.O.
HAVE YOU BEEN DRINKING?
CHLOROPHYLL.
I HEREBY IRREVOCABLY APPOINT YOU CHAIRMAN AND C.E.O. OF STARK INDUSTRIES, EFFECTIVE IMMEDIATELY.
I'VE ACTUALLY GIVEN THIS A FAIR AMOUNT OF THOUGHT. TRYING TO FIGURE OUT WHO A WORTHY SUCCESSOR WOULD BE. AND THEN I REALIZED...
...IT'S YOU. IT'S ALWAYS BEEN YOU.
CONGRATULATIONS.
DON'T THINK. DRINK!
I...I DON'T KNOW WHAT TO THINK.
IRON

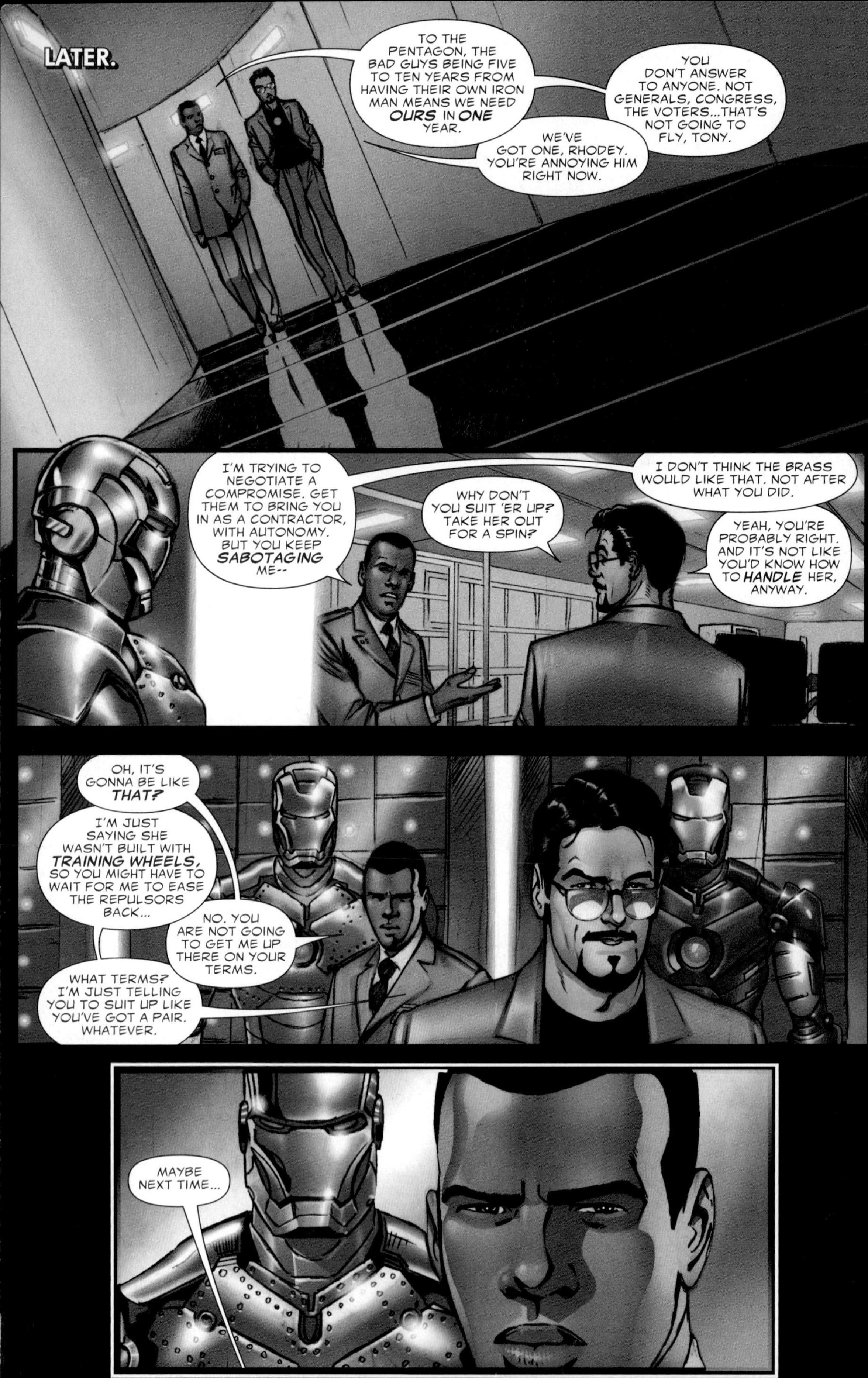
LATER.
TO THE PENTAGON, THE BAD GUYS BEING FIVE TO TEN YEARS FROM HAVING THEIR OWN IRON MAN MEANS WE NEED OURS IN ONE YEAR.
YOU DON'T ANSWER TO ANYONE. NOT GENERALS, CONGRESS, THE VOTERS...THAT'S NOT GOING TO FLY, TONY.
WE'VE GOT ONE, RHODEY. YOU'RE ANNOYING HIM RIGHT NOW.
I'M TRYING TO NEGOTIATE A COMPROMISE. GET THEM TO BRING YOU IN AS A CONTRACTOR, WITH AUTONOMY. BUT YOU KEEP SABOTAGING ME--
WHY DON'T YOU SUIT 'ER UP? TAKE HER OUT FOR A SPIN?
I DON'T THINK THE BRASS WOULD LIKE THAT. NOT AFTER WHAT YOU DID.
YEAH, YOU'RE PROBABLY RIGHT. AND IT'S NOT LIKE YOU'D KNOW HOW TO HANDLE HER, ANYWAY.
OH, IT'S GONNA BE LIKE THAT?
I'M JUST SAYING SHE WASN'T BUILT WITH TRAINING WHEELS, SO YOU MIGHT HAVE TO WAIT FOR ME TO EASE THE REPULSORS BACK...
NO. YOU ARE NOT GOING TO GET ME UP THERE ON YOUR TERMS.
WHAT TERMS? I'M JUST TELLING YOU TO SUIT UP LIKE YOU'VE GOT A PAIR. WHATEVER.
MAYBE NEXT TIME...

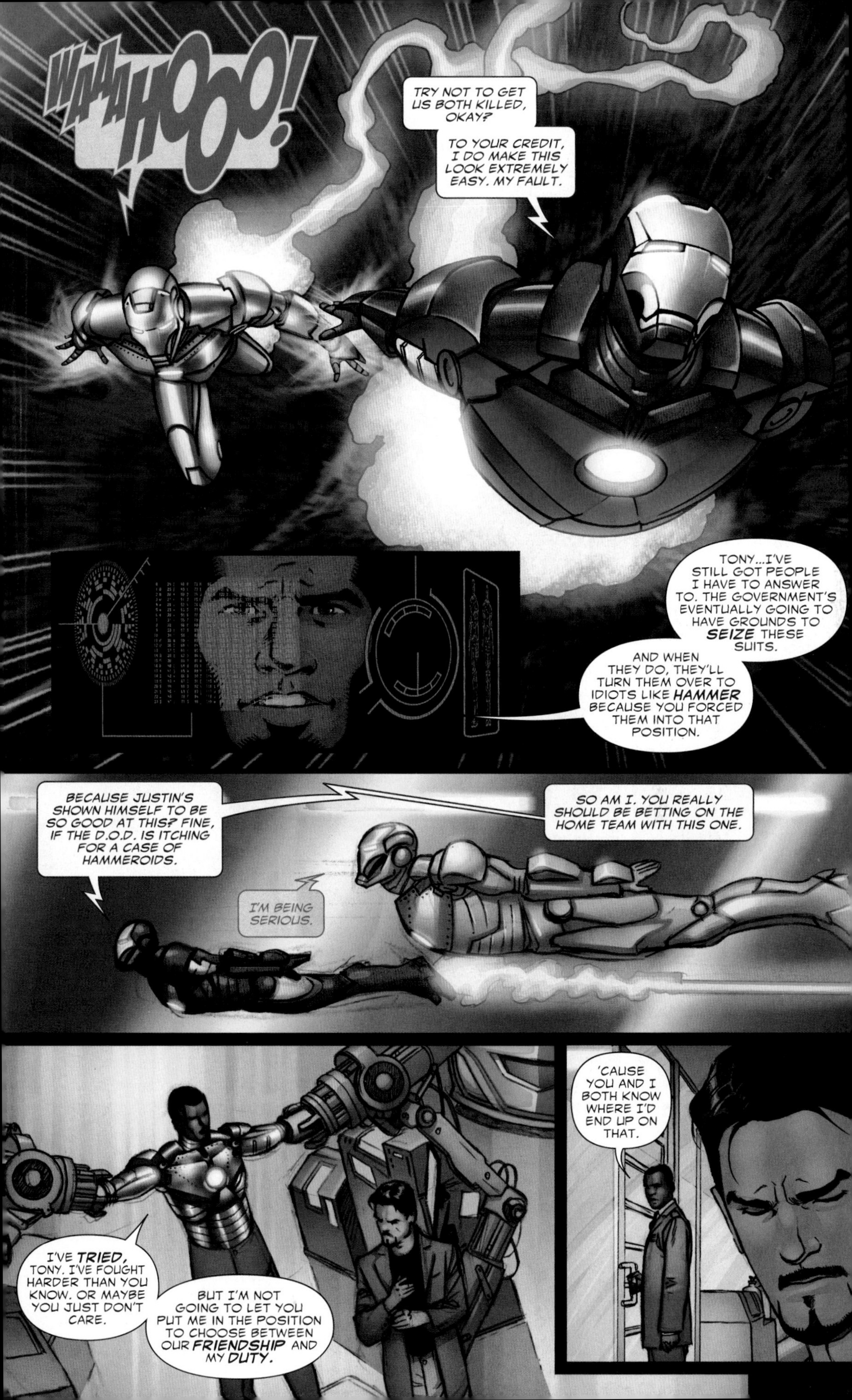
WAAAHOOO!
TRY NOT TO GET US BOTH KILLED, OKAY?
TO YOUR CREDIT, I DO MAKE THIS LOOK EXTREMELY EASY. MY FAULT.
TONY...I'VE STILL GOT PEOPLE I HAVE TO ANSWER TO. THE GOVERNMENT'S EVENTUALLY GOING TO HAVE GROUNDS TO SEIZE THESE SUITS.
AND WHEN THEY DO, THEY'LL TURN THEM OVER TO IDIOTS LIKE HAMMER BECAUSE YOU FORCED THEM INTO THAT POSITION.
BECAUSE JUSTIN'S SHOWN HIMSELF TO BE SO GOOD AT THIS? FINE, IF THE D.O.D. IS ITCHING FOR A CASE OF HAMMEROIDS.
I'M BEING SERIOUS.
SO AM I. YOU REALLY SHOULD BE BETTING ON THE HOME TEAM WITH THIS ONE.
I'VE TRIED, TONY. I'VE FOUGHT HARDER THAN YOU KNOW. OR MAYBE YOU JUST DON'T CARE.
BUT I'M NOT GOING TO LET YOU PUT ME IN THE POSITION TO CHOOSE BETWEEN OUR FRIENDSHIP AND MY DUTY.
'CAUSE YOU AND I BOTH KNOW WHERE I'D END UP ON THAT.

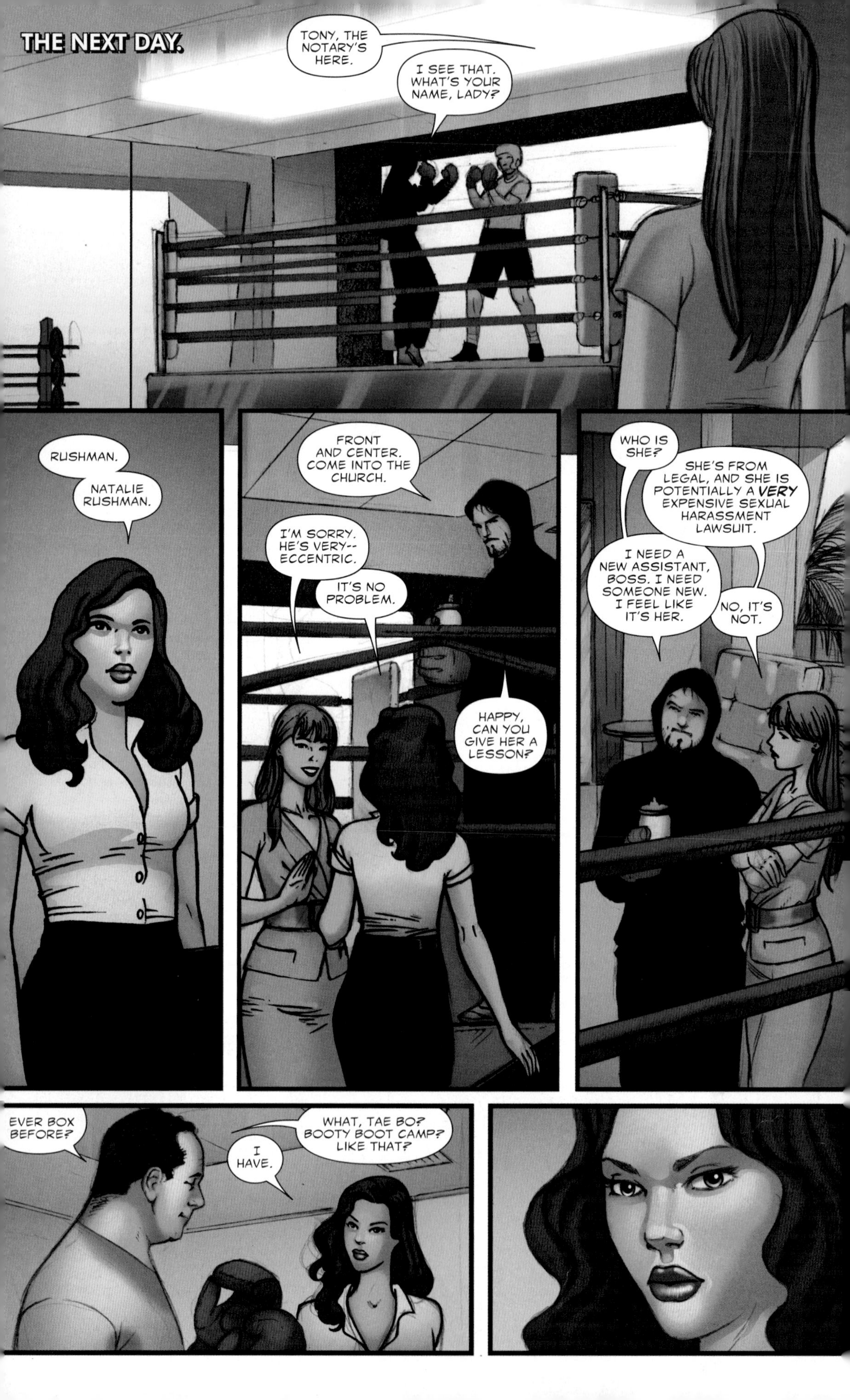
THE NEXT DAY.
TONY, THE NOTARY'S HERE.
I SEE THAT. WHAT'S YOUR NAME, LADY?
RUSHMAN.
NATALIE RUSHMAN.
FRONT AND CENTER. COME INTO THE CHURCH.
I'M SORRY. HE'S VERY-- ECCENTRIC.
IT'S NO PROBLEM.
HAPPY, CAN YOU GIVE HER A LESSON?
WHO IS SHE?
SHE'S FROM LEGAL, AND SHE IS POTENTIALLY A VERY EXPENSIVE SEXUAL HARASSMENT LAWSUIT.
I NEED A NEW ASSISTANT, BOSS. I NEED SOMEONE NEW. I FEEL LIKE IT'S HER.
NO, IT'S NOT.
EVER BOX BEFORE?
I HAVE.
WHAT, TAE BO? BOOTY BOOT CAMP? LIKE THAT?

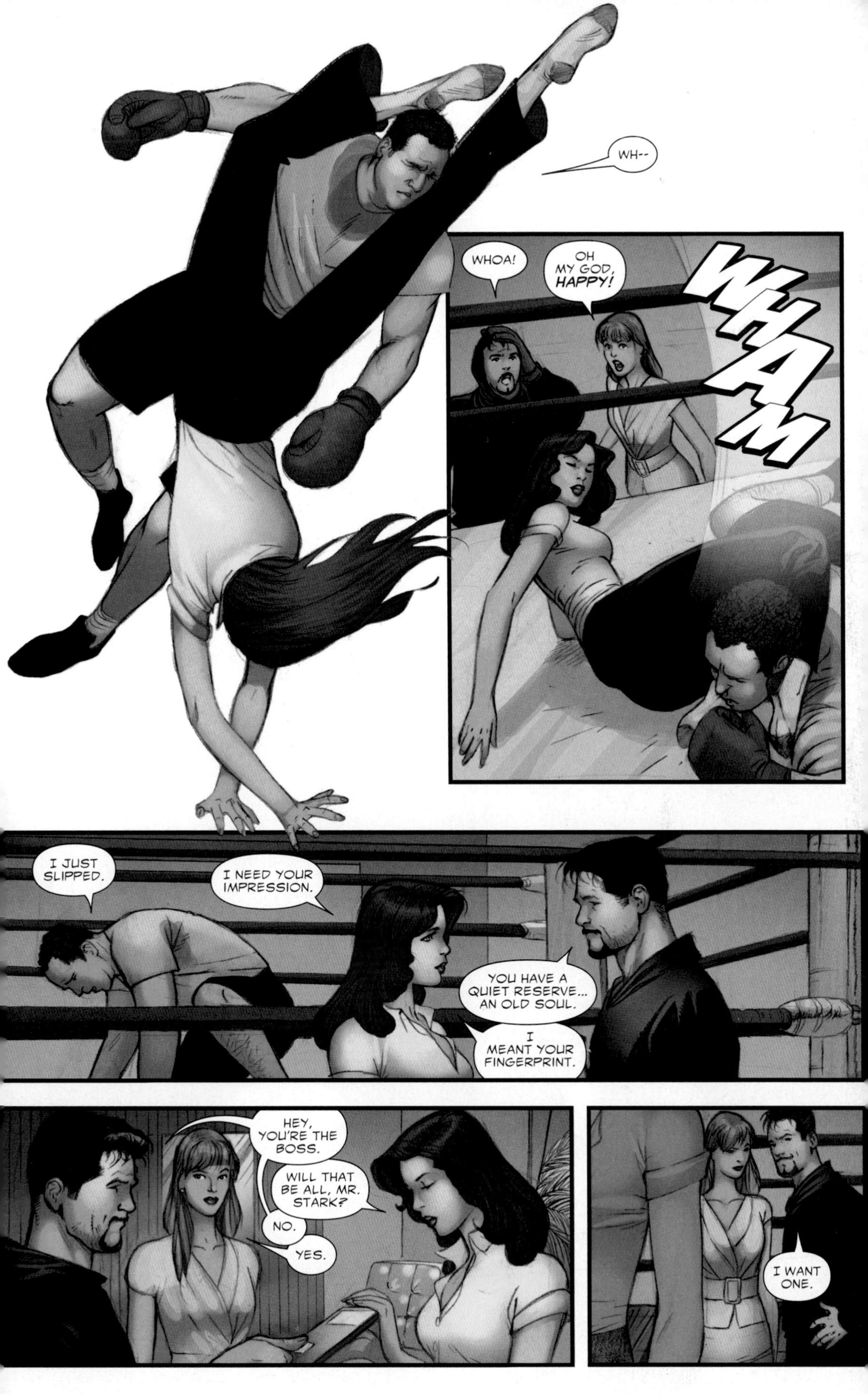
WH--
WHOA!
OH MY GOD, HAPPY!
WHAM
I JUST SLIPPED.
I NEED YOUR IMPRESSION.
YOU HAVE A QUIET RESERVE... AN OLD SOUL.
I MEANT YOUR FINGERPRINT.
HEY, YOU'RE THE BOSS.
WILL THAT BE ALL, MR. STARK?
NO.
YES.
I WANT ONE.

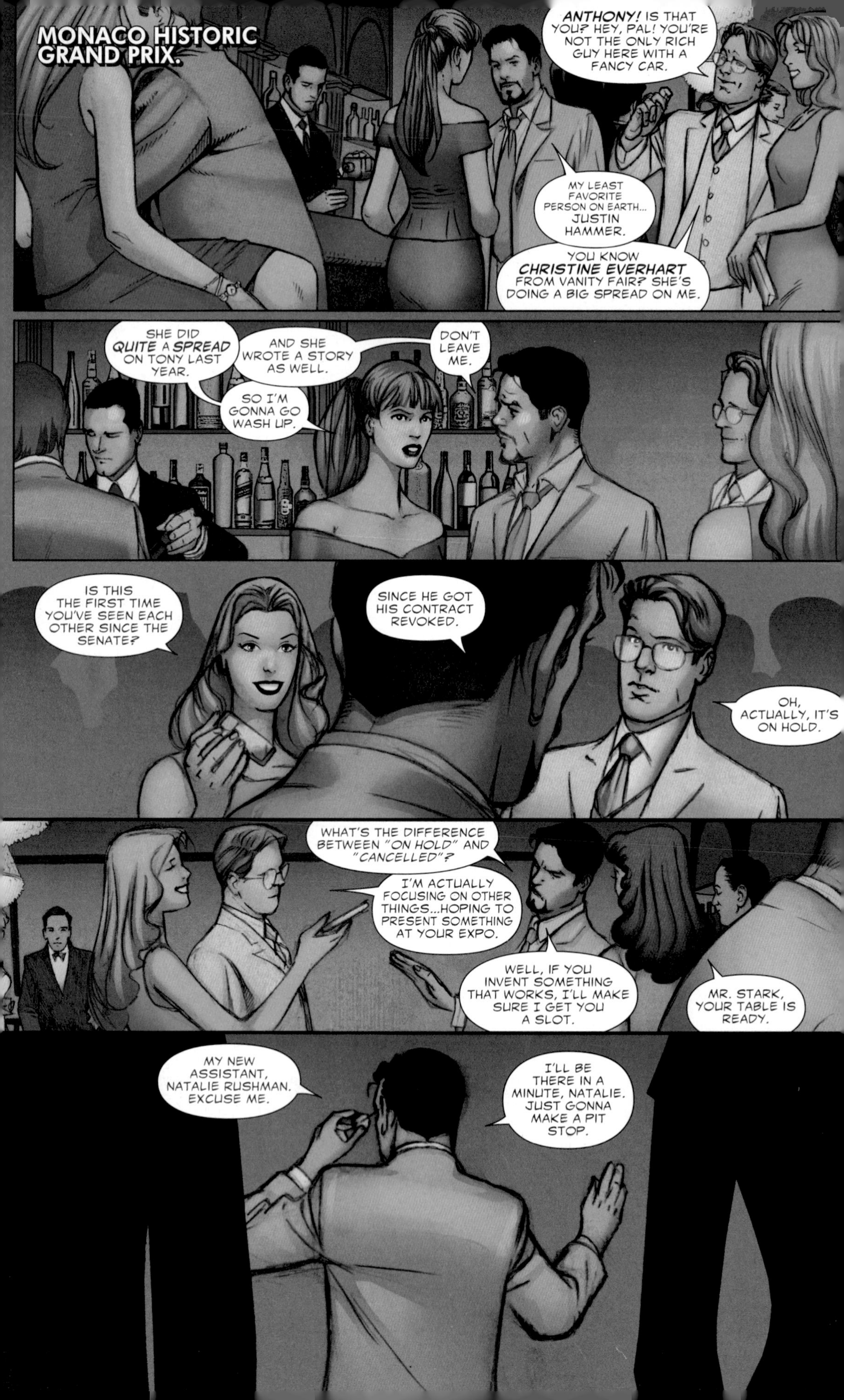
MONACO HISTORIC GRAND PRIX.
ANTHONY! IS THAT YOU? HEY, PAL! YOU'RE NOT THE ONLY RICH GUY HERE WITH A FANCY CAR.
MY LEAST FAVORITE PERSON ON EARTH... JUSTIN HAMMER.
YOU KNOW CHRISTINE EVERHART FROM VANITY FAIR? SHE'S DOING A BIG SPREAD ON ME.
SHE DID QUITE A SPREAD ON TONY LAST YEAR.
AND SHE WROTE A STORY AS WELL.
DON'T LEAVE ME.
SO I'M GONNA GO WASH UP.
IS THIS THE FIRST TIME YOU'VE SEEN EACH OTHER SINCE THE SENATE?
SINCE HE GOT HIS CONTRACT REVOKED.
OH, ACTUALLY, IT'S ON HOLD.
WHAT'S THE DIFFERENCE BETWEEN "ON HOLD" AND "CANCELLED"?
I'M ACTUALLY FOCUSING ON OTHER THINGS...HOPING TO PRESENT SOMETHING AT YOUR EXPO.
WELL, IF YOU INVENT SOMETHING THAT WORKS, I'LL MAKE SURE I GET YOU A SLOT.
MR. STARK, YOUR TABLE IS READY.
MY NEW ASSISTANT, NATALIE RUSHMAN. EXCUSE ME.
I'LL BE THERE IN A MINUTE, NATALIE. JUST GONNA MAKE A PIT STOP.

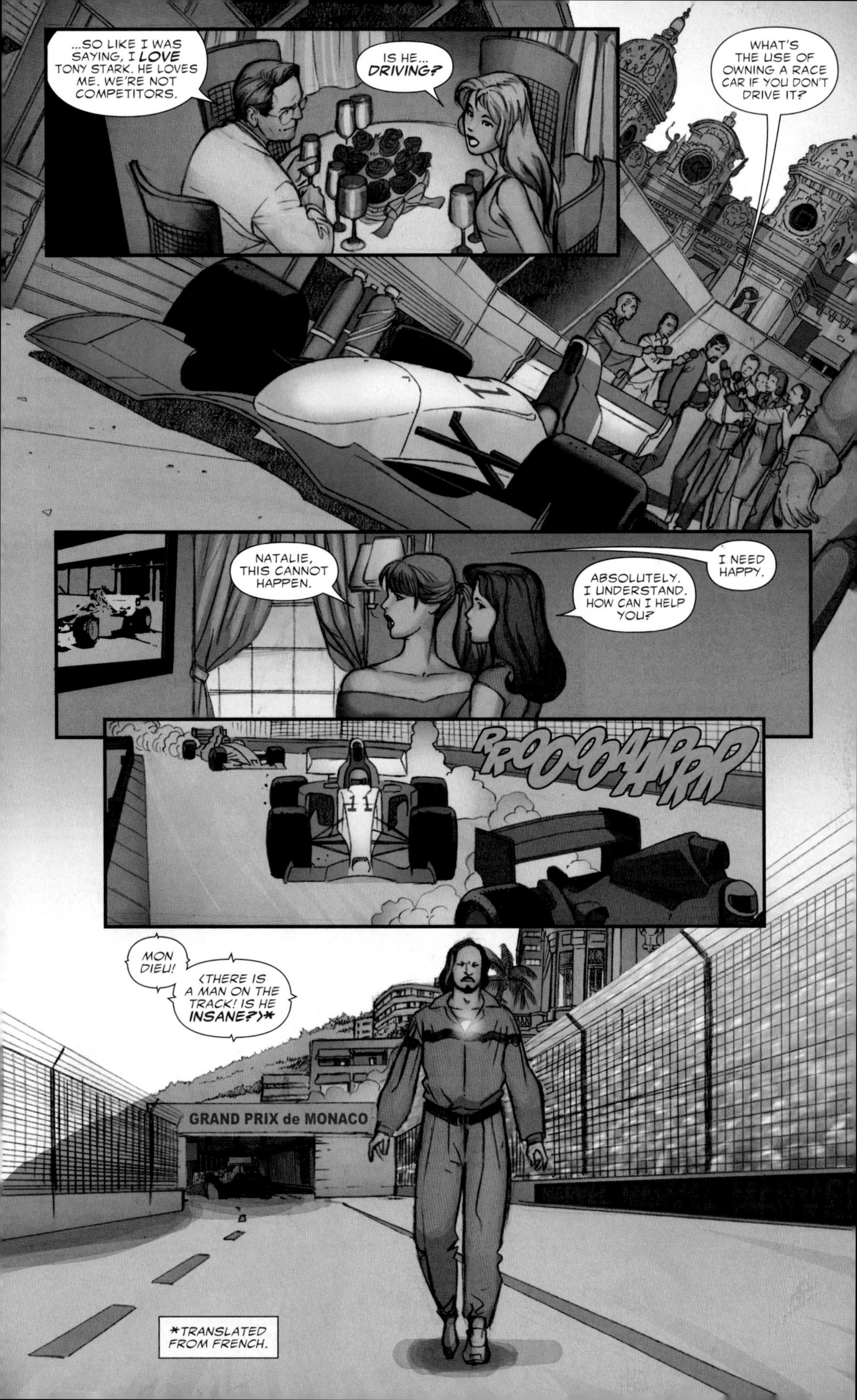
...SO LIKE I WAS SAYING, I LOVE TONY STARK. HE LOVES ME. WE'RE NOT COMPETITORS.
IS HE... DRIVING?
WHAT'S THE USE OF OWNING A RACE CAR IF YOU DON'T DRIVE IT?
NATALIE, THIS CANNOT HAPPEN.
ABSOLUTELY. I UNDERSTAND. HOW CAN I HELP YOU?
I NEED HAPPY.
RROOOOAARRR
MON DIEU!
<THERE IS A MAN ON THE TRACK! IS HE INSANE?>*
GRAND PRIX de MONACO
*TRANSLATED FROM FRENCH.

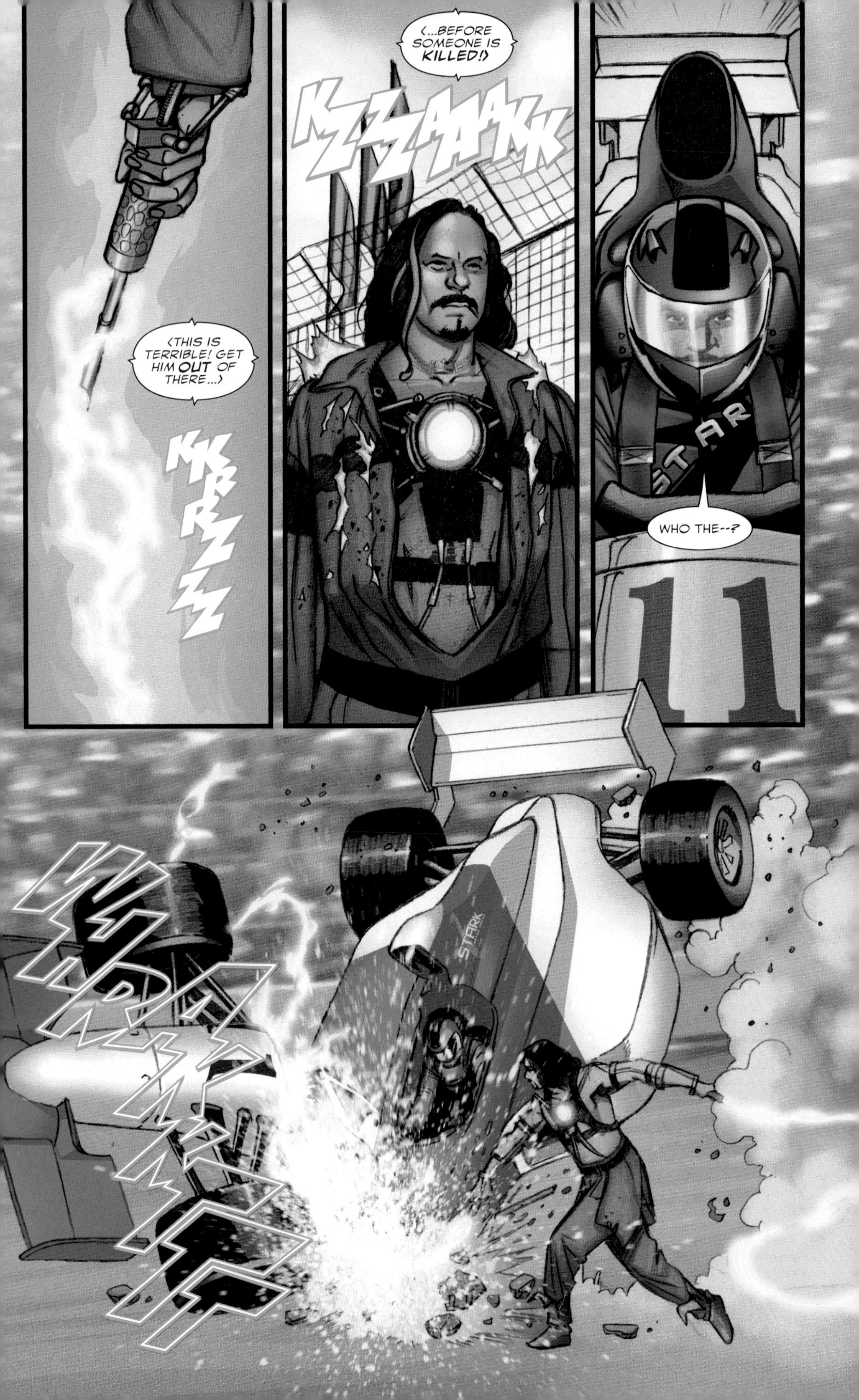

‹THIS IS TERRIBLE! GET HIM OUT OF THERE...›
KKRRZZZ
‹...BEFORE SOMEONE IS KILLED!›
KZZZAAAKK
STAR
WHO THE--?
11
STARK

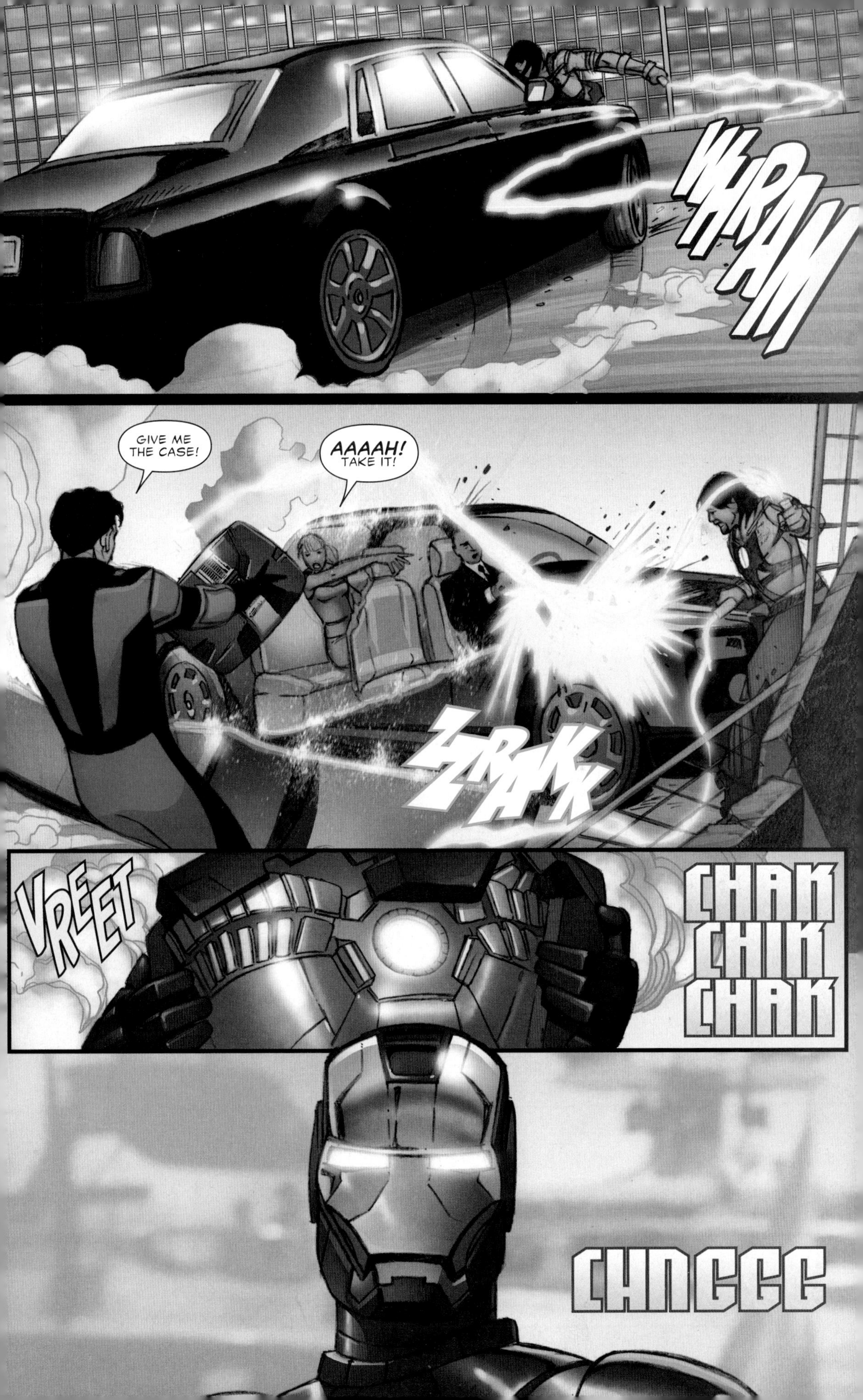
WHRAM
GIVE ME THE CASE!
AAAAH! TAKE IT!
ZZRAKK
VREET
CHAK CHIK CHAK
CHNGGG

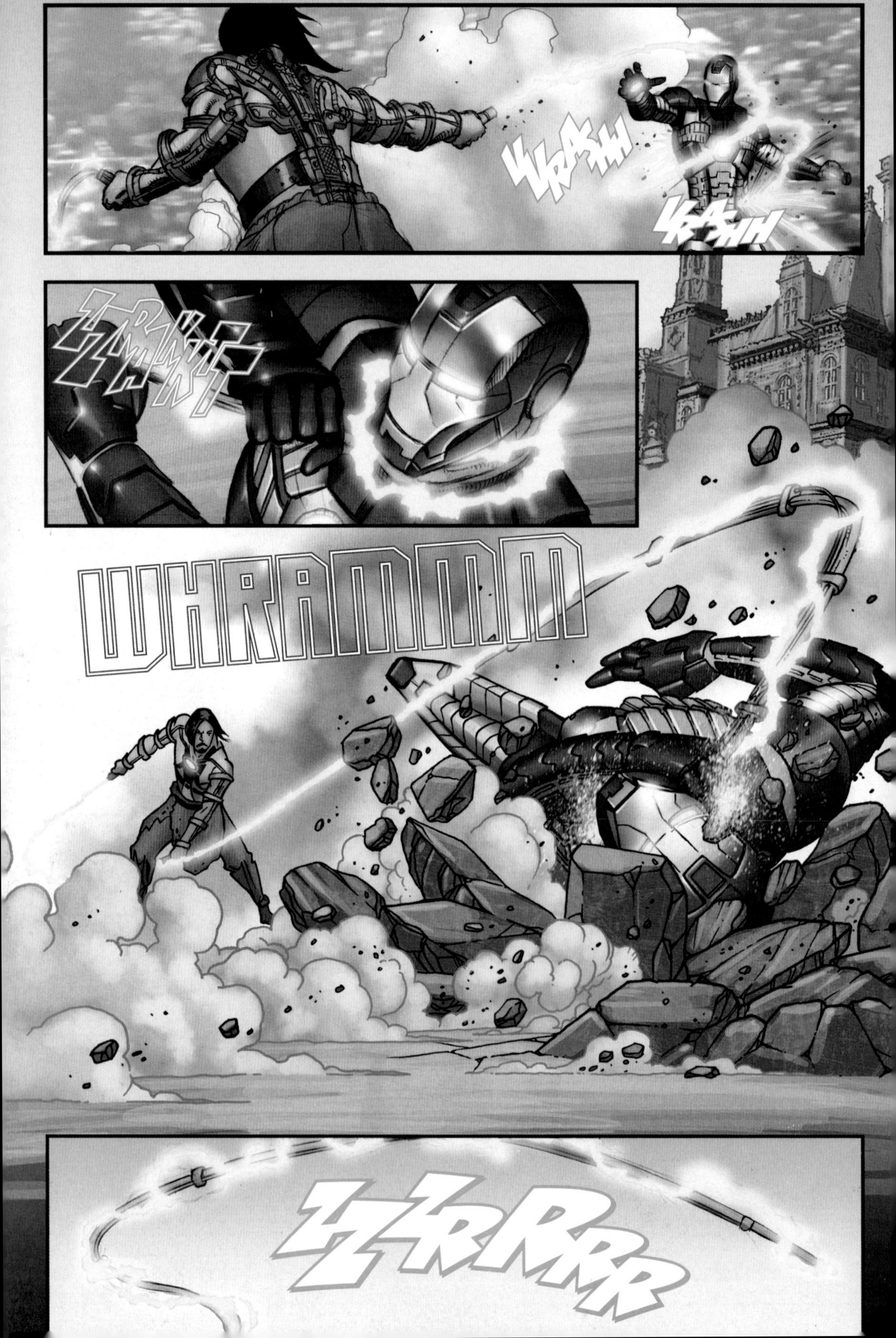
KRASHH
KRASHH
WHRAMMM
ZZRRRR

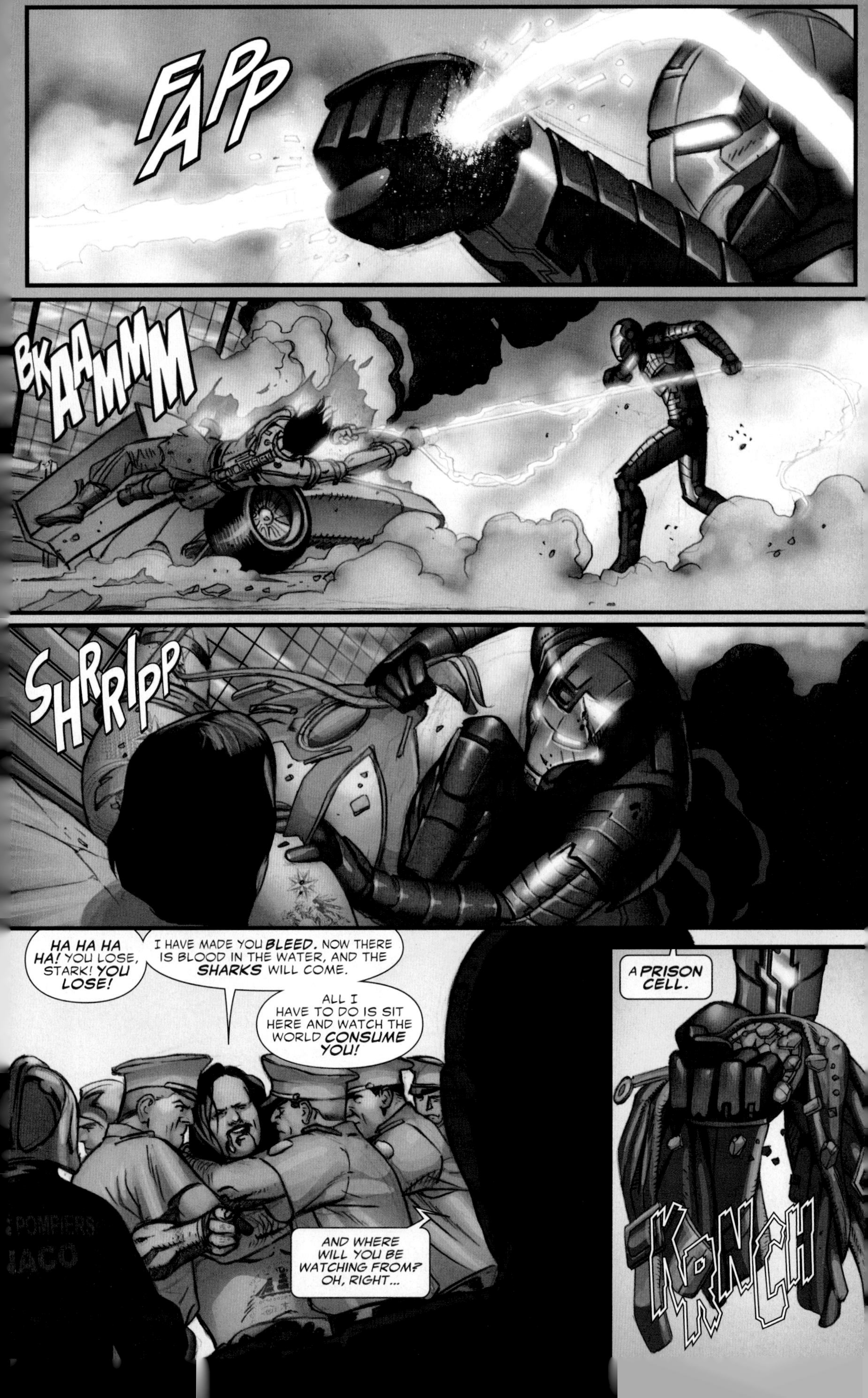
FAPP
BKAAMMMM
SHRRIPP
HA HA HA HA! YOU LOSE, STARK! YOU LOSE!
I HAVE MADE YOU BLEED. NOW THERE IS BLOOD IN THE WATER, AND THE SHARKS WILL COME.
ALL I HAVE TO DO IS SIT HERE AND WATCH THE WORLD CONSUME YOU!
AND WHERE WILL YOU BE WATCHING FROM? OH, RIGHT...
A PRISON CELL.
KRNCH

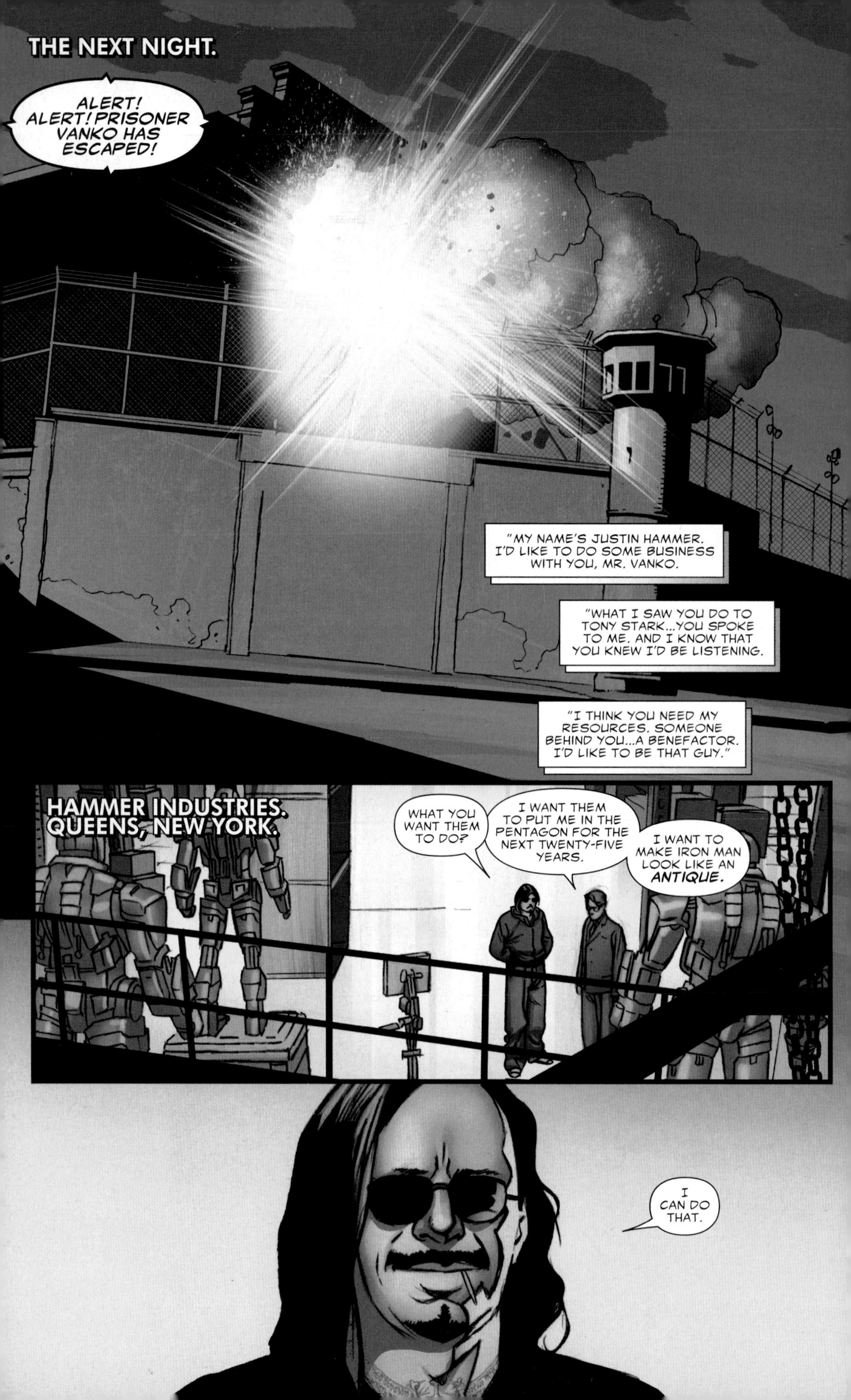

THE NEXT NIGHT.
ALERT! ALERT! PRISONER VANKO HAS ESCAPED!
"MY NAME'S JUSTIN HAMMER. I'D LIKE TO DO SOME BUSINESS WITH YOU, MR. VANKO.
"WHAT I SAW YOU DO TO TONY STARK...YOU SPOKE TO ME. AND I KNOW THAT YOU KNEW I'D BE LISTENING.
"I THINK YOU NEED MY RESOURCES. SOMEONE BEHIND YOU...A BENEFACTOR. I'D LIKE TO BE THAT GUY."
HAMMER INDUSTRIES. QUEENS, NEW YORK.
WHAT YOU WANT THEM TO DO?
I WANT THEM TO PUT ME IN THE PENTAGON FOR THE NEXT TWENTY-FIVE YEARS.
I WANT TO MAKE IRON MAN LOOK LIKE AN ANTIQUE.
I CAN DO THAT.

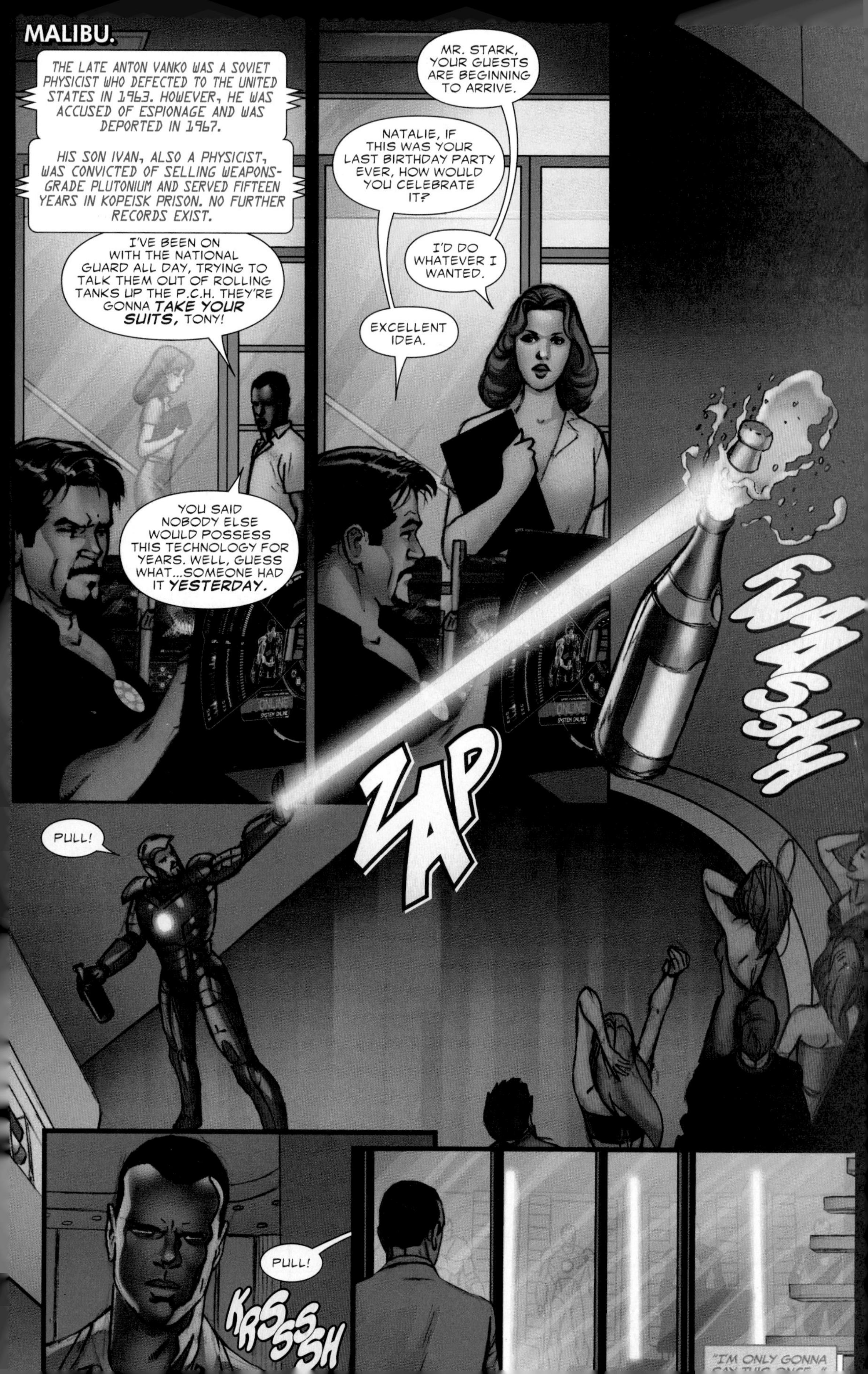

MALIBU.
THE LATE ANTON VANKO WAS A SOVIET PHYSICIST WHO DEFECTED TO THE UNITED STATES IN 1963. HOWEVER, HE WAS ACCUSED OF ESPIONAGE AND WAS DEPORTED IN 1967.
HIS SON IVAN, ALSO A PHYSICIST, WAS CONVICTED OF SELLING WEAPONS-GRADE PLUTONIUM AND SERVED FIFTEEN YEARS IN KOPEISK PRISON. NO FURTHER RECORDS EXIST.
I'VE BEEN ON WITH THE NATIONAL GUARD ALL DAY, TRYING TO TALK THEM OUT OF ROLLING TANKS UP THE P.C.H. THEY'RE GONNA TAKE YOUR SUITS, TONY!
YOU SAID NOBODY ELSE WOULD POSSESS THIS TECHNOLOGY FOR YEARS. WELL, GUESS WHAT...SOMEONE HAD IT YESTERDAY.
MR. STARK, YOUR GUESTS ARE BEGINNING TO ARRIVE.
NATALIE, IF THIS WAS YOUR LAST BIRTHDAY PARTY EVER, HOW WOULD YOU CELEBRATE IT?
I'D DO WHATEVER I WANTED.
EXCELLENT IDEA.
FWASSHH
ZAP
PULL!
PULL!
KRSSSSH
"I'M ONLY GONNA

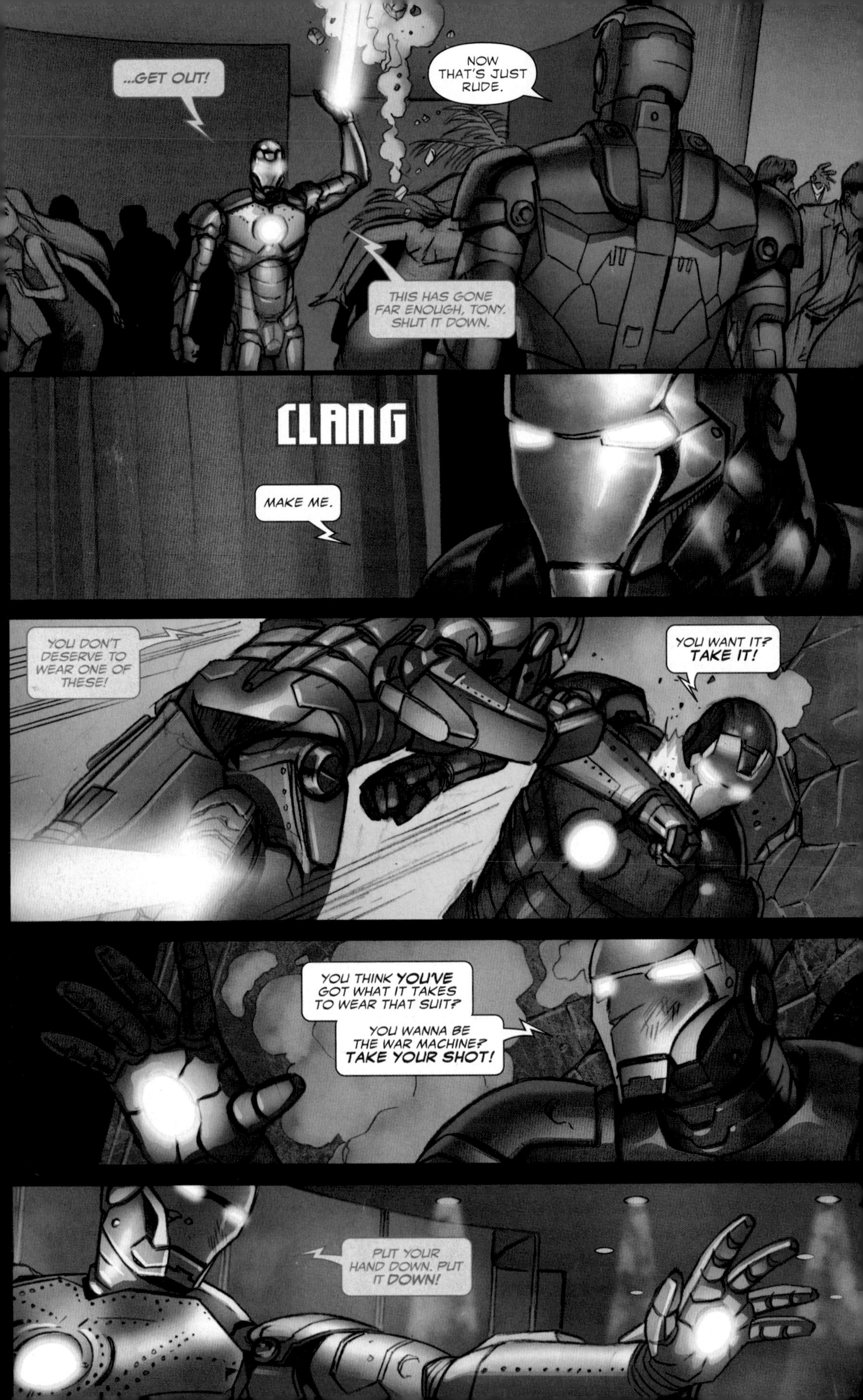
...GET OUT!
NOW THAT'S JUST RUDE.
THIS HAS GONE FAR ENOUGH, TONY. SHUT IT DOWN.
CLANG
MAKE ME.
YOU DON'T DESERVE TO WEAR ONE OF THESE!
YOU WANT IT? TAKE IT!
YOU THINK YOU'VE GOT WHAT IT TAKES TO WEAR THAT SUIT?
YOU WANNA BE THE WAR MACHINE? TAKE YOUR SHOT!
PUT YOUR HAND DOWN. PUT IT DOWN!

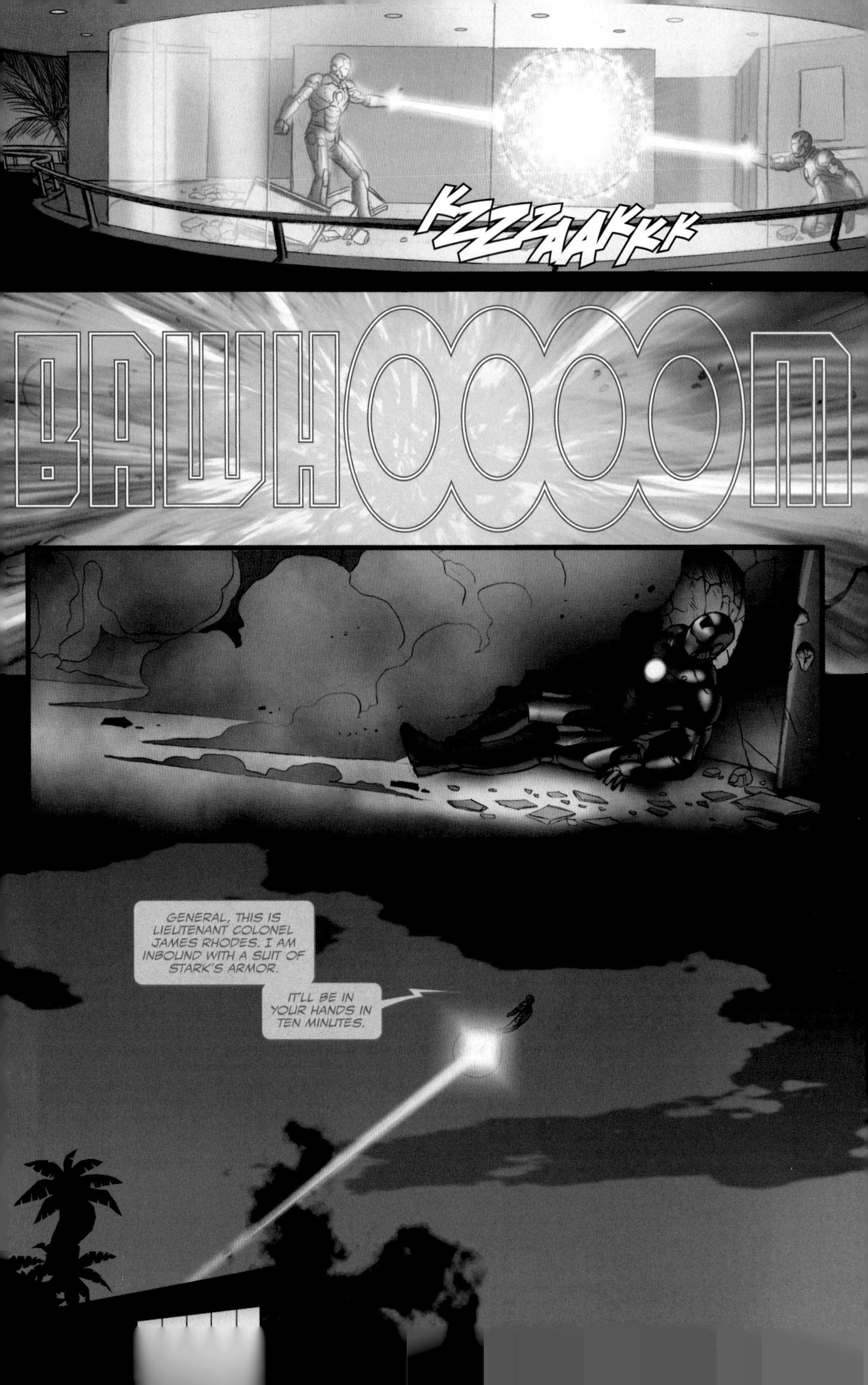
KZZZAAKKK
BAWHOOOOM
GENERAL, THIS IS LIEUTENANT COLONEL JAMES RHODES. I AM INBOUND WITH A SUIT OF STARK'S ARMOR.
IT'LL BE IN YOUR HANDS IN TEN MINUTES.

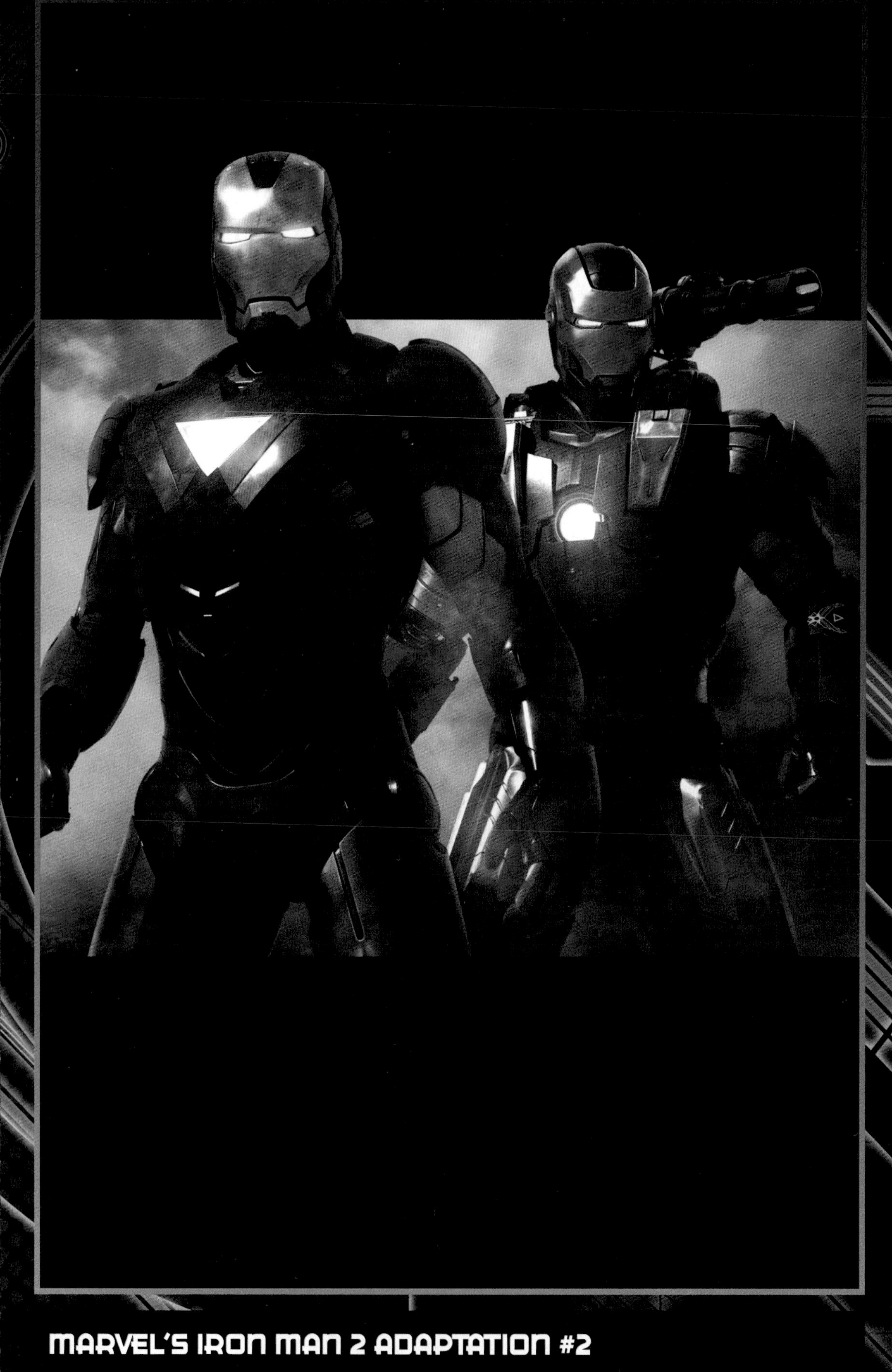

MARVEL'S IRON MAN 2 ADAPTATION #2

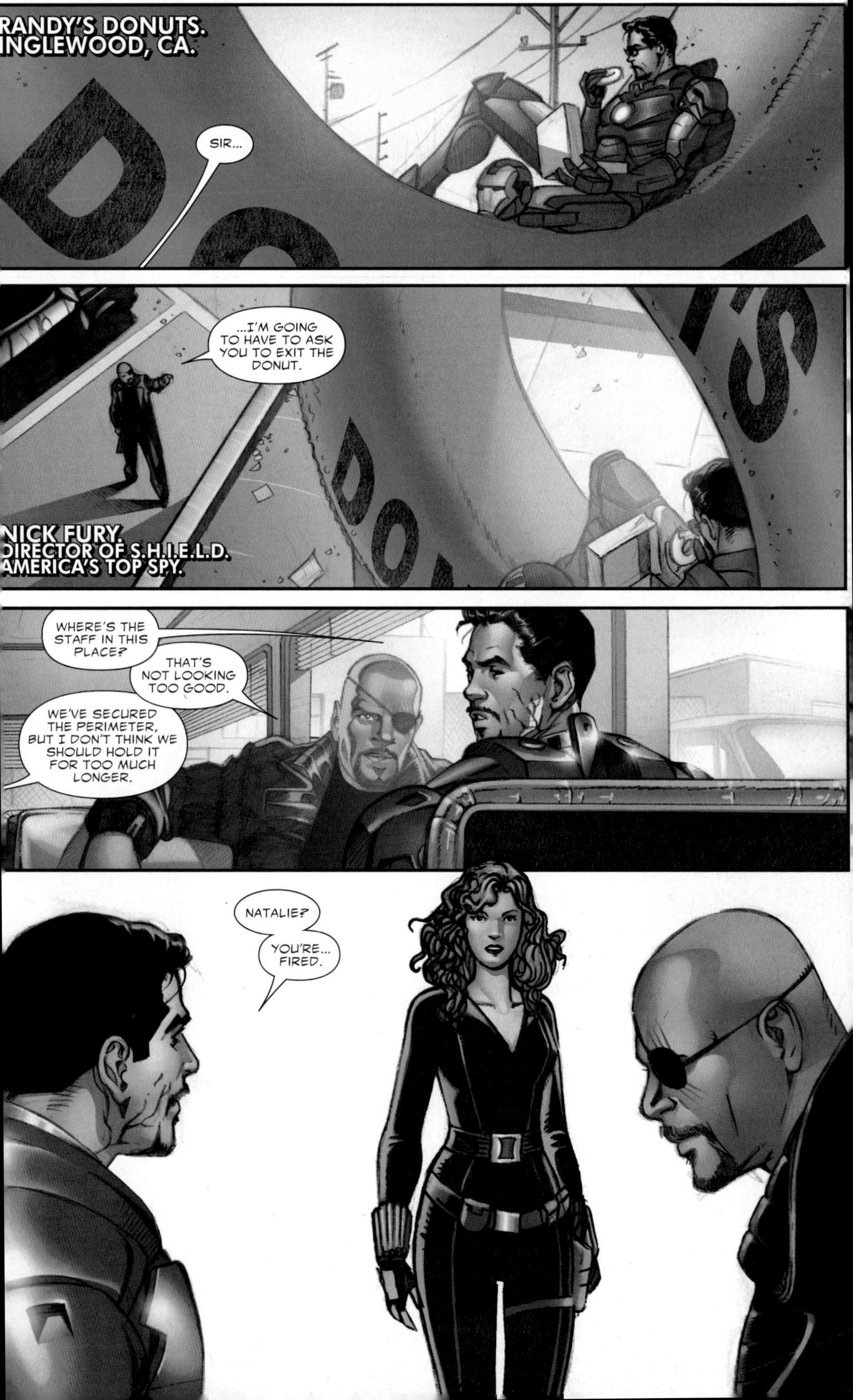

RANDY'S DONUTS.
INGLEWOOD, CA.
SIR...
...I'M GOING TO HAVE TO ASK YOU TO EXIT THE DONUT.
NICK FURY.
DIRECTOR OF S.H.I.E.L.D.
AMERICA'S TOP SPY.
WHERE'S THE STAFF IN THIS PLACE?
THAT'S NOT LOOKING TOO GOOD.
WE'VE SECURED THE PERIMETER, BUT I DON'T THINK WE SHOULD HOLD IT FOR TOO MUCH LONGER.
NATALIE?
YOU'RE... FIRED.

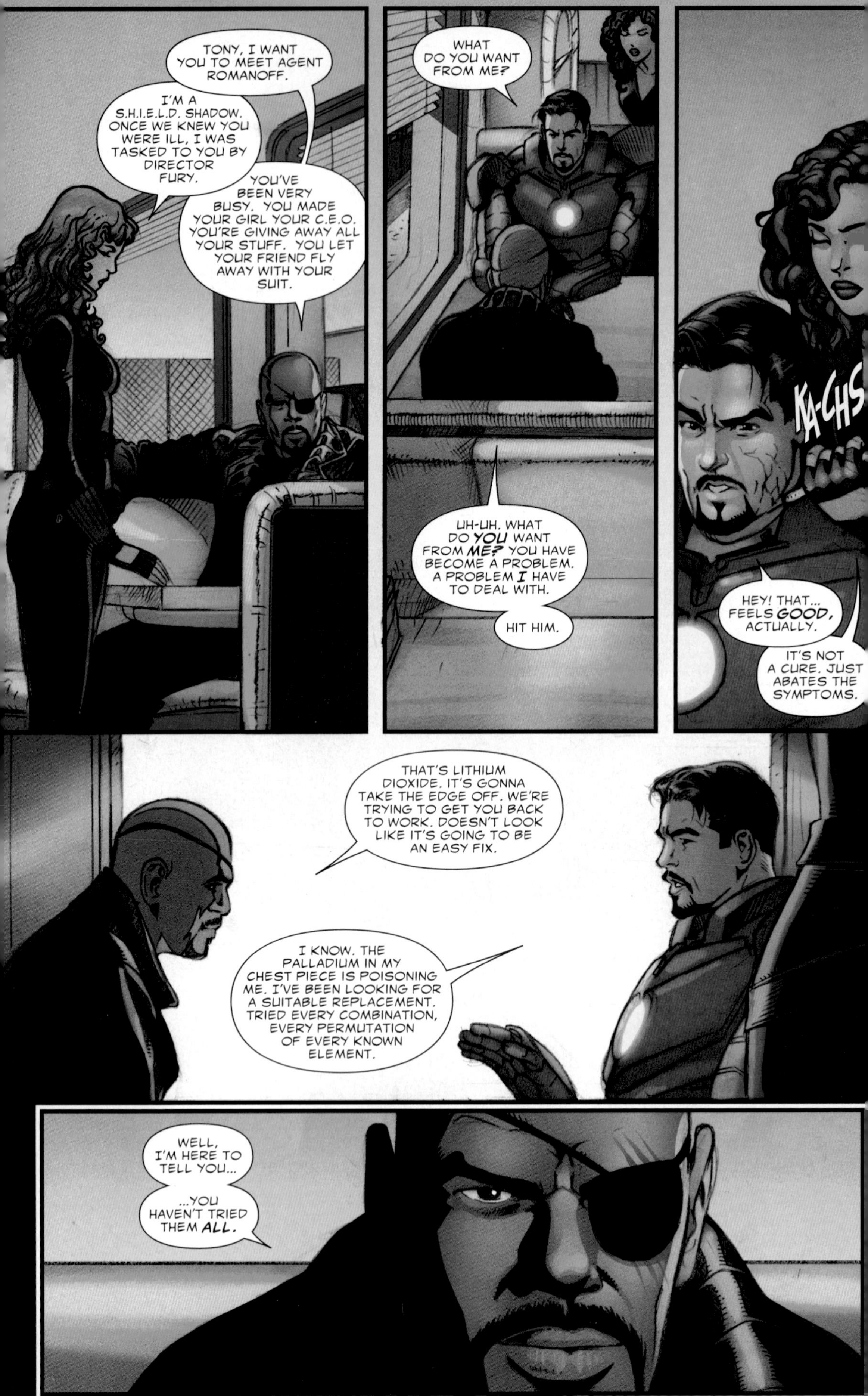
TONY, I WANT YOU TO MEET AGENT ROMANOFF.
I'M A S.H.I.E.L.D. SHADOW. ONCE WE KNEW YOU WERE ILL, I WAS TASKED TO YOU BY DIRECTOR FURY.
YOU'VE BEEN VERY BUSY. YOU MADE YOUR GIRL YOUR C.E.O. YOU'RE GIVING AWAY ALL YOUR STUFF. YOU LET YOUR FRIEND FLY AWAY WITH YOUR SUIT.
WHAT DO YOU WANT FROM ME?
UH-UH. WHAT DO *YOU* WANT FROM *ME?* YOU HAVE BECOME A PROBLEM. A PROBLEM *I* HAVE TO DEAL WITH.
HIT HIM.
KA-CHS
HEY! THAT... FEELS *GOOD,* ACTUALLY.
IT'S NOT A CURE. JUST ABATES THE SYMPTOMS.
THAT'S LITHIUM DIOXIDE. IT'S GONNA TAKE THE EDGE OFF. WE'RE TRYING TO GET YOU BACK TO WORK. DOESN'T LOOK LIKE IT'S GOING TO BE AN EASY FIX.
I KNOW. THE PALLADIUM IN MY CHEST PIECE IS POISONING ME. I'VE BEEN LOOKING FOR A SUITABLE REPLACEMENT. TRIED EVERY COMBINATION, EVERY PERMUTATION OF EVERY KNOWN ELEMENT.
WELL, I'M HERE TO TELL YOU...
...YOU HAVEN'T TRIED THEM *ALL.*

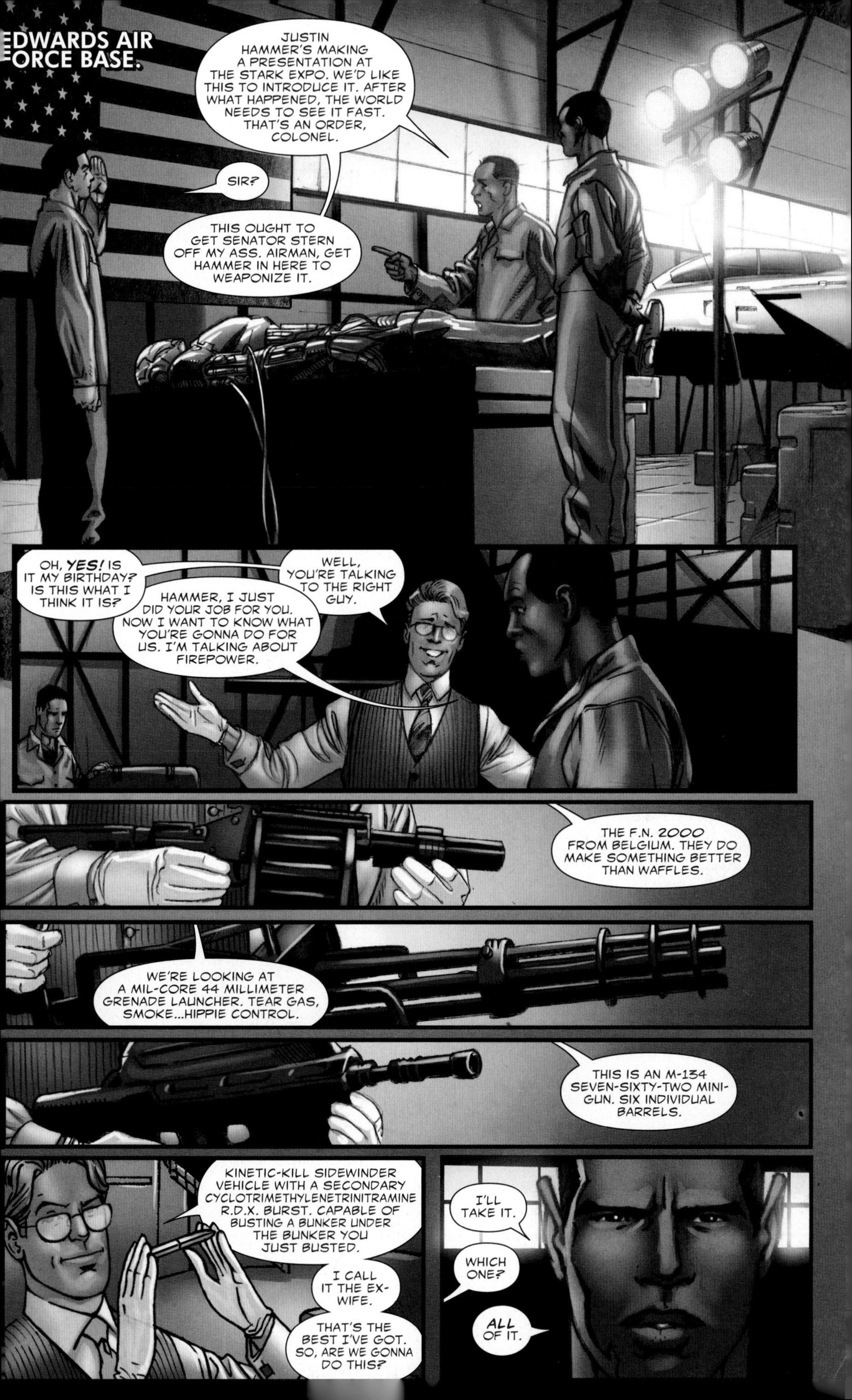

EDWARDS AIR FORCE BASE.
JUSTIN HAMMER'S MAKING A PRESENTATION AT THE STARK EXPO. WE'D LIKE THIS TO INTRODUCE IT. AFTER WHAT HAPPENED, THE WORLD NEEDS TO SEE IT FAST. THAT'S AN ORDER, COLONEL.
SIR?
THIS OUGHT TO GET SENATOR STERN OFF MY ASS. AIRMAN, GET HAMMER IN HERE TO WEAPONIZE IT.
OH, YES! IS IT MY BIRTHDAY? IS THIS WHAT I THINK IT IS?
HAMMER, I JUST DID YOUR JOB FOR YOU. NOW I WANT TO KNOW WHAT YOU'RE GONNA DO FOR US. I'M TALKING ABOUT FIREPOWER.
WELL, YOU'RE TALKING TO THE RIGHT GUY.
THE F.N. 2000 FROM BELGIUM. THEY DO MAKE SOMETHING BETTER THAN WAFFLES.
WE'RE LOOKING AT A MIL-CORE 44 MILLIMETER GRENADE LAUNCHER. TEAR GAS, SMOKE...HIPPIE CONTROL.
THIS IS AN M-134 SEVEN-SIXTY-TWO MINI-GUN. SIX INDIVIDUAL BARRELS.
KINETIC-KILL SIDEWINDER VEHICLE WITH A SECONDARY CYCLOTRIMETHYLENETRINITRAMINE R.D.X. BURST. CAPABLE OF BUSTING A BUNKER UNDER THE BUNKER YOU JUST BUSTED.
I CALL IT THE EX-WIFE.
THAT'S THE BEST I'VE GOT. SO, ARE WE GONNA DO THIS?
I'LL TAKE IT.
WHICH ONE?
ALL OF IT.

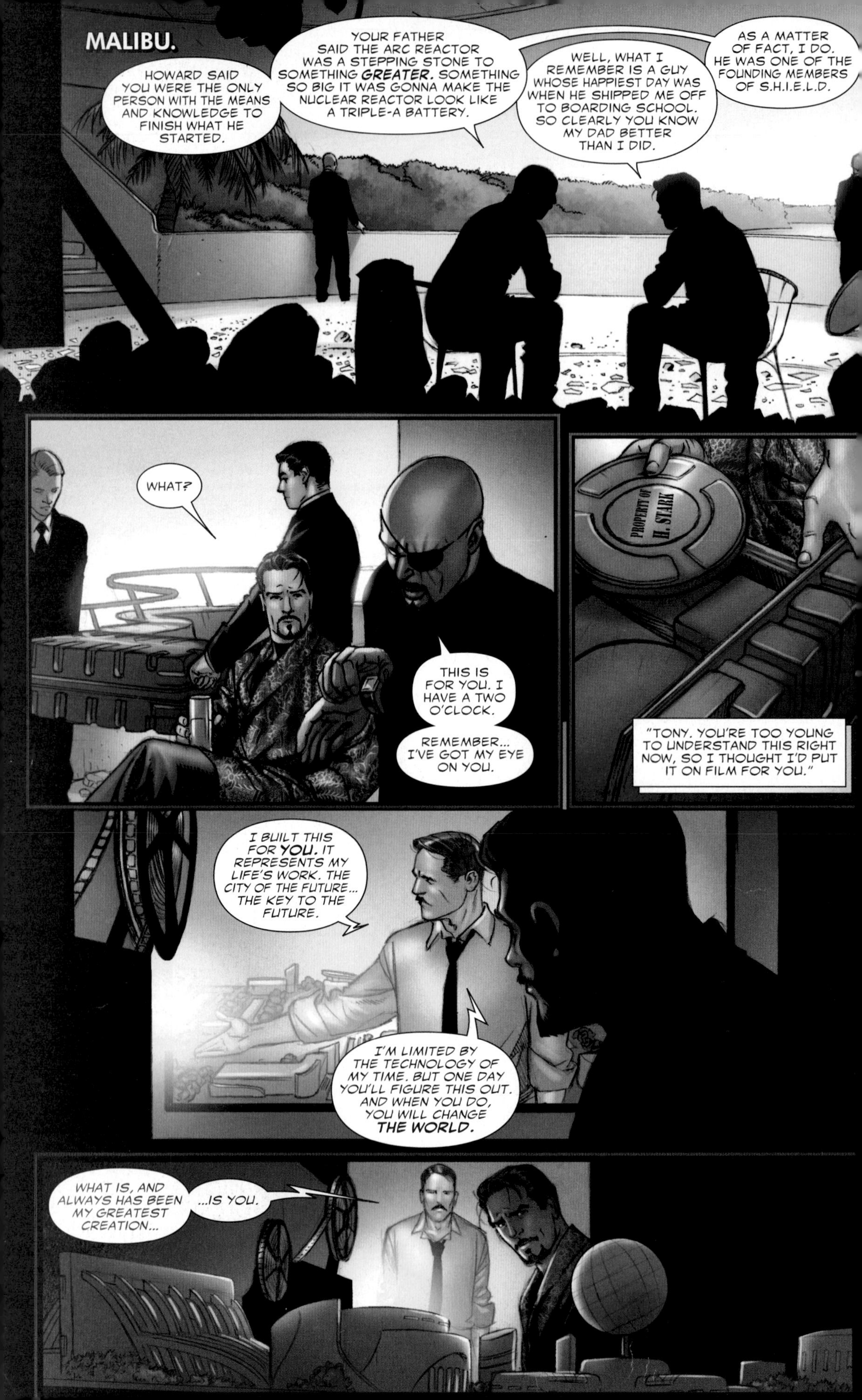
MALIBU.
HOWARD SAID YOU WERE THE ONLY PERSON WITH THE MEANS AND KNOWLEDGE TO FINISH WHAT HE STARTED.
YOUR FATHER SAID THE ARC REACTOR WAS A STEPPING STONE TO SOMETHING GREATER. SOMETHING SO BIG IT WAS GONNA MAKE THE NUCLEAR REACTOR LOOK LIKE A TRIPLE-A BATTERY.
WELL, WHAT I REMEMBER IS A GUY WHOSE HAPPIEST DAY WAS WHEN HE SHIPPED ME OFF TO BOARDING SCHOOL. SO CLEARLY YOU KNOW MY DAD BETTER THAN I DID.
AS A MATTER OF FACT, I DO. HE WAS ONE OF THE FOUNDING MEMBERS OF S.H.I.E.L.D.
WHAT?
THIS IS FOR YOU. I HAVE A TWO O'CLOCK.
REMEMBER... I'VE GOT MY EYE ON YOU.
PROPERTY OF H. STARK
"TONY. YOU'RE TOO YOUNG TO UNDERSTAND THIS RIGHT NOW, SO I THOUGHT I'D PUT IT ON FILM FOR YOU."
I BUILT THIS FOR YOU. IT REPRESENTS MY LIFE'S WORK. THE CITY OF THE FUTURE... THE KEY TO THE FUTURE.
I'M LIMITED BY THE TECHNOLOGY OF MY TIME. BUT ONE DAY YOU'LL FIGURE THIS OUT. AND WHEN YOU DO, YOU WILL CHANGE THE WORLD.
WHAT IS, AND ALWAYS HAS BEEN MY GREATEST CREATION...
...IS YOU.

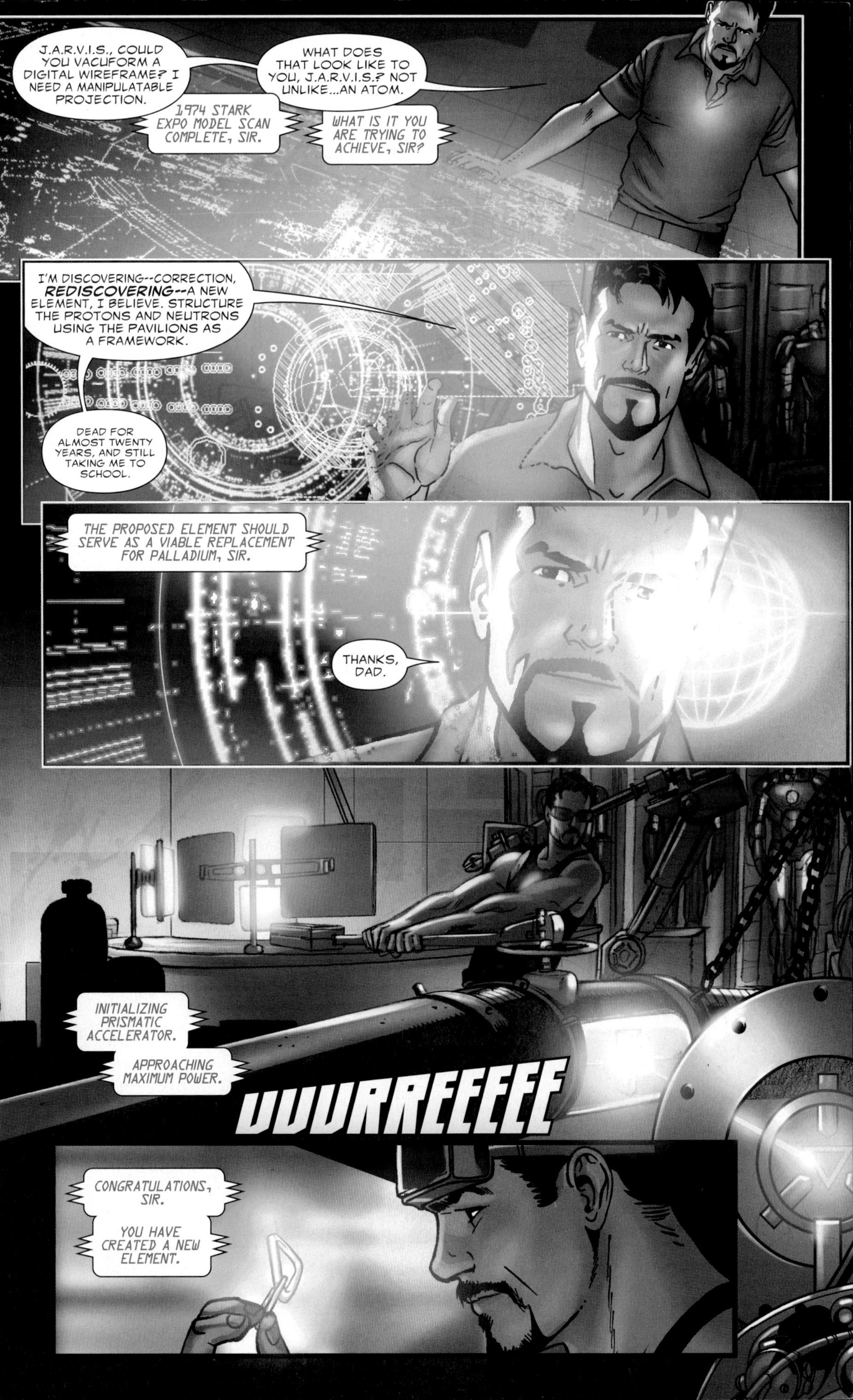
J.A.R.V.I.S., COULD YOU VACUFORM A DIGITAL WIREFRAME? I NEED A MANIPULATABLE PROJECTION.
1974 STARK EXPO MODEL SCAN COMPLETE, SIR.
WHAT DOES THAT LOOK LIKE TO YOU, J.A.R.V.I.S.? NOT UNLIKE...AN ATOM.
WHAT IS IT YOU ARE TRYING TO ACHIEVE, SIR?
I'M DISCOVERING--CORRECTION, REDISCOVERING--A NEW ELEMENT, I BELIEVE. STRUCTURE THE PROTONS AND NEUTRONS USING THE PAVILIONS AS A FRAMEWORK.
DEAD FOR ALMOST TWENTY YEARS, AND STILL TAKING ME TO SCHOOL.
THE PROPOSED ELEMENT SHOULD SERVE AS A VIABLE REPLACEMENT FOR PALLADIUM, SIR.
THANKS, DAD.
INITIALIZING PRISMATIC ACCELERATOR.
APPROACHING MAXIMUM POWER.
VUURREEEEE
CONGRATULATIONS, SIR.
YOU HAVE CREATED A NEW ELEMENT.

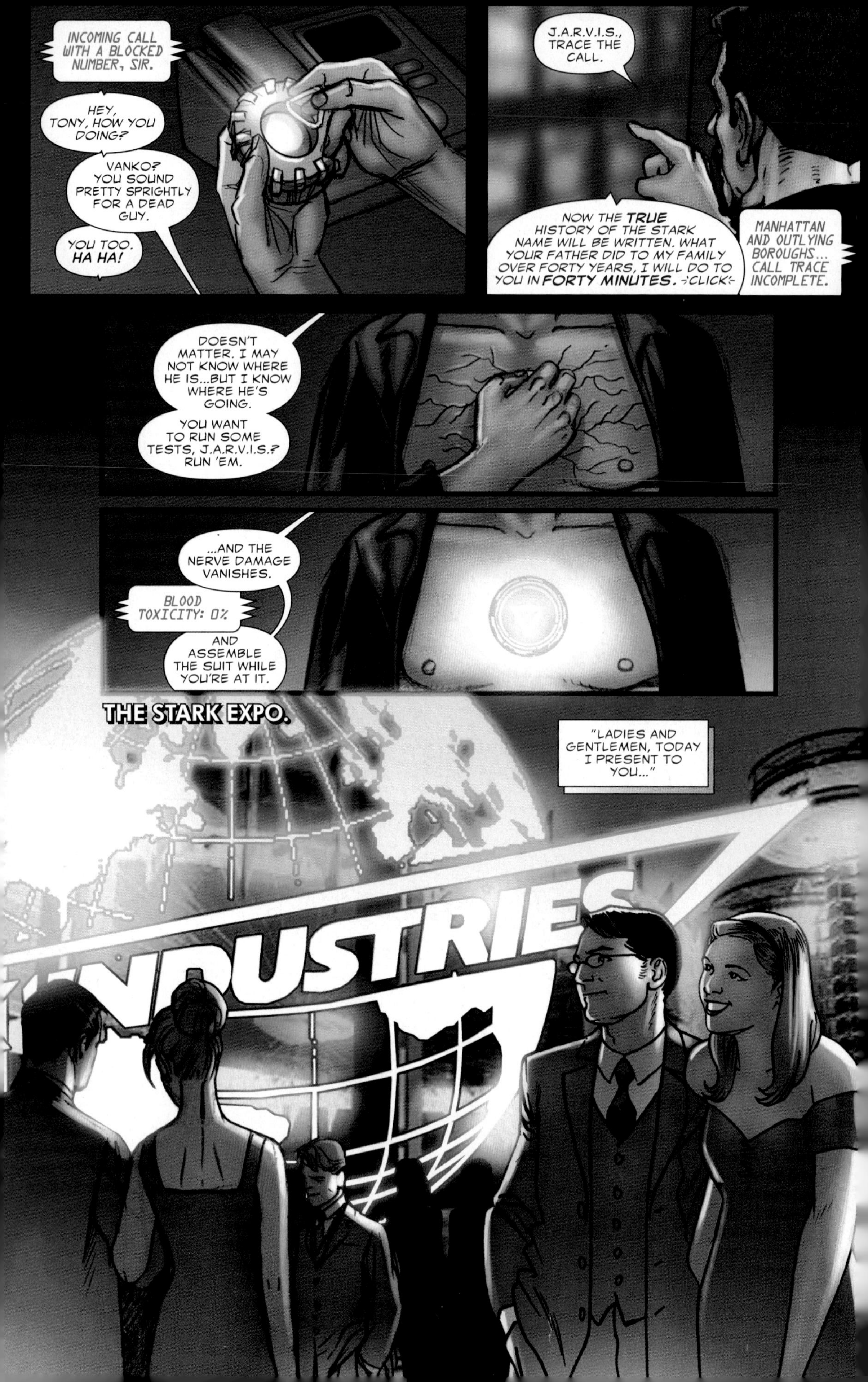
INCOMING CALL WITH A BLOCKED NUMBER, SIR.
HEY, TONY, HOW YOU DOING?
VANKO? YOU SOUND PRETTY SPRIGHTLY FOR A DEAD GUY.
YOU TOO. HA HA!
J.A.R.V.I.S., TRACE THE CALL.
NOW THE TRUE HISTORY OF THE STARK NAME WILL BE WRITTEN. WHAT YOUR FATHER DID TO MY FAMILY OVER FORTY YEARS, I WILL DO TO YOU IN FORTY MINUTES. CLICK
MANHATTAN AND OUTLYING BOROUGHS... CALL TRACE INCOMPLETE.
DOESN'T MATTER. I MAY NOT KNOW WHERE HE IS...BUT I KNOW WHERE HE'S GOING.
YOU WANT TO RUN SOME TESTS, J.A.R.V.I.S.? RUN 'EM.
...AND THE NERVE DAMAGE VANISHES.
BLOOD TOXICITY: 0%
AND ASSEMBLE THE SUIT WHILE YOU'RE AT IT.
THE STARK EXPO.
"LADIES AND GENTLEMEN, TODAY I PRESENT TO YOU..."
INDUSTRIES

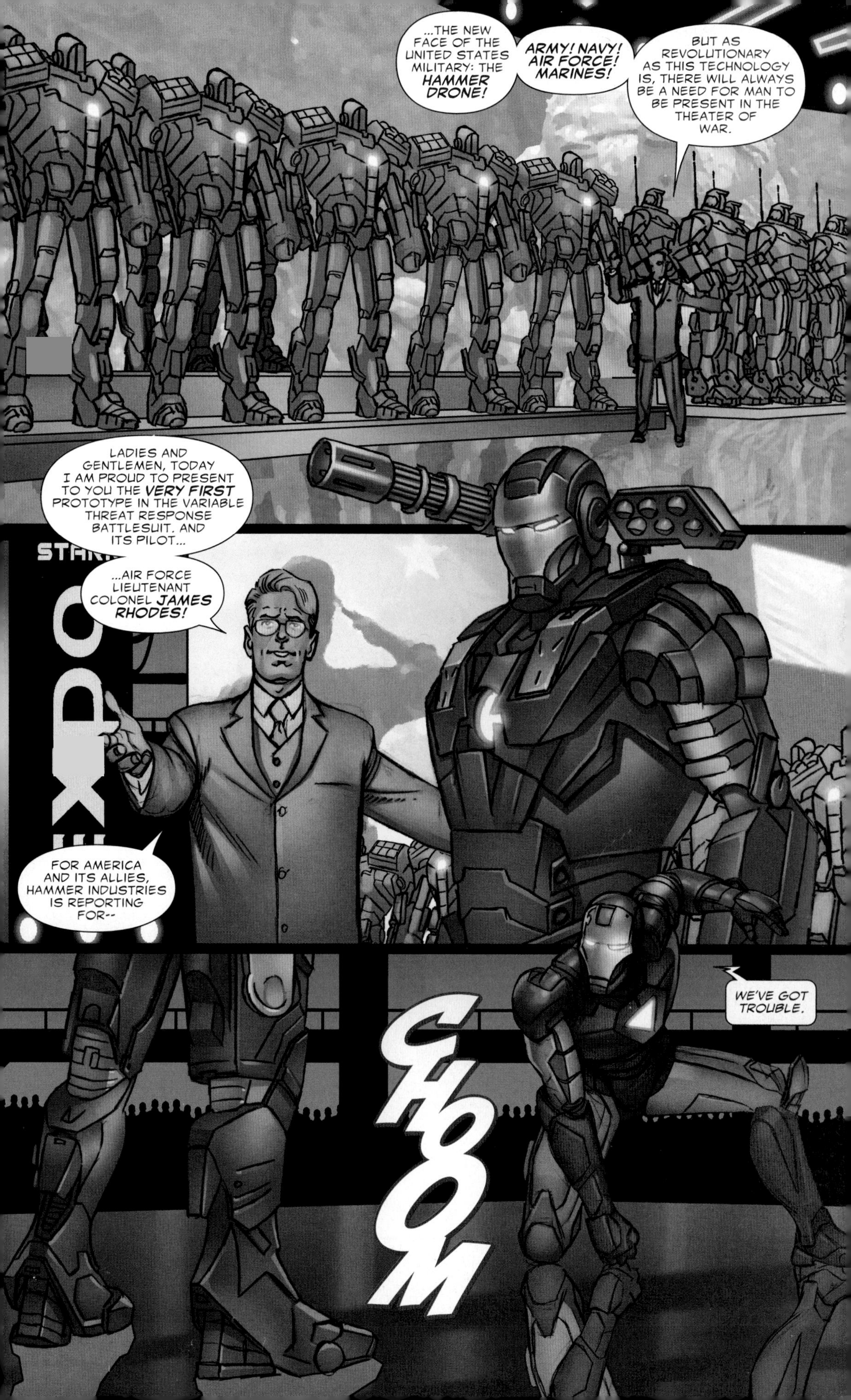

...THE NEW FACE OF THE UNITED STATES MILITARY: THE *HAMMER DRONE!*
ARMY! NAVY! AIR FORCE! MARINES!
BUT AS REVOLUTIONARY AS THIS TECHNOLOGY IS, THERE WILL ALWAYS BE A NEED FOR MAN TO BE PRESENT IN THE THEATER OF WAR.
LADIES AND GENTLEMEN, TODAY I AM PROUD TO PRESENT TO YOU THE *VERY FIRST* PROTOTYPE IN THE VARIABLE THREAT RESPONSE BATTLESUIT. AND ITS PILOT...
...AIR FORCE LIEUTENANT COLONEL *JAMES RHODES!*
FOR AMERICA AND ITS ALLIES, HAMMER INDUSTRIES IS REPORTING FOR--
CHOOM
WE'VE GOT TROUBLE.

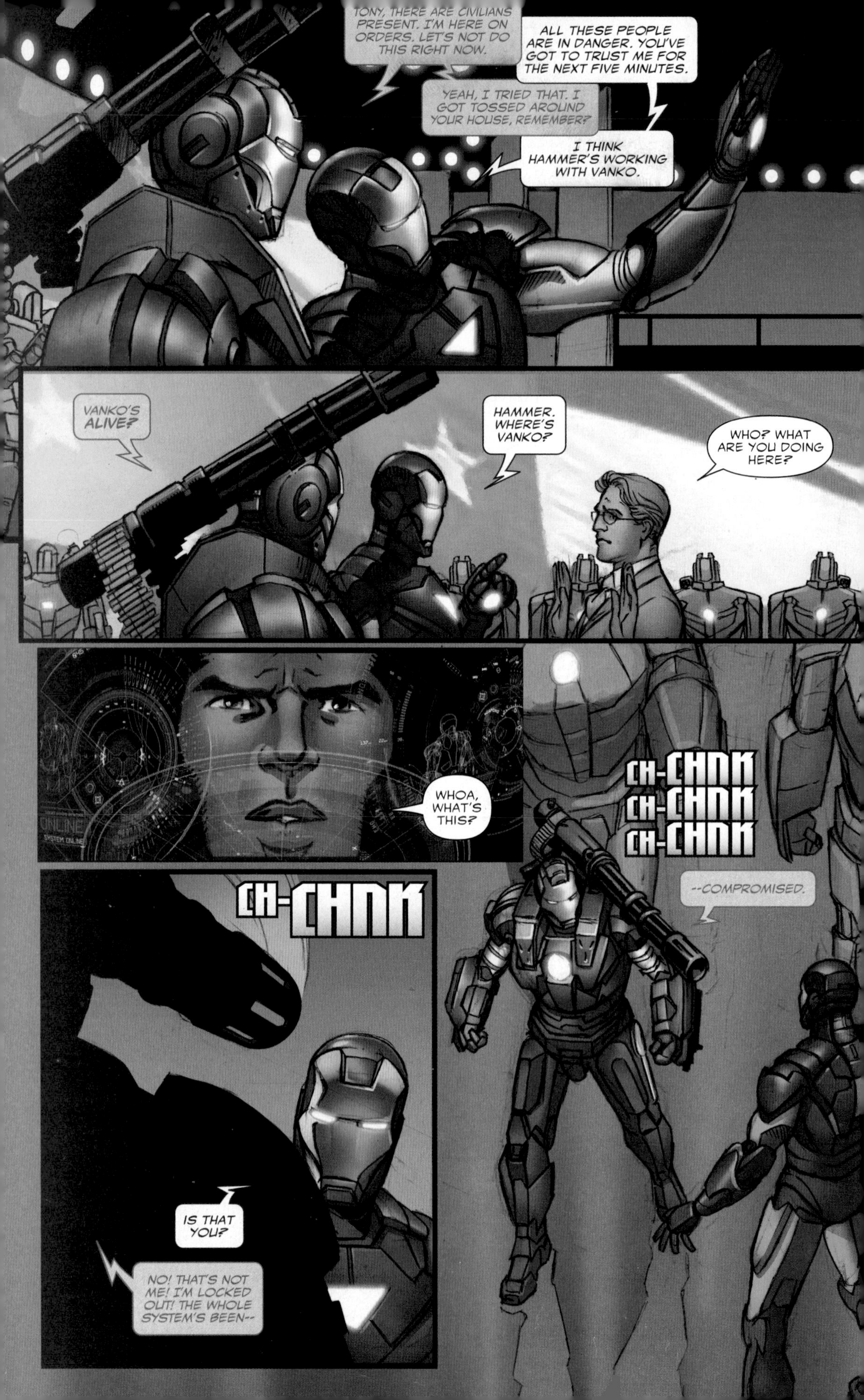
TONY, THERE ARE CIVILIANS PRESENT. I'M HERE ON ORDERS. LET'S NOT DO THIS RIGHT NOW.
ALL THESE PEOPLE ARE IN DANGER. YOU'VE GOT TO TRUST ME FOR THE NEXT FIVE MINUTES.
YEAH, I TRIED THAT. I GOT TOSSED AROUND YOUR HOUSE, REMEMBER?
I THINK HAMMER'S WORKING WITH VANKO.
VANKO'S ALIVE?
HAMMER. WHERE'S VANKO?
WHO? WHAT ARE YOU DOING HERE?
WHOA, WHAT'S THIS?
CH-CHNK
CH-CHNK
CH-CHNK
CH-CHNK
--COMPROMISED.
IS THAT YOU?
NO! THAT'S NOT ME! I'M LOCKED OUT! THE WHOLE SYSTEM'S BEEN--

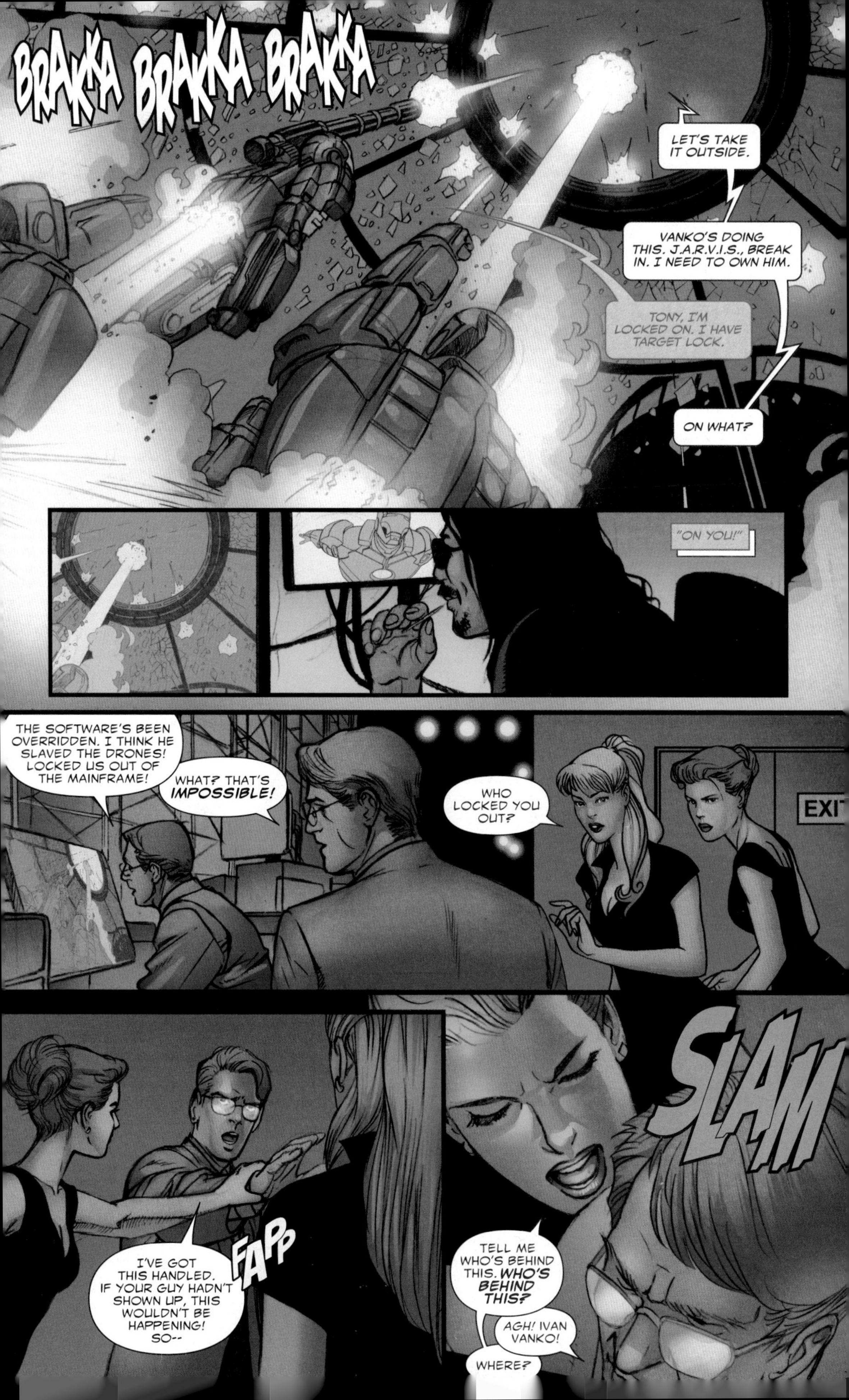
BRAKKA BRAKKA BRAKKA
LET'S TAKE IT OUTSIDE.
VANKO'S DOING THIS. J.A.R.V.I.S., BREAK IN. I NEED TO OWN HIM.
TONY, I'M LOCKED ON. I HAVE TARGET LOCK.
ON WHAT?
"ON YOU!"
THE SOFTWARE'S BEEN OVERRIDDEN. I THINK HE SLAVED THE DRONES! LOCKED US OUT OF THE MAINFRAME!
WHAT? THAT'S *IMPOSSIBLE!*
WHO LOCKED YOU OUT?
EXIT
I'VE GOT THIS HANDLED. IF YOUR GUY HADN'T SHOWN UP, THIS WOULDN'T BE HAPPENING! SO--
FAPP
SLAM
TELL ME WHO'S BEHIND THIS. *WHO'S BEHIND THIS?*
AGH! IVAN VANKO!
WHERE?

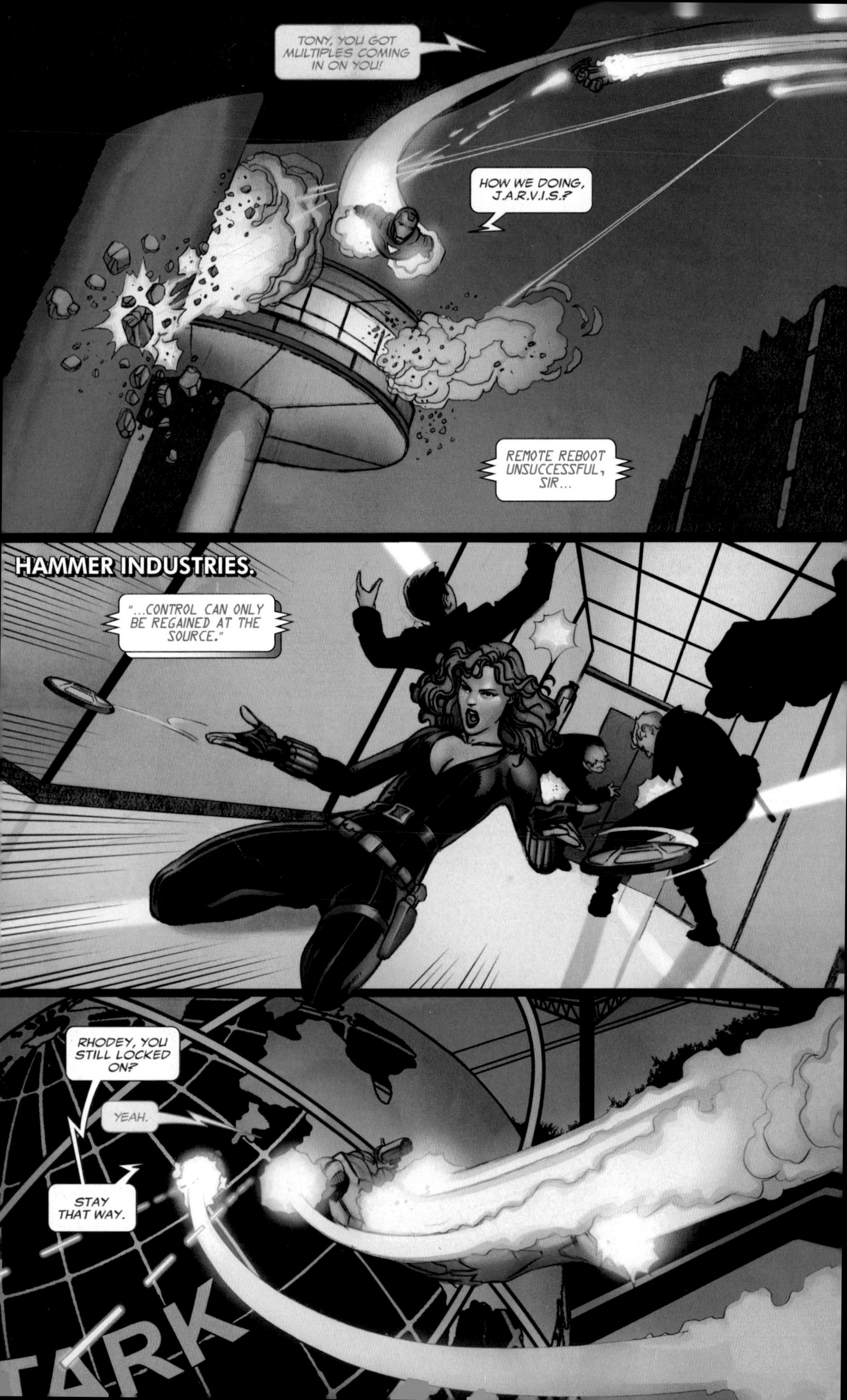
TONY, YOU GOT MULTIPLES COMING IN ON YOU!
HOW WE DOING, J.A.R.V.I.S.?
REMOTE REBOOT UNSUCCESSFUL, SIR...
HAMMER INDUSTRIES.
"...CONTROL CAN ONLY BE REGAINED AT THE SOURCE."
RHODEY, YOU STILL LOCKED ON?
YEAH.
STAY THAT WAY.

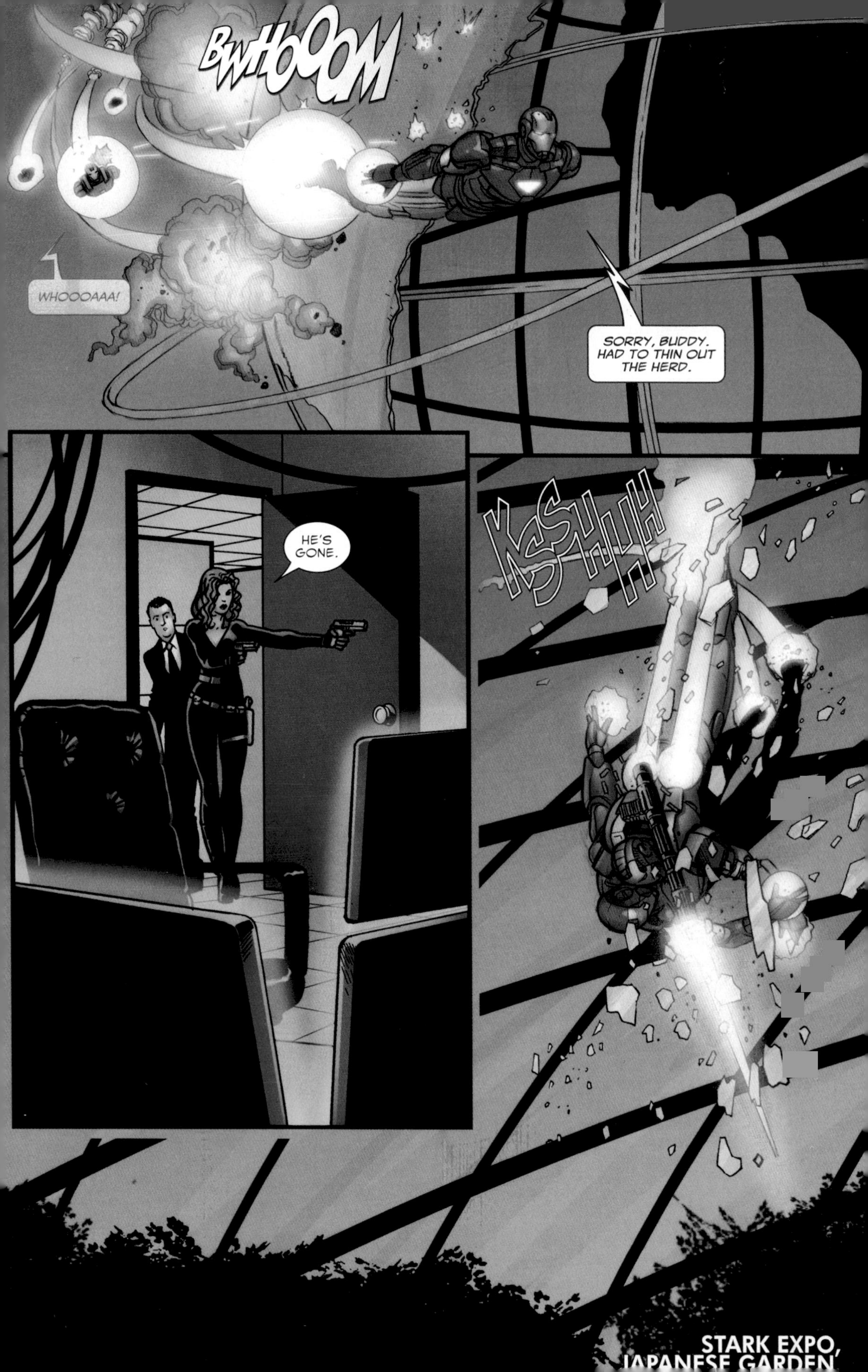
BWHOOOM
WHOOOAAA!
SORRY, BUDDY. HAD TO THIN OUT THE HERD.
HE'S GONE.
KSHHH
STARK EXPO,
JAPANESE GARDEN

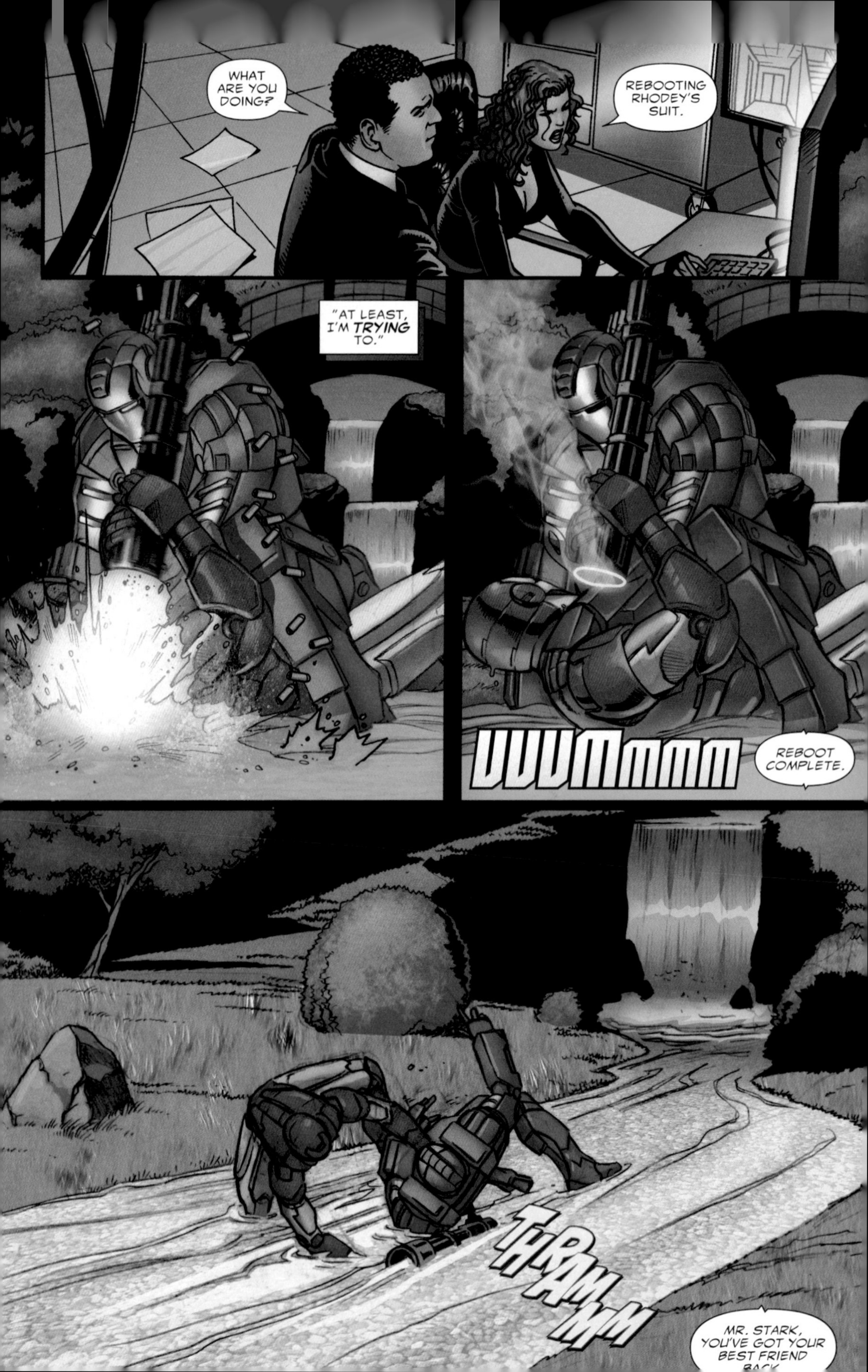
WHAT ARE YOU DOING?
REBOOTING RHODEY'S SUIT.
"AT LEAST, I'M TRYING TO."
VVVMMMM
REBOOT COMPLETE.
THRAMMM
MR. STARK, YOU'VE GOT YOUR BEST FRIEND

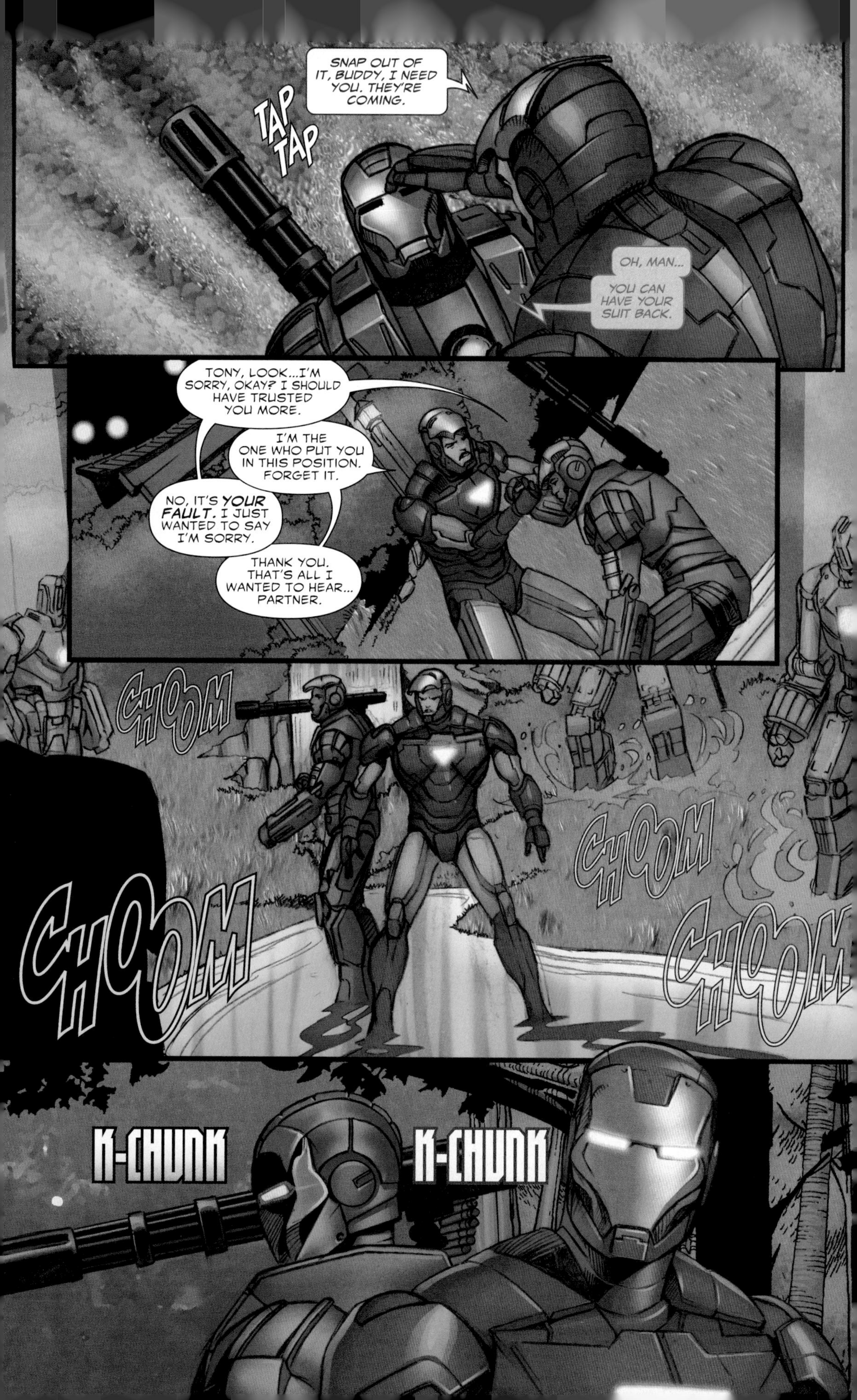

SNAP OUT OF IT, BUDDY, I NEED YOU. THEY'RE COMING.
TAP TAP
OH, MAN...
YOU CAN HAVE YOUR SUIT BACK.
TONY, LOOK...I'M SORRY, OKAY? I SHOULD HAVE TRUSTED YOU MORE.
I'M THE ONE WHO PUT YOU IN THIS POSITION. FORGET IT.
NO, IT'S YOUR FAULT. I JUST WANTED TO SAY I'M SORRY.
THANK YOU. THAT'S ALL I WANTED TO HEAR... PARTNER.
CHOOM
CHOOM
CHOOM
CHOOM
K-CHUNK
K-CHUNK

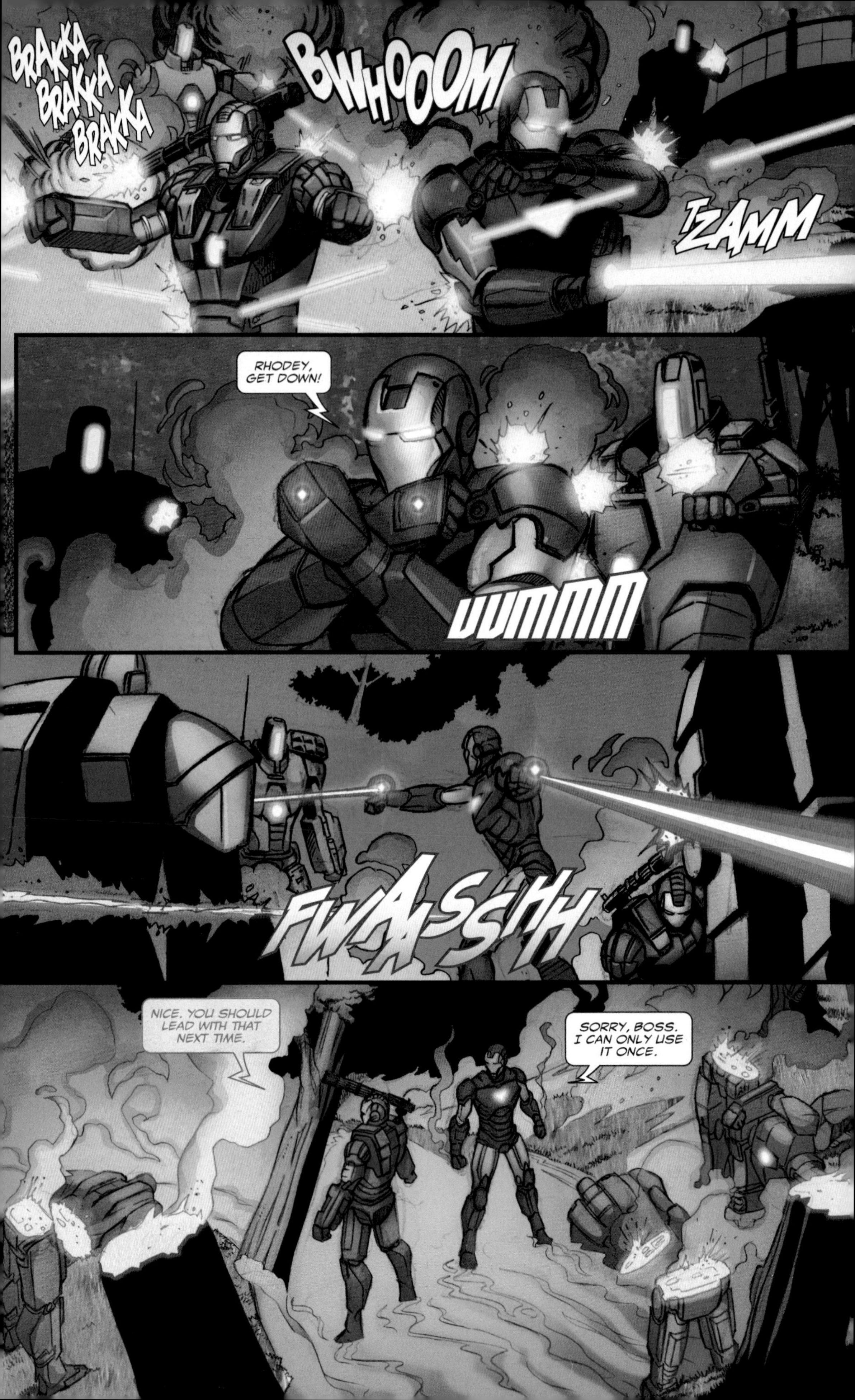
BRAKKA BRAKKA BRAKKA
BWHOOOM
TZAMM
RHODEY, GET DOWN!
VUMMM
FWASSHH
NICE. YOU SHOULD LEAD WITH THAT NEXT TIME.
SORRY, BOSS. I CAN ONLY USE IT ONCE.

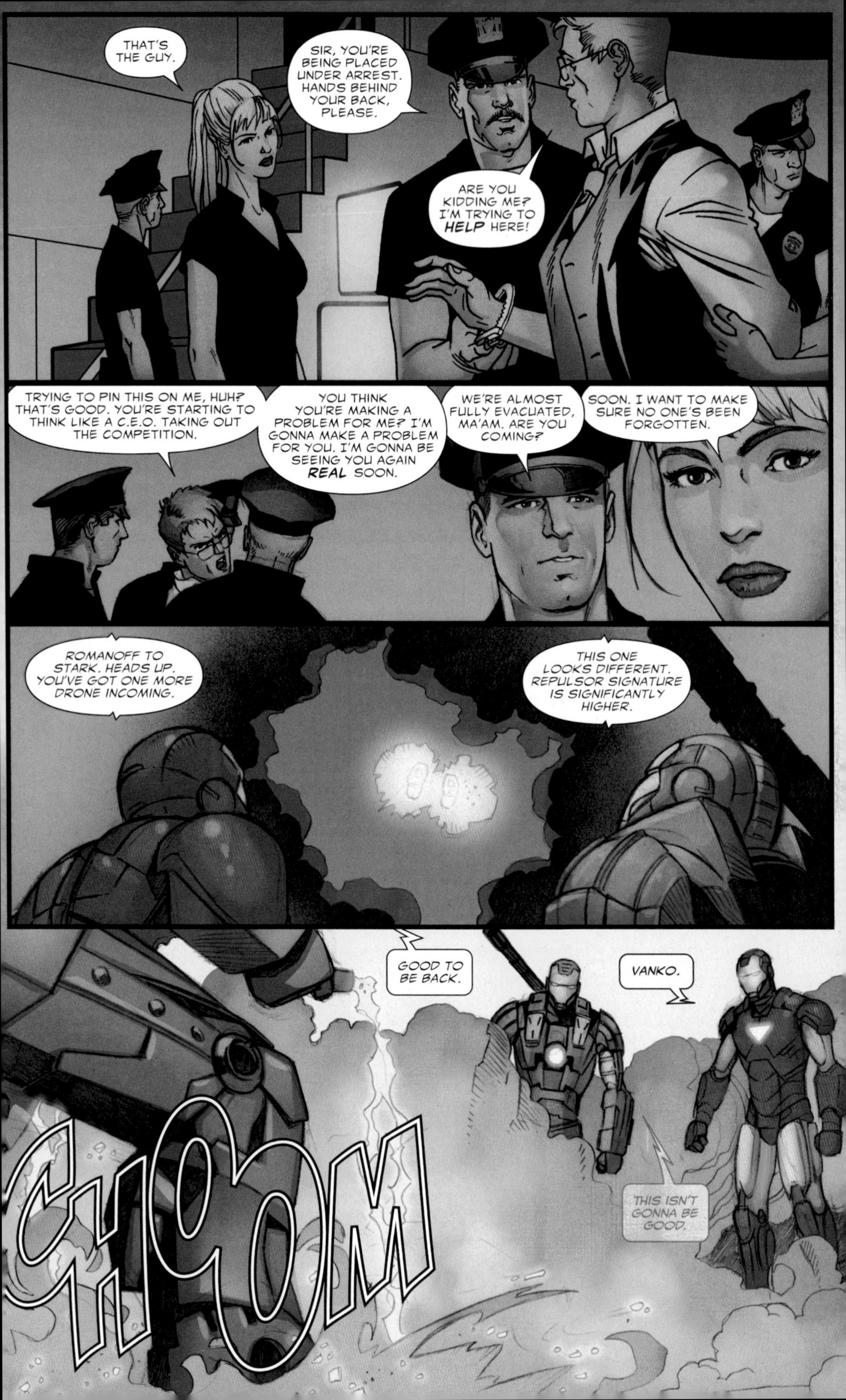
THAT'S THE GUY.
SIR, YOU'RE BEING PLACED UNDER ARREST. HANDS BEHIND YOUR BACK, PLEASE.
ARE YOU KIDDING ME? I'M TRYING TO **HELP** HERE!
TRYING TO PIN THIS ON ME, HUH? THAT'S GOOD. YOU'RE STARTING TO THINK LIKE A C.E.O. TAKING OUT THE COMPETITION.
YOU THINK YOU'RE MAKING A PROBLEM FOR ME? I'M GONNA MAKE A PROBLEM FOR YOU. I'M GONNA BE SEEING YOU AGAIN **REAL** SOON.
WE'RE ALMOST FULLY EVACUATED, MA'AM. ARE YOU COMING?
SOON. I WANT TO MAKE SURE NO ONE'S BEEN FORGOTTEN.
ROMANOFF TO STARK. HEADS UP. YOU'VE GOT ONE MORE DRONE INCOMING.
THIS ONE LOOKS DIFFERENT. REPULSOR SIGNATURE IS SIGNIFICANTLY HIGHER.
CHOOM
GOOD TO BE BACK.
VANKO.
THIS ISN'T GONNA BE GOOD.

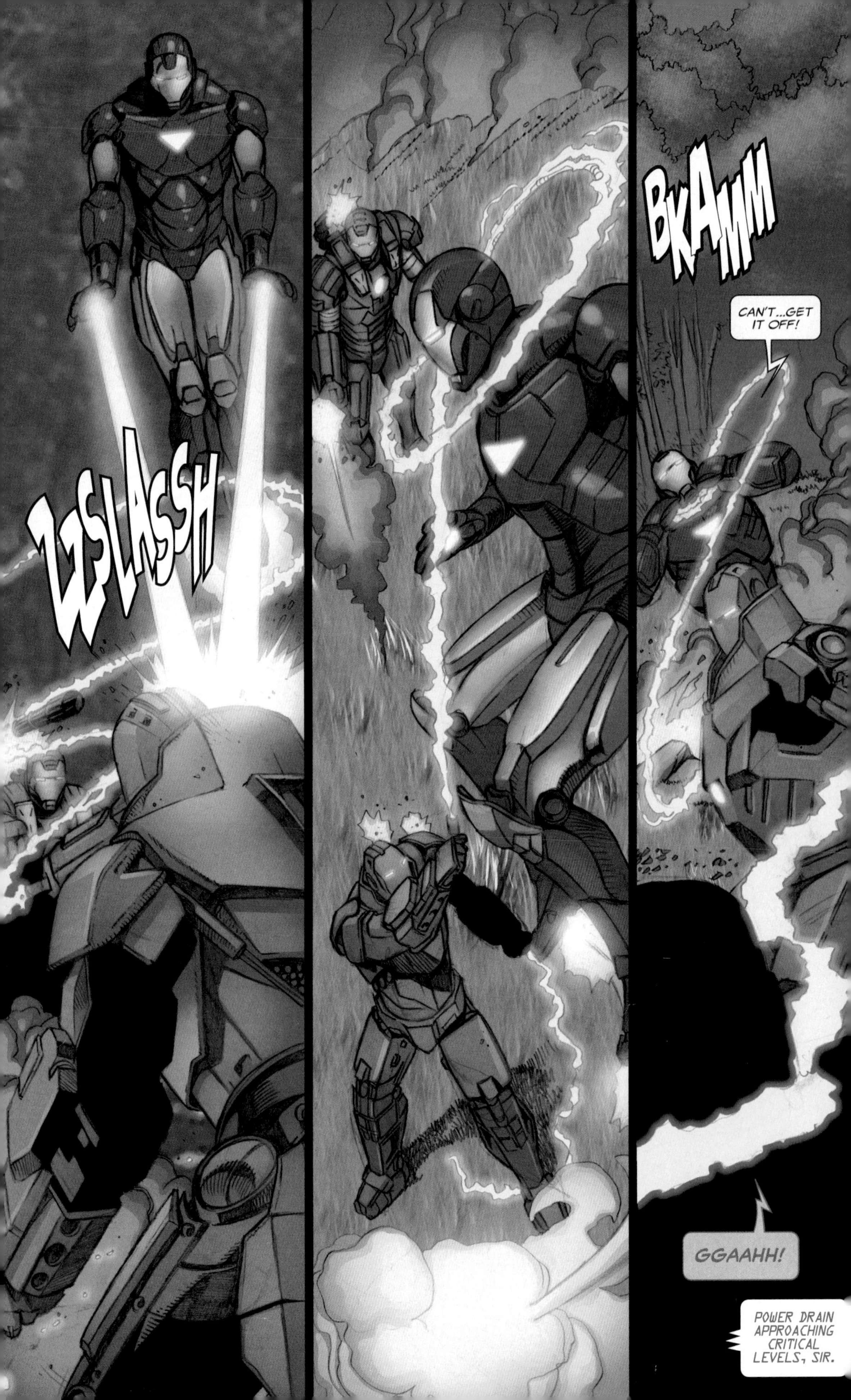
ZZSLASSH
BKAMM
CAN'T...GET IT OFF!
GGAAHH!
POWER DRAIN APPROACHING CRITICAL LEVELS, SIR.

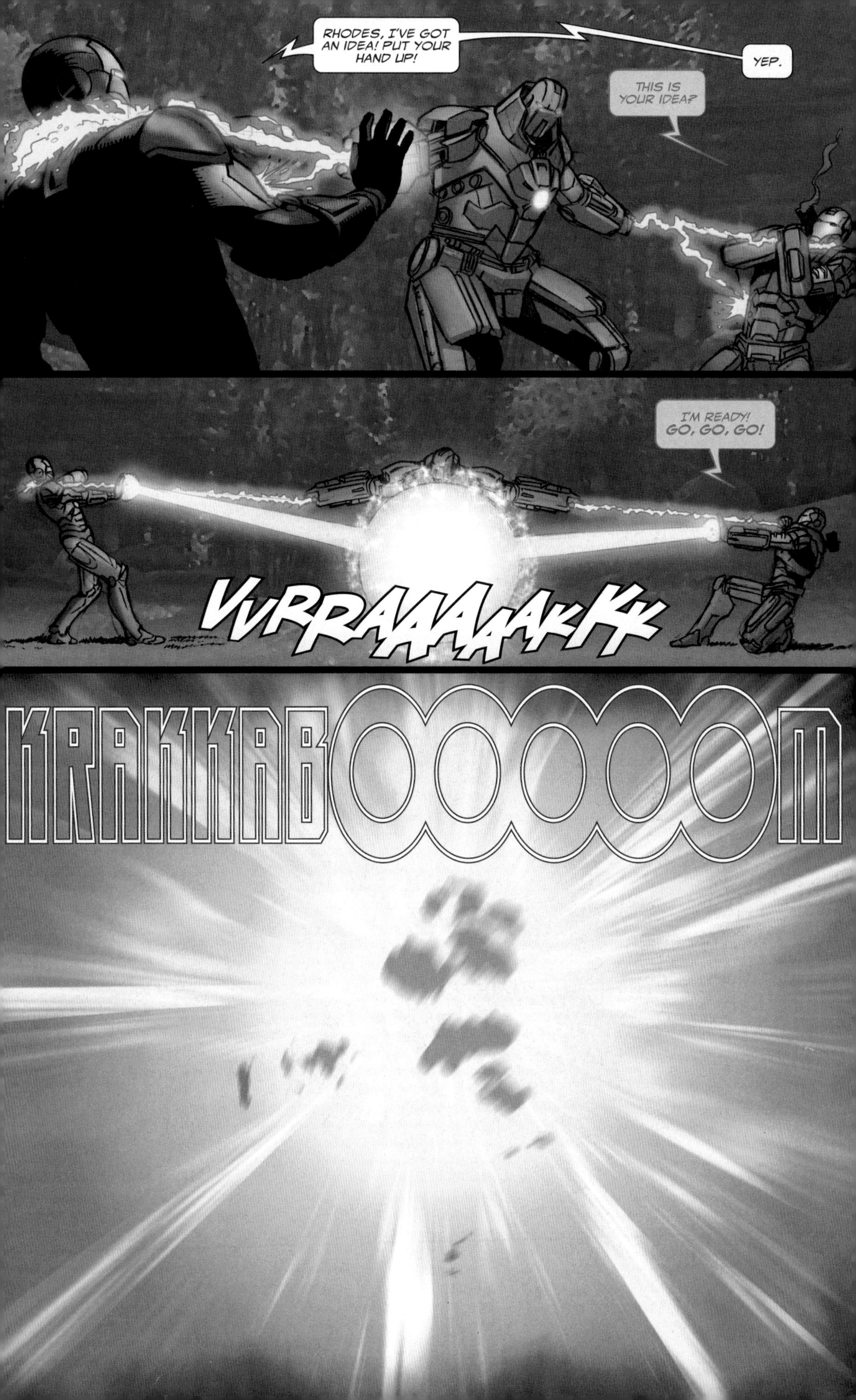
RHODES, I'VE GOT AN IDEA! PUT YOUR HAND UP!
YEP.
THIS IS YOUR IDEA?
I'M READY! GO, GO, GO!
VVRRAAAAAAKKK
KRAKKABOOOOOOM

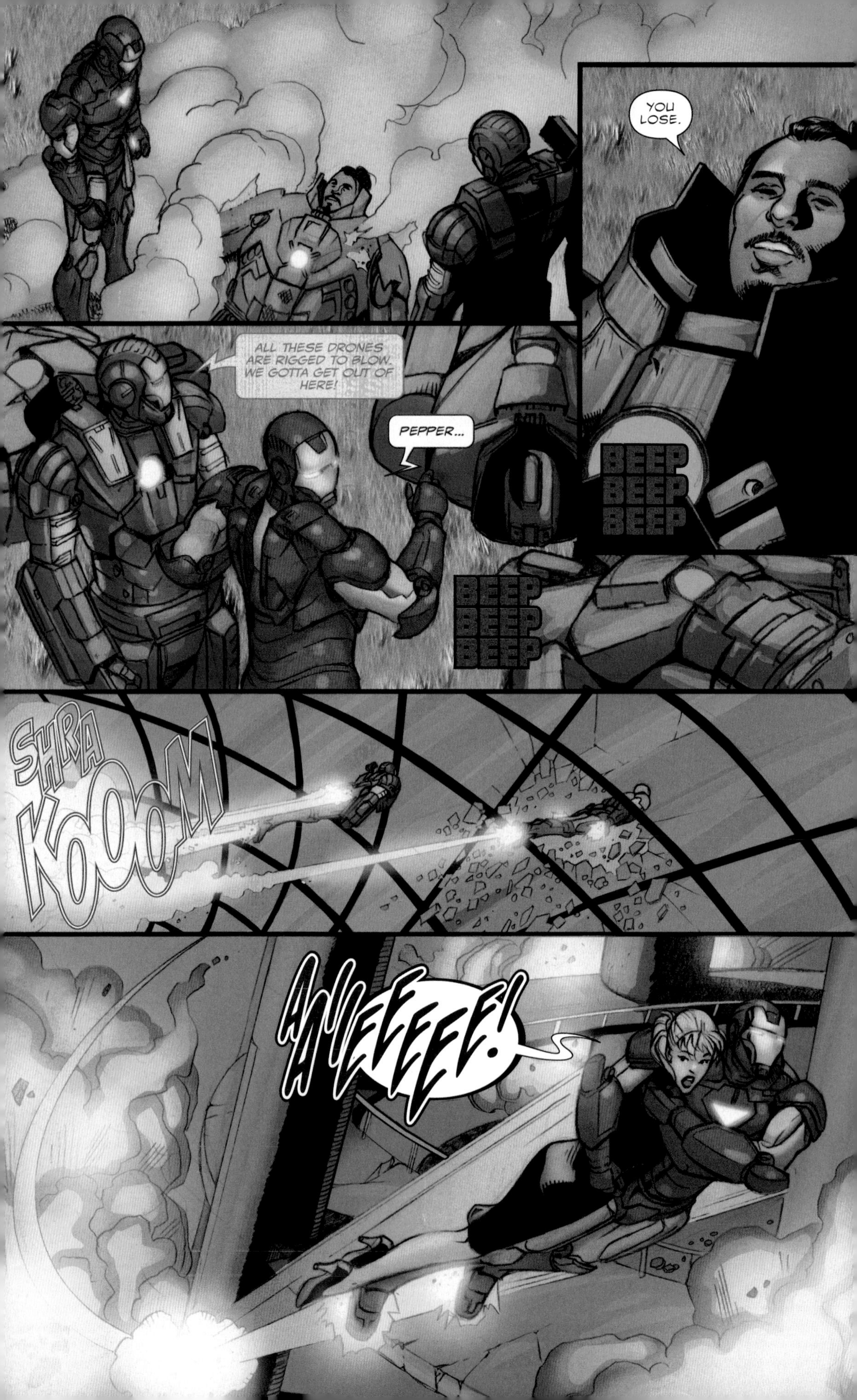
YOU LOSE.
ALL THESE DRONES ARE RIGGED TO BLOW. WE GOTTA GET OUT OF HERE!
PEPPER...
BEEP BEEP BEEP
BEEP BEEP BEEP
SHRA KOOOOM
AAIIEEEEE!

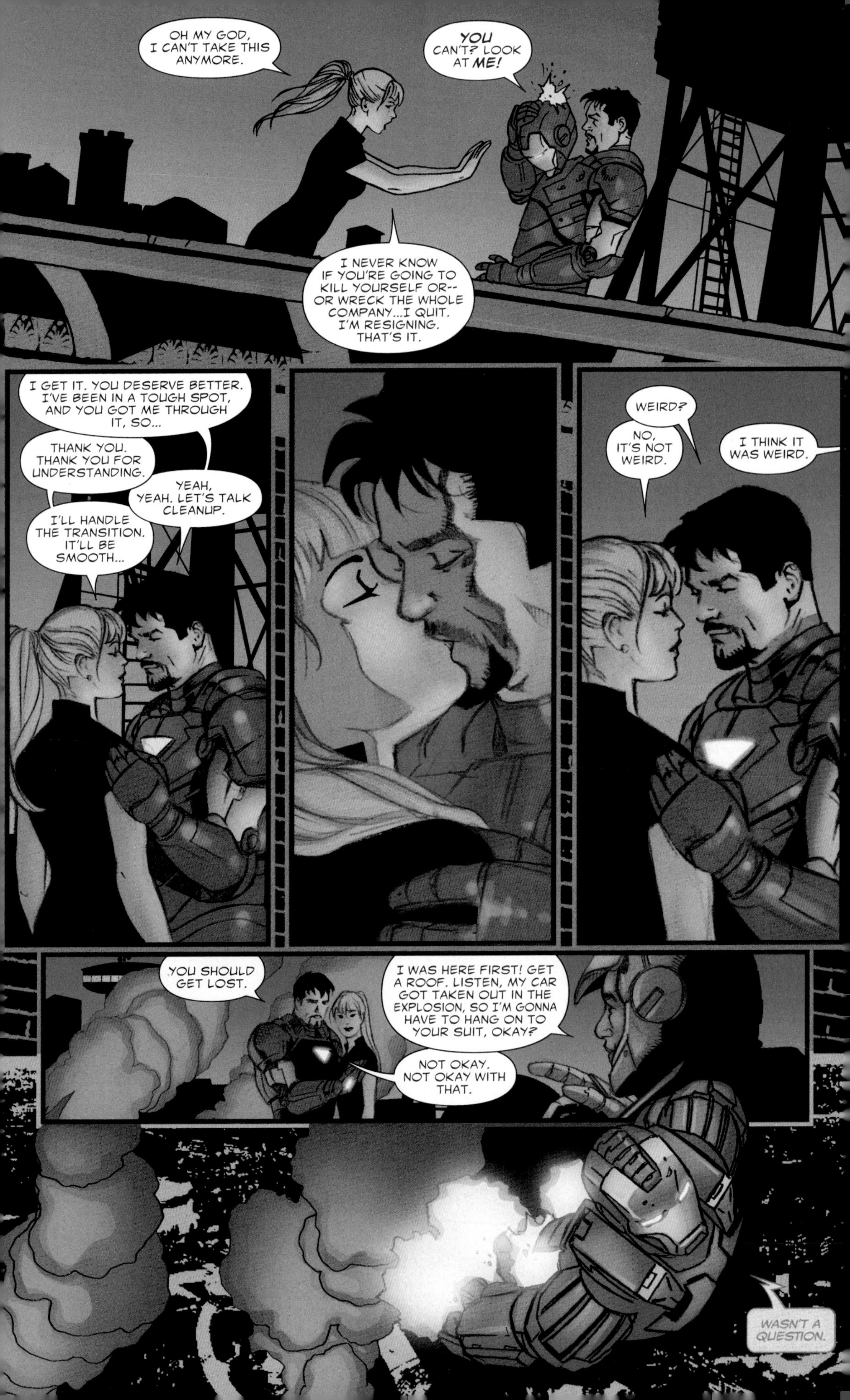
OH MY GOD, I CAN'T TAKE THIS ANYMORE.
YOU CAN'T? LOOK AT ME!
I NEVER KNOW IF YOU'RE GOING TO KILL YOURSELF OR-- OR WRECK THE WHOLE COMPANY...I QUIT. I'M RESIGNING. THAT'S IT.
I GET IT. YOU DESERVE BETTER. I'VE BEEN IN A TOUGH SPOT, AND YOU GOT ME THROUGH IT, SO...
THANK YOU. THANK YOU FOR UNDERSTANDING.
YEAH, YEAH. LET'S TALK CLEANUP.
I'LL HANDLE THE TRANSITION. IT'LL BE SMOOTH...
WEIRD?
NO, IT'S NOT WEIRD.
I THINK IT WAS WEIRD.
YOU SHOULD GET LOST.
I WAS HERE FIRST! GET A ROOF. LISTEN, MY CAR GOT TAKEN OUT IN THE EXPLOSION, SO I'M GONNA HAVE TO HANG ON TO YOUR SUIT, OKAY?
NOT OKAY. NOT OKAY WITH THAT.
WASN'T A QUESTION.

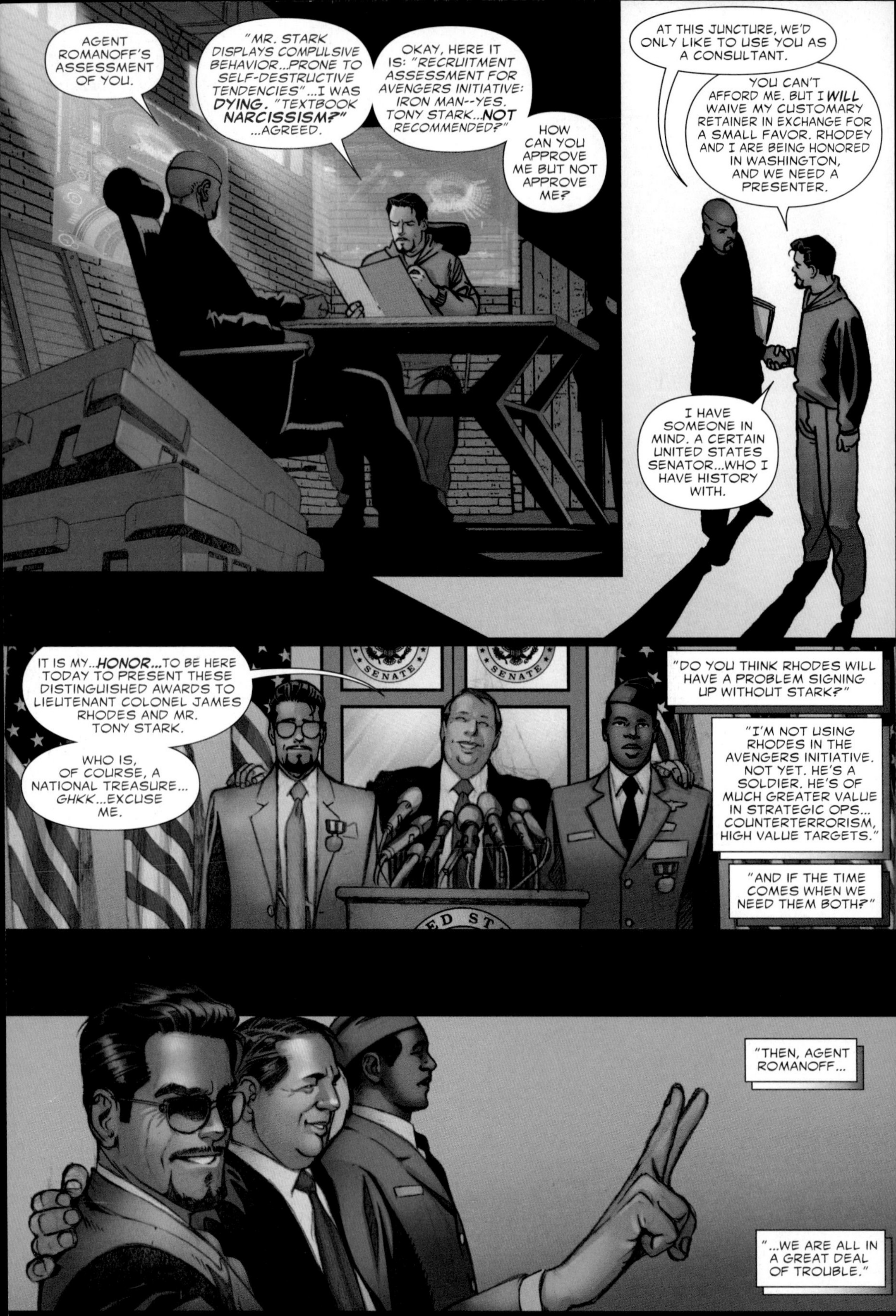
AGENT ROMANOFF'S ASSESSMENT OF YOU.
"MR. STARK DISPLAYS COMPULSIVE BEHAVIOR...PRONE TO SELF-DESTRUCTIVE TENDENCIES"...I WAS DYING. "TEXTBOOK NARCISSISM?" ...AGREED.
OKAY, HERE IT IS: "RECRUITMENT ASSESSMENT FOR AVENGERS INITIATIVE: IRON MAN--YES. TONY STARK...NOT RECOMMENDED?"
HOW CAN YOU APPROVE ME BUT NOT APPROVE ME?
AT THIS JUNCTURE, WE'D ONLY LIKE TO USE YOU AS A CONSULTANT.
YOU CAN'T AFFORD ME. BUT I WILL WAIVE MY CUSTOMARY RETAINER IN EXCHANGE FOR A SMALL FAVOR. RHODEY AND I ARE BEING HONORED IN WASHINGTON, AND WE NEED A PRESENTER.
I HAVE SOMEONE IN MIND. A CERTAIN UNITED STATES SENATOR...WHO I HAVE HISTORY WITH.
IT IS MY...HONOR...TO BE HERE TODAY TO PRESENT THESE DISTINGUISHED AWARDS TO LIEUTENANT COLONEL JAMES RHODES AND MR. TONY STARK.
WHO IS, OF COURSE, A NATIONAL TREASURE... GHKK...EXCUSE ME.
SENATE
SENATE
"DO YOU THINK RHODES WILL HAVE A PROBLEM SIGNING UP WITHOUT STARK?"
"I'M NOT USING RHODES IN THE AVENGERS INITIATIVE. NOT YET. HE'S A SOLDIER. HE'S OF MUCH GREATER VALUE IN STRATEGIC OPS... COUNTERTERRORISM, HIGH VALUE TARGETS."
"AND IF THE TIME COMES WHEN WE NEED THEM BOTH?"
"THEN, AGENT ROMANOFF...
"...WE ARE ALL IN A GREAT DEAL OF TROUBLE."

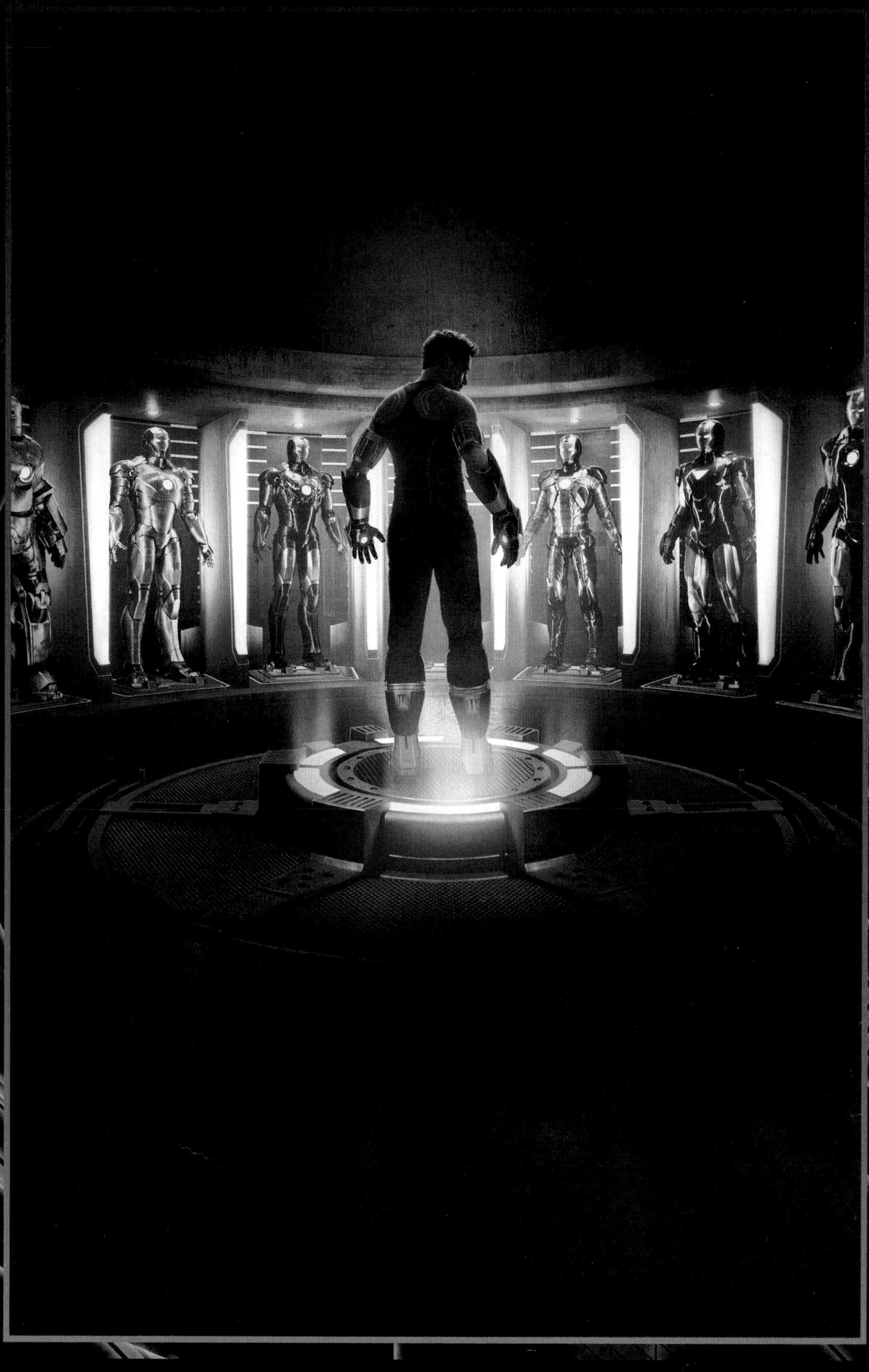

MARVEL'S IRON MAN 3 PRELUDE #1

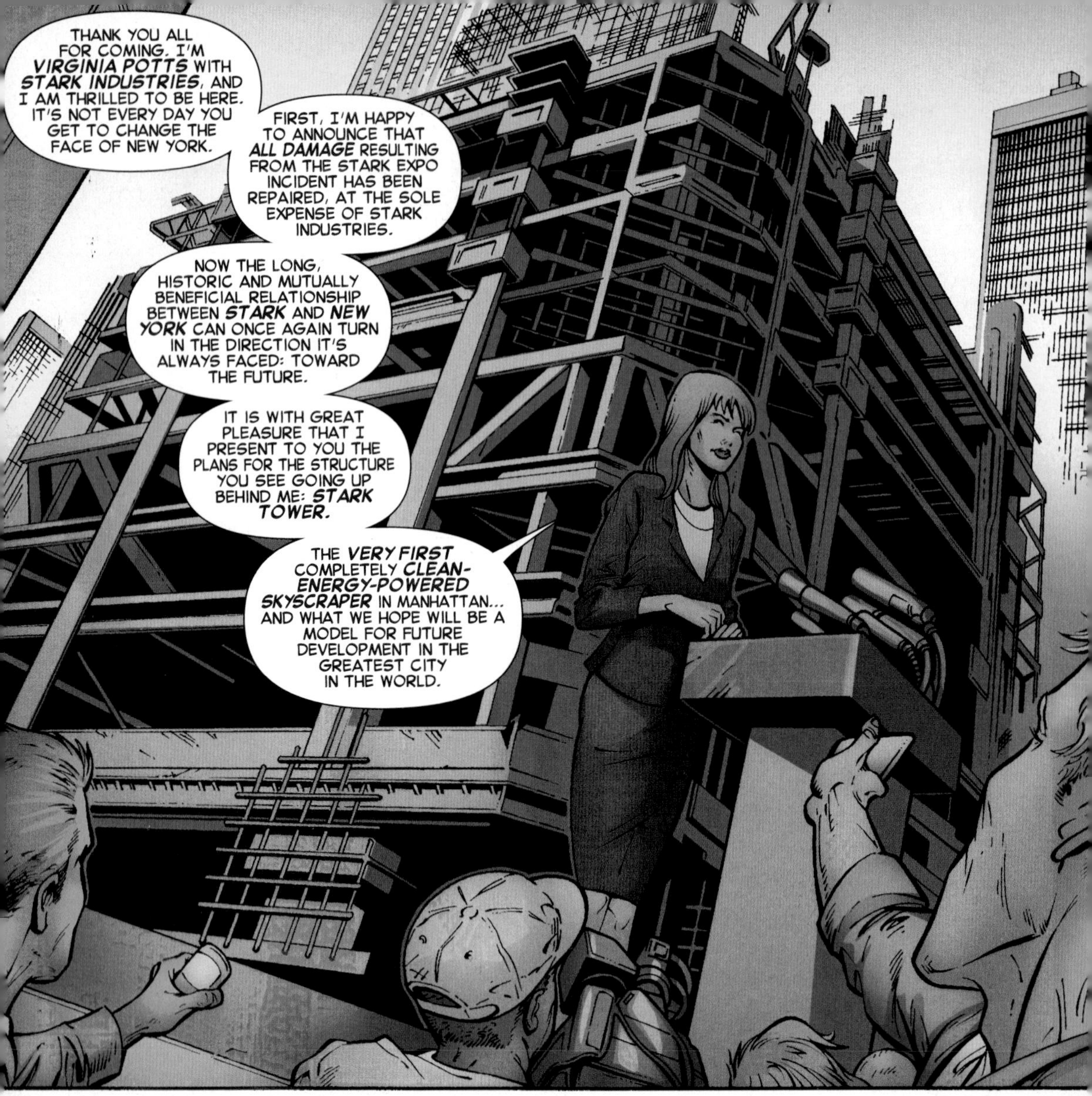
THANK YOU ALL FOR COMING. I'M VIRGINIA POTTS WITH STARK INDUSTRIES, AND I AM THRILLED TO BE HERE. IT'S NOT EVERY DAY YOU GET TO CHANGE THE FACE OF NEW YORK.
FIRST, I'M HAPPY TO ANNOUNCE THAT ALL DAMAGE RESULTING FROM THE STARK EXPO INCIDENT HAS BEEN REPAIRED, AT THE SOLE EXPENSE OF STARK INDUSTRIES.
NOW THE LONG, HISTORIC AND MUTUALLY BENEFICIAL RELATIONSHIP BETWEEN STARK AND NEW YORK CAN ONCE AGAIN TURN IN THE DIRECTION IT'S ALWAYS FACED: TOWARD THE FUTURE.
IT IS WITH GREAT PLEASURE THAT I PRESENT TO YOU THE PLANS FOR THE STRUCTURE YOU SEE GOING UP BEHIND ME: STARK TOWER.
THE VERY FIRST COMPLETELY CLEAN-ENERGY-POWERED SKYSCRAPER IN MANHATTAN... AND WHAT WE HOPE WILL BE A MODEL FOR FUTURE DEVELOPMENT IN THE GREATEST CITY IN THE WORLD.

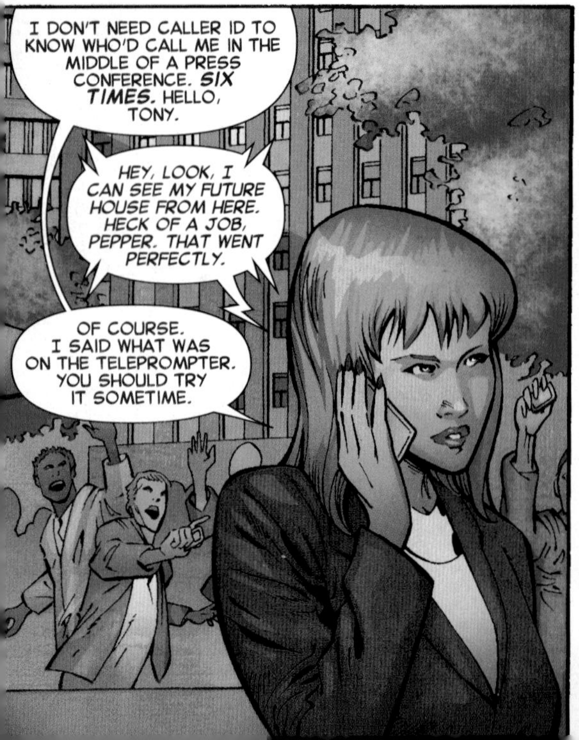
I DON'T NEED CALLER ID TO KNOW WHO'D CALL ME IN THE MIDDLE OF A PRESS CONFERENCE. SIX TIMES. HELLO, TONY.
HEY, LOOK, I CAN SEE MY FUTURE HOUSE FROM HERE. HECK OF A JOB, PEPPER. THAT WENT PERFECTLY.
OF COURSE. I SAID WHAT WAS ON THE TELEPROMPTER. YOU SHOULD TRY IT SOMETIME.

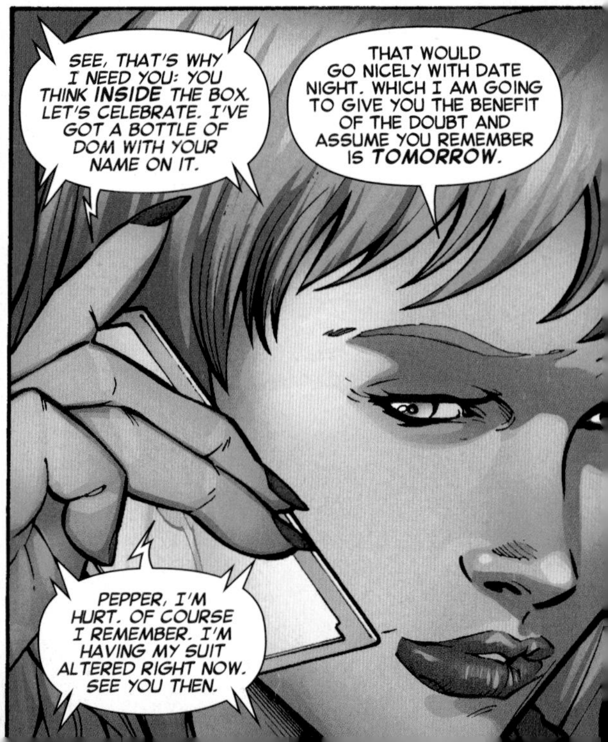
SEE, THAT'S WHY I NEED YOU: YOU THINK INSIDE THE BOX. LET'S CELEBRATE. I'VE GOT A BOTTLE OF DOM WITH YOUR NAME ON IT.
THAT WOULD GO NICELY WITH DATE NIGHT. WHICH I AM GOING TO GIVE YOU THE BENEFIT OF THE DOUBT AND ASSUME YOU REMEMBER IS TOMORROW.
PEPPER, I'M HURT. OF COURSE I REMEMBER. I'M HAVING MY SUIT ALTERED RIGHT NOW. SEE YOU THEN.

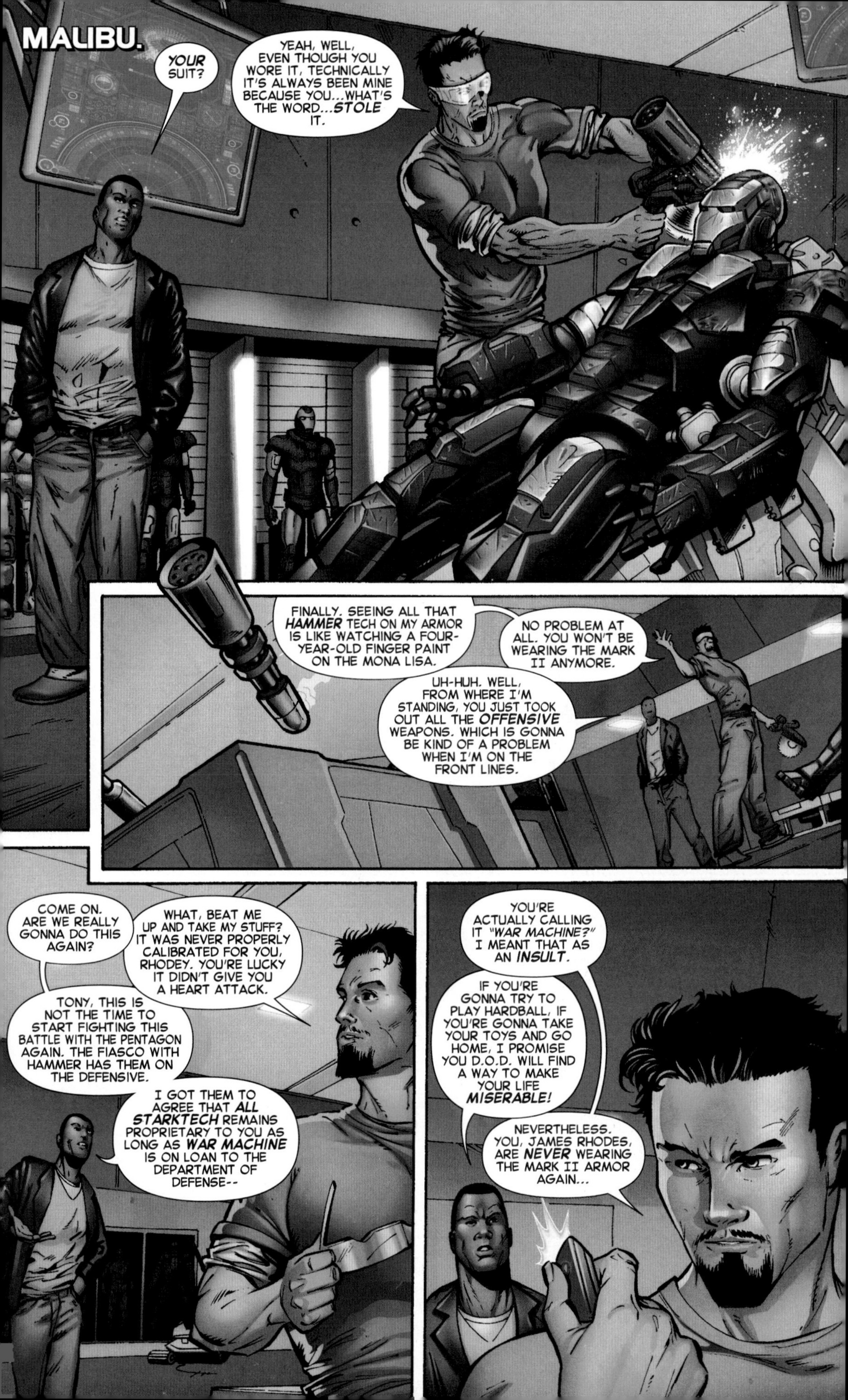
MALIBU.
YOUR SUIT?
YEAH, WELL, EVEN THOUGH YOU WORE IT, TECHNICALLY IT'S ALWAYS BEEN MINE BECAUSE YOU...WHAT'S THE WORD...STOLE IT.
FINALLY. SEEING ALL THAT HAMMER TECH ON MY ARMOR IS LIKE WATCHING A FOUR-YEAR-OLD FINGER PAINT ON THE MONA LISA.
NO PROBLEM AT ALL. YOU WON'T BE WEARING THE MARK II ANYMORE.
UH-HUH. WELL, FROM WHERE I'M STANDING, YOU JUST TOOK OUT ALL THE OFFENSIVE WEAPONS. WHICH IS GONNA BE KIND OF A PROBLEM WHEN I'M ON THE FRONT LINES.
COME ON. ARE WE REALLY GONNA DO THIS AGAIN?
WHAT, BEAT ME UP AND TAKE MY STUFF? IT WAS NEVER PROPERLY CALIBRATED FOR YOU, RHODEY. YOU'RE LUCKY IT DIDN'T GIVE YOU A HEART ATTACK.
TONY, THIS IS NOT THE TIME TO START FIGHTING THIS BATTLE WITH THE PENTAGON AGAIN. THE FIASCO WITH HAMMER HAS THEM ON THE DEFENSIVE.
I GOT THEM TO AGREE THAT ALL STARKTECH REMAINS PROPRIETARY TO YOU AS LONG AS WAR MACHINE IS ON LOAN TO THE DEPARTMENT OF DEFENSE--
YOU'RE ACTUALLY CALLING IT "WAR MACHINE?" I MEANT THAT AS AN INSULT.
IF YOU'RE GONNA TRY TO PLAY HARDBALL, IF YOU'RE GONNA TAKE YOUR TOYS AND GO HOME, I PROMISE YOU D.O.D. WILL FIND A WAY TO MAKE YOUR LIFE MISERABLE!
NEVERTHELESS. YOU, JAMES RHODES, ARE NEVER WEARING THE MARK II ARMOR AGAIN...

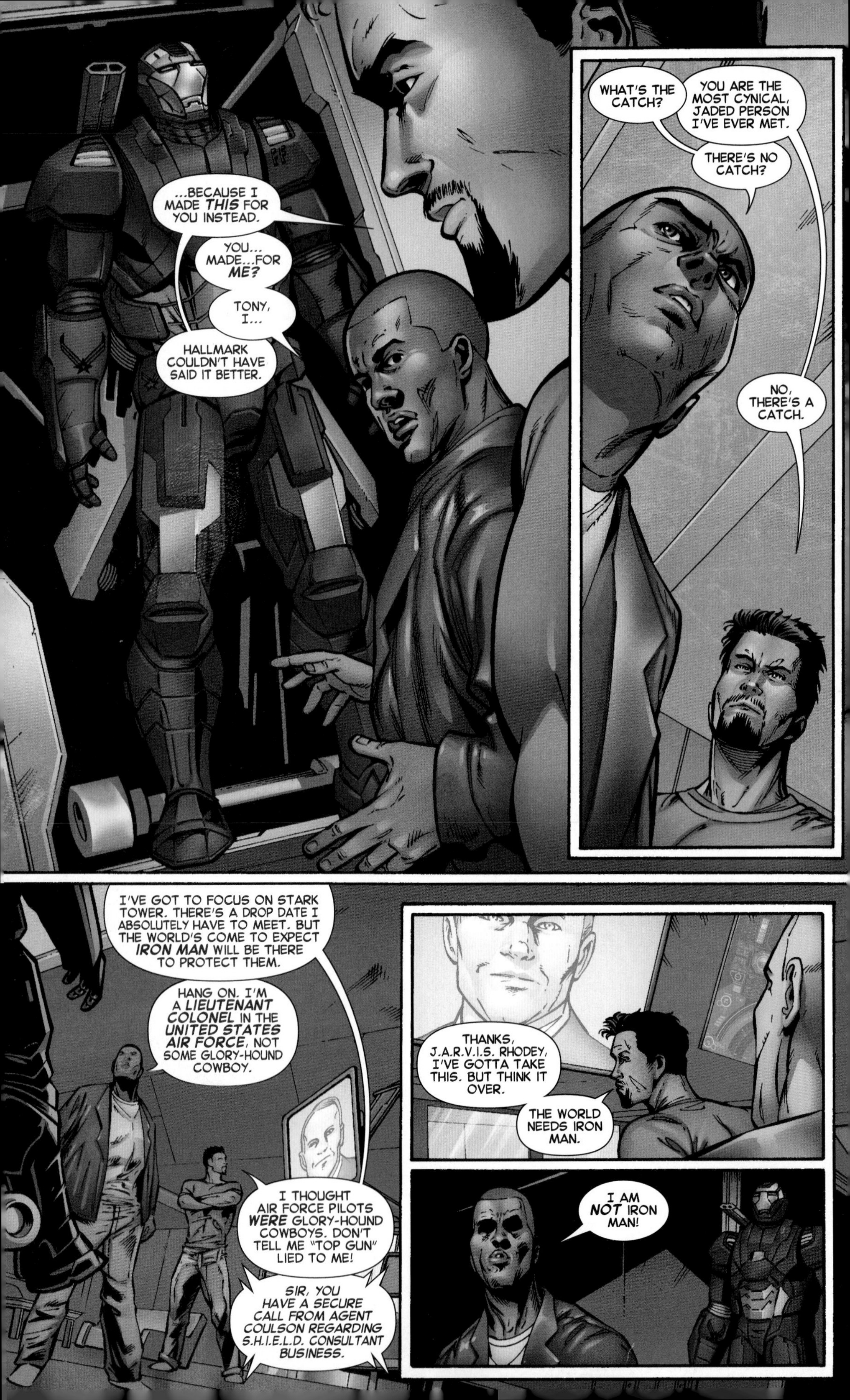

...BECAUSE I MADE THIS FOR YOU INSTEAD.
YOU... MADE...FOR ME?
TONY, I...
HALLMARK COULDN'T HAVE SAID IT BETTER.
WHAT'S THE CATCH?
YOU ARE THE MOST CYNICAL, JADED PERSON I'VE EVER MET.
THERE'S NO CATCH?
NO, THERE'S A CATCH.
I'VE GOT TO FOCUS ON STARK TOWER. THERE'S A DROP DATE I ABSOLUTELY HAVE TO MEET. BUT THE WORLD'S COME TO EXPECT IRON MAN WILL BE THERE TO PROTECT THEM.
HANG ON. I'M A LIEUTENANT COLONEL IN THE UNITED STATES AIR FORCE, NOT SOME GLORY-HOUND COWBOY.
I THOUGHT AIR FORCE PILOTS WERE GLORY-HOUND COWBOYS. DON'T TELL ME "TOP GUN" LIED TO ME!
SIR, YOU HAVE A SECURE CALL FROM AGENT COULSON REGARDING S.H.I.E.L.D. CONSULTANT BUSINESS.
THANKS, J.A.R.V.I.S. RHODEY, I'VE GOTTA TAKE THIS. BUT THINK IT OVER.
THE WORLD NEEDS IRON MAN.
I AM NOT IRON MAN!

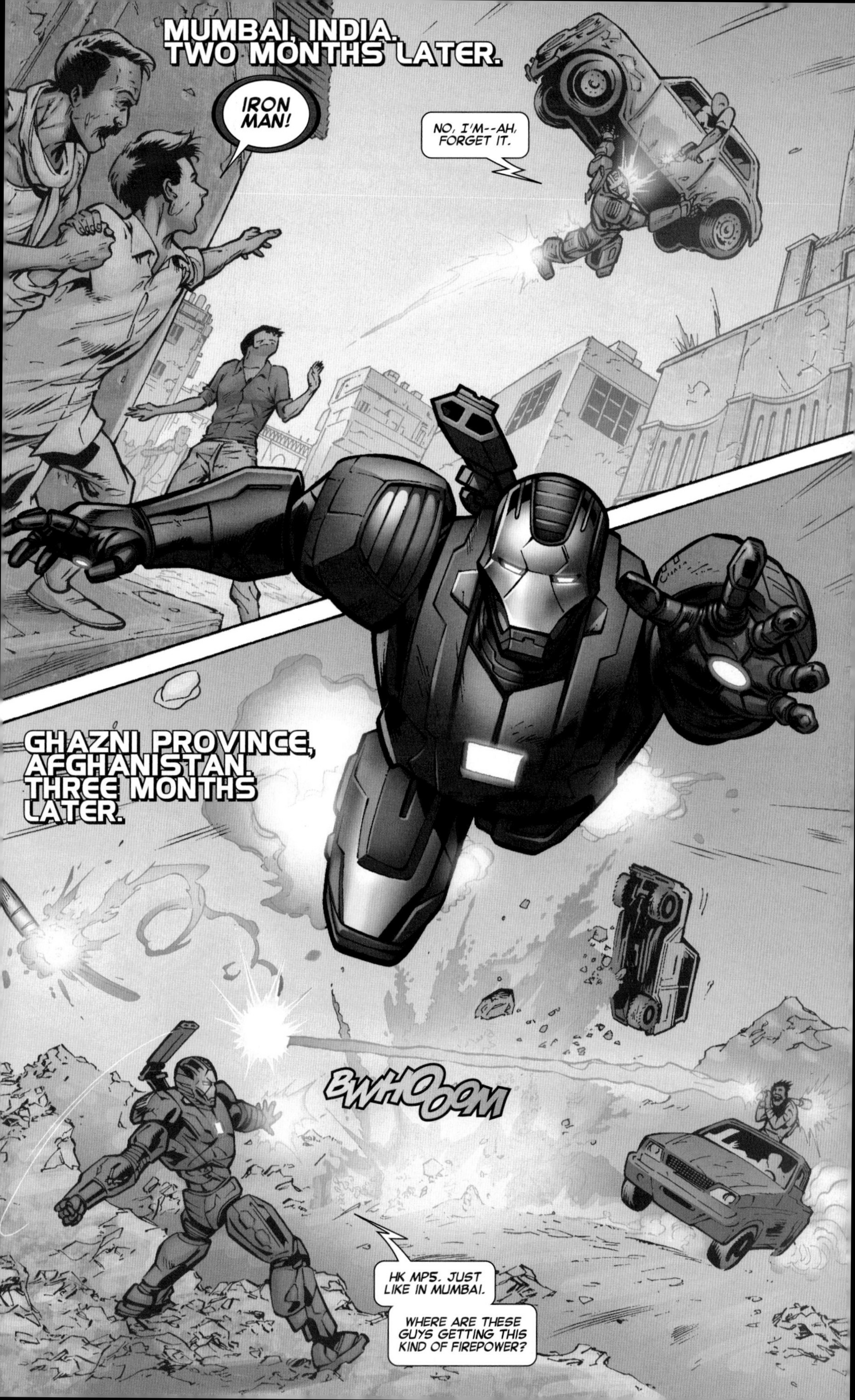
MUMBAI, INDIA. TWO MONTHS LATER.
IRON MAN!
NO, I'M--AH, FORGET IT.
GHAZNI PROVINCE, AFGHANISTAN. THREE MONTHS LATER.
BWHOOOOM
HK MP5. JUST LIKE IN MUMBAI.
WHERE ARE THESE GUYS GETTING THIS KIND OF FIREPOWER?

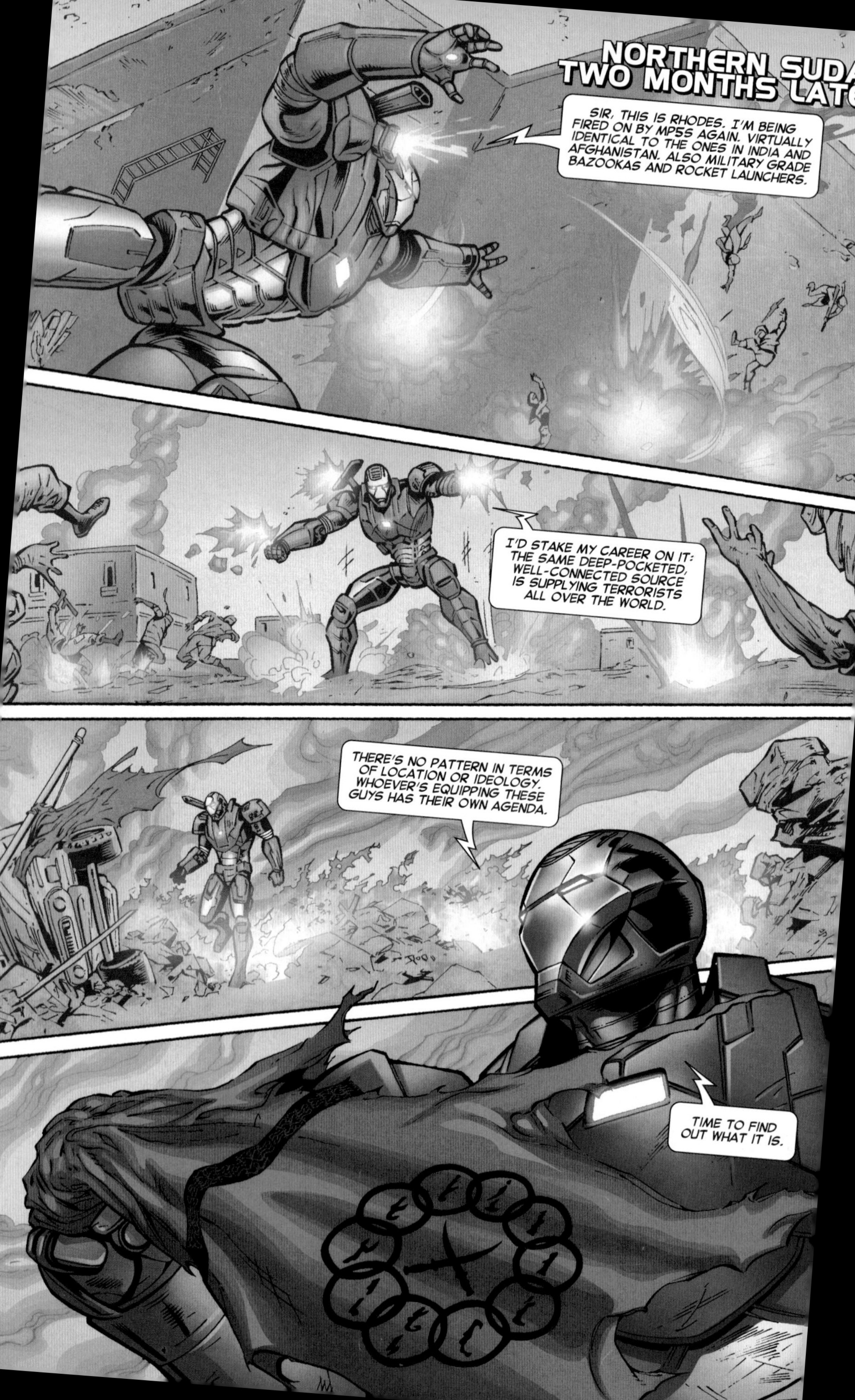
NORTHERN SUDA
TWO MONTHS LAT
SIR, THIS IS RHODES. I'M BEING FIRED ON BY MP5S AGAIN. VIRTUALLY IDENTICAL TO THE ONES IN INDIA AND AFGHANISTAN. ALSO MILITARY GRADE BAZOOKAS AND ROCKET LAUNCHERS.
I'D STAKE MY CAREER ON IT: THE SAME DEEP-POCKETED, WELL-CONNECTED SOURCE IS SUPPLYING TERRORISTS ALL OVER THE WORLD.
THERE'S NO PATTERN IN TERMS OF LOCATION OR IDEOLOGY. WHOEVER'S EQUIPPING THESE GUYS HAS THEIR OWN AGENDA.
TIME TO FIND OUT WHAT IT IS.

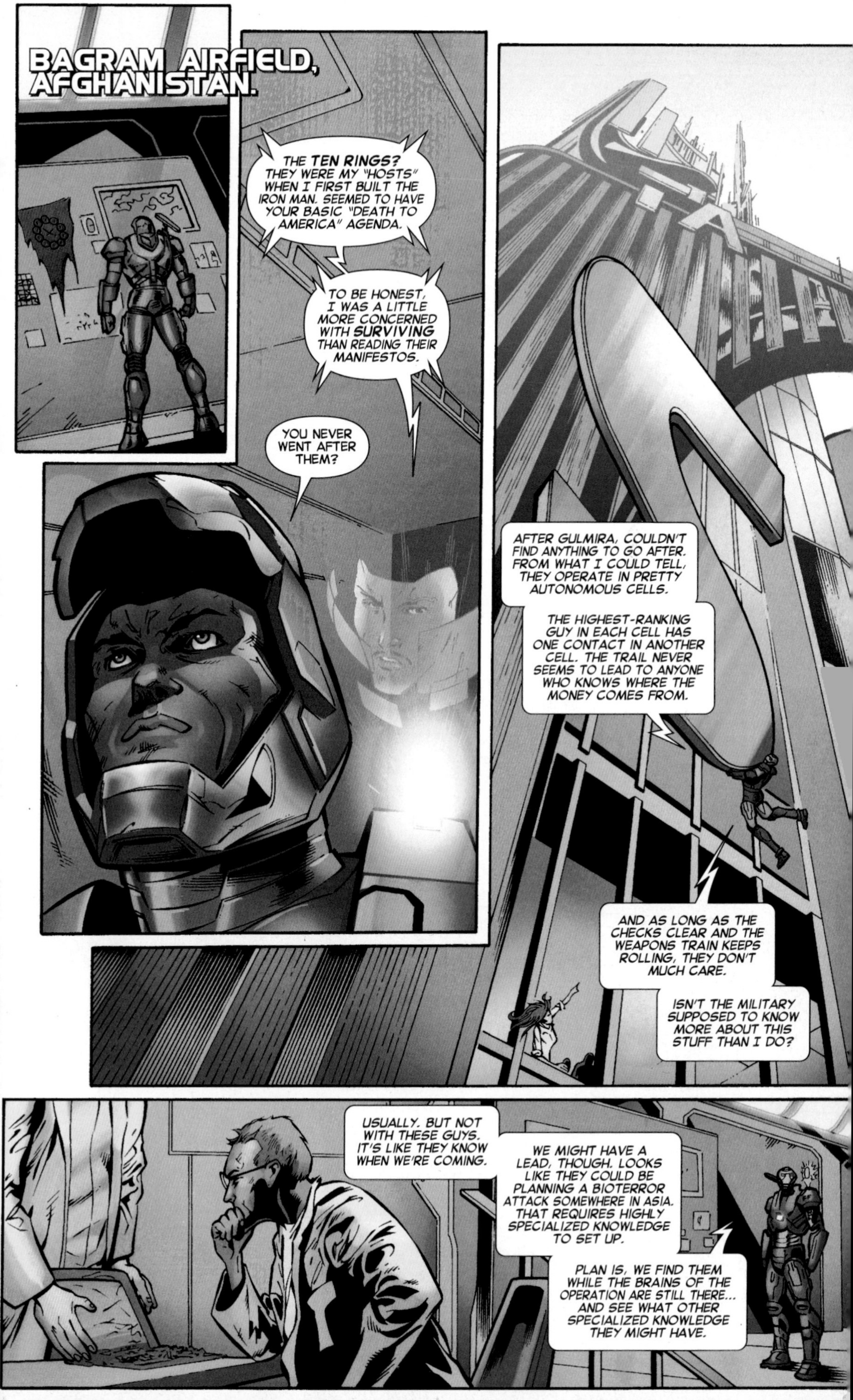
BAGRAM AIRFIELD, AFGHANISTAN.
THE TEN RINGS? THEY WERE MY "HOSTS" WHEN I FIRST BUILT THE IRON MAN. SEEMED TO HAVE YOUR BASIC "DEATH TO AMERICA" AGENDA.
TO BE HONEST, I WAS A LITTLE MORE CONCERNED WITH SURVIVING THAN READING THEIR MANIFESTOS.
YOU NEVER WENT AFTER THEM?
AFTER GULMIRA, COULDN'T FIND ANYTHING TO GO AFTER. FROM WHAT I COULD TELL, THEY OPERATE IN PRETTY AUTONOMOUS CELLS.
THE HIGHEST-RANKING GUY IN EACH CELL HAS ONE CONTACT IN ANOTHER CELL. THE TRAIL NEVER SEEMS TO LEAD TO ANYONE WHO KNOWS WHERE THE MONEY COMES FROM.
AND AS LONG AS THE CHECKS CLEAR AND THE WEAPONS TRAIN KEEPS ROLLING, THEY DON'T MUCH CARE.
ISN'T THE MILITARY SUPPOSED TO KNOW MORE ABOUT THIS STUFF THAN I DO?
USUALLY. BUT NOT WITH THESE GUYS. IT'S LIKE THEY KNOW WHEN WE'RE COMING.
WE MIGHT HAVE A LEAD, THOUGH. LOOKS LIKE THEY COULD BE PLANNING A BIOTERROR ATTACK SOMEWHERE IN ASIA. THAT REQUIRES HIGHLY SPECIALIZED KNOWLEDGE TO SET UP.
PLAN IS, WE FIND THEM WHILE THE BRAINS OF THE OPERATION ARE STILL THERE... AND SEE WHAT OTHER SPECIALIZED KNOWLEDGE THEY MIGHT HAVE.

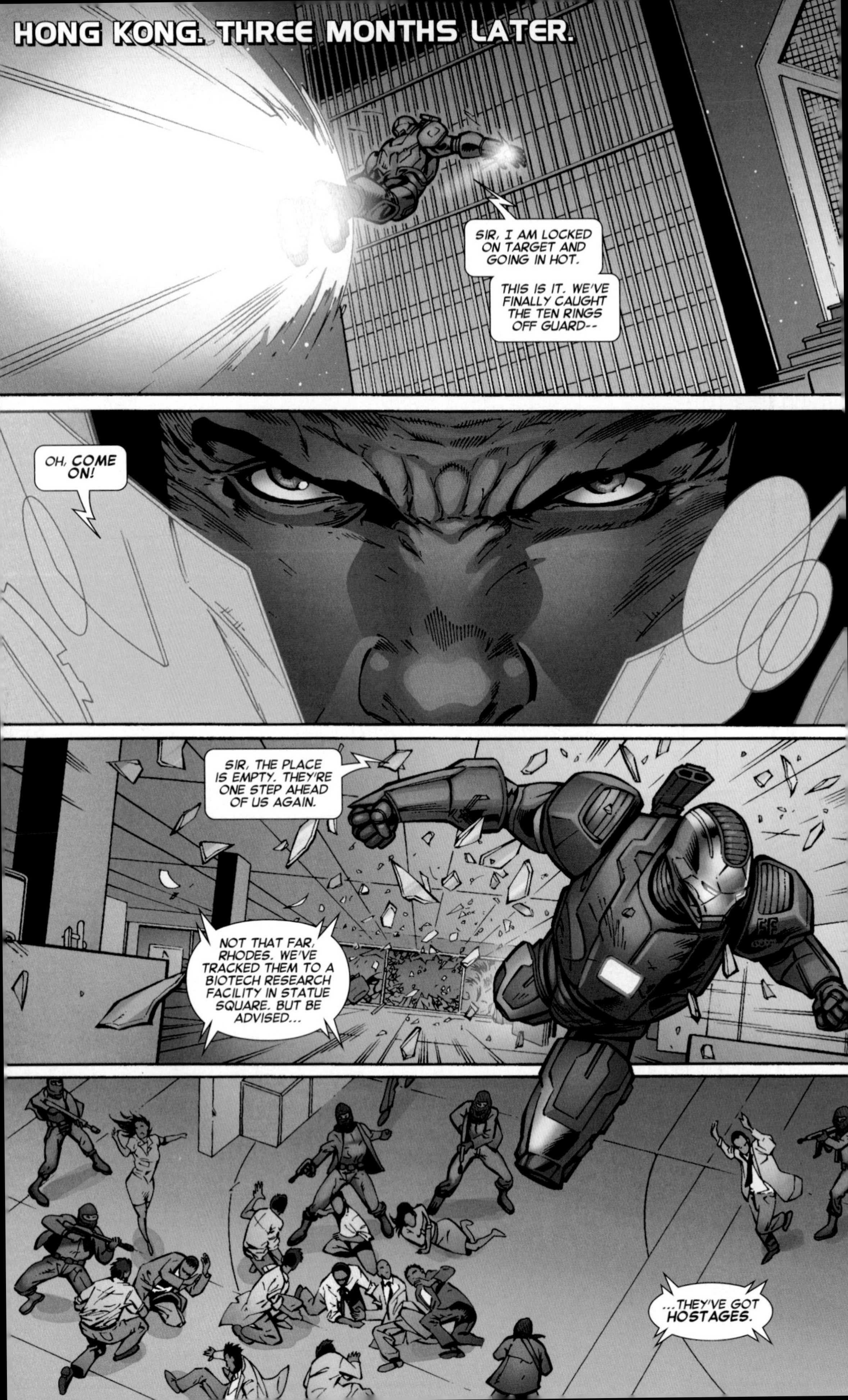
HONG KONG. THREE MONTHS LATER.
SIR, I AM LOCKED ON TARGET AND GOING IN HOT.
THIS IS IT. WE'VE FINALLY CAUGHT THE TEN RINGS OFF GUARD--
OH, COME ON!
SIR, THE PLACE IS EMPTY. THEY'RE ONE STEP AHEAD OF US AGAIN.
NOT THAT FAR, RHODES. WE'VE TRACKED THEM TO A BIOTECH RESEARCH FACILITY IN STATUE SQUARE. BUT BE ADVISED...
...THEY'VE GOT HOSTAGES.

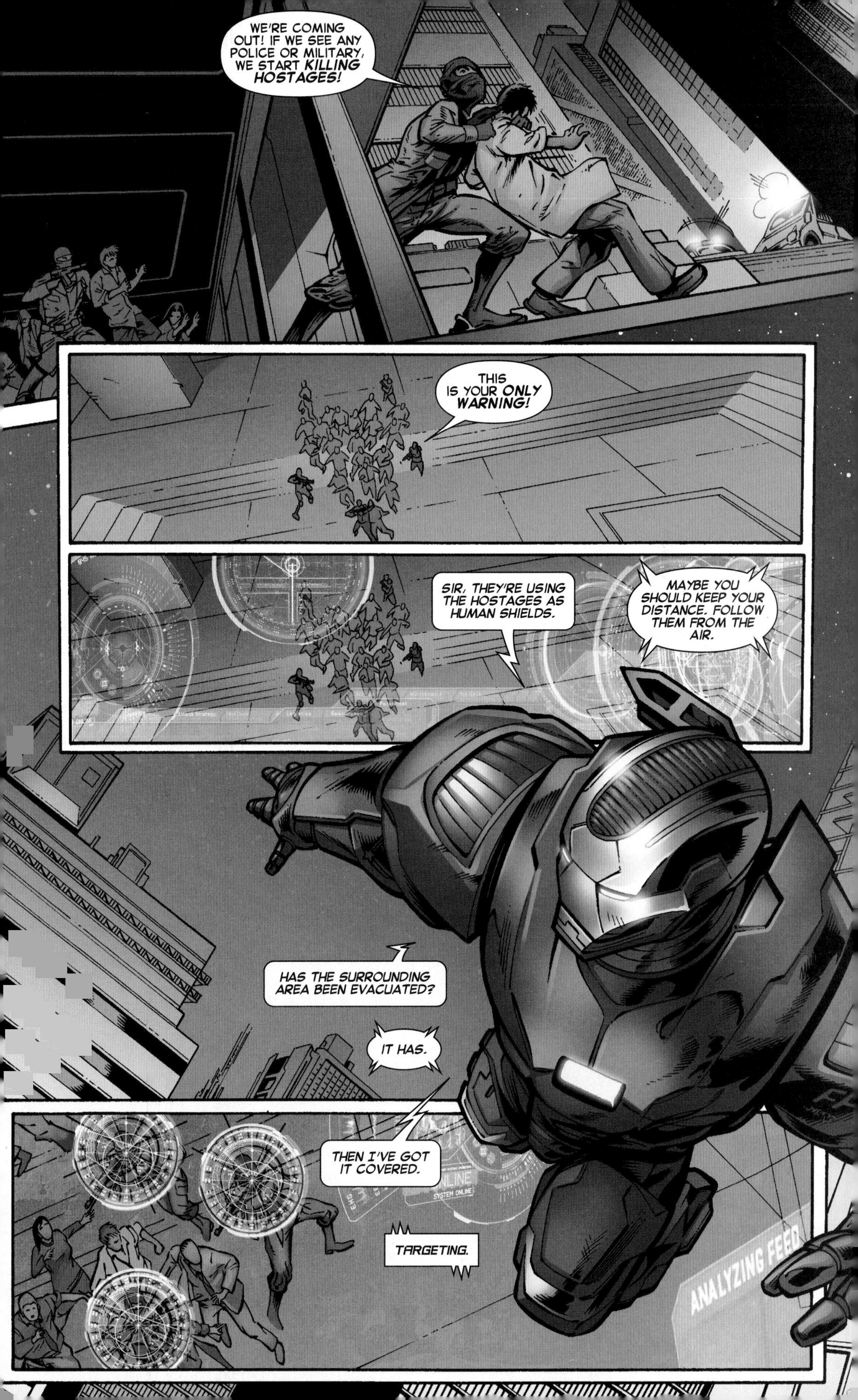
WE'RE COMING OUT! IF WE SEE ANY POLICE OR MILITARY, WE START KILLING HOSTAGES!
THIS IS YOUR ONLY WARNING!
SIR, THEY'RE USING THE HOSTAGES AS HUMAN SHIELDS.
MAYBE YOU SHOULD KEEP YOUR DISTANCE. FOLLOW THEM FROM THE AIR.
HAS THE SURROUNDING AREA BEEN EVACUATED?
IT HAS.
THEN I'VE GOT IT COVERED.
TARGETING.
SYSTEM ONLINE
ANALYZING FEED

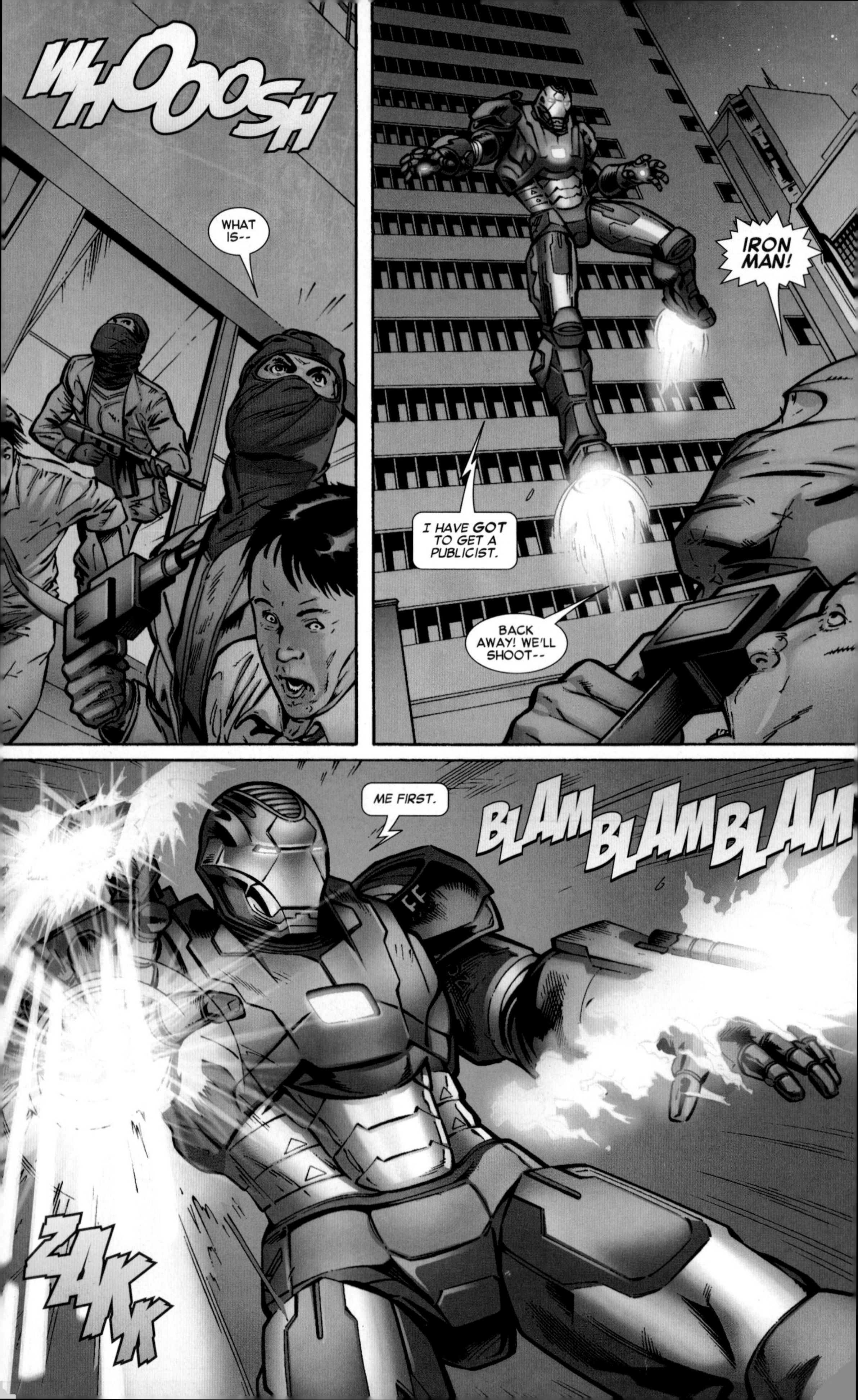
WHOOOOSH
WHAT IS--
IRON MAN!
I HAVE GOT TO GET A PUBLICIST.
BACK AWAY! WE'LL SHOOT--
ME FIRST.
BLAM BLAM BLAM
ZAKK

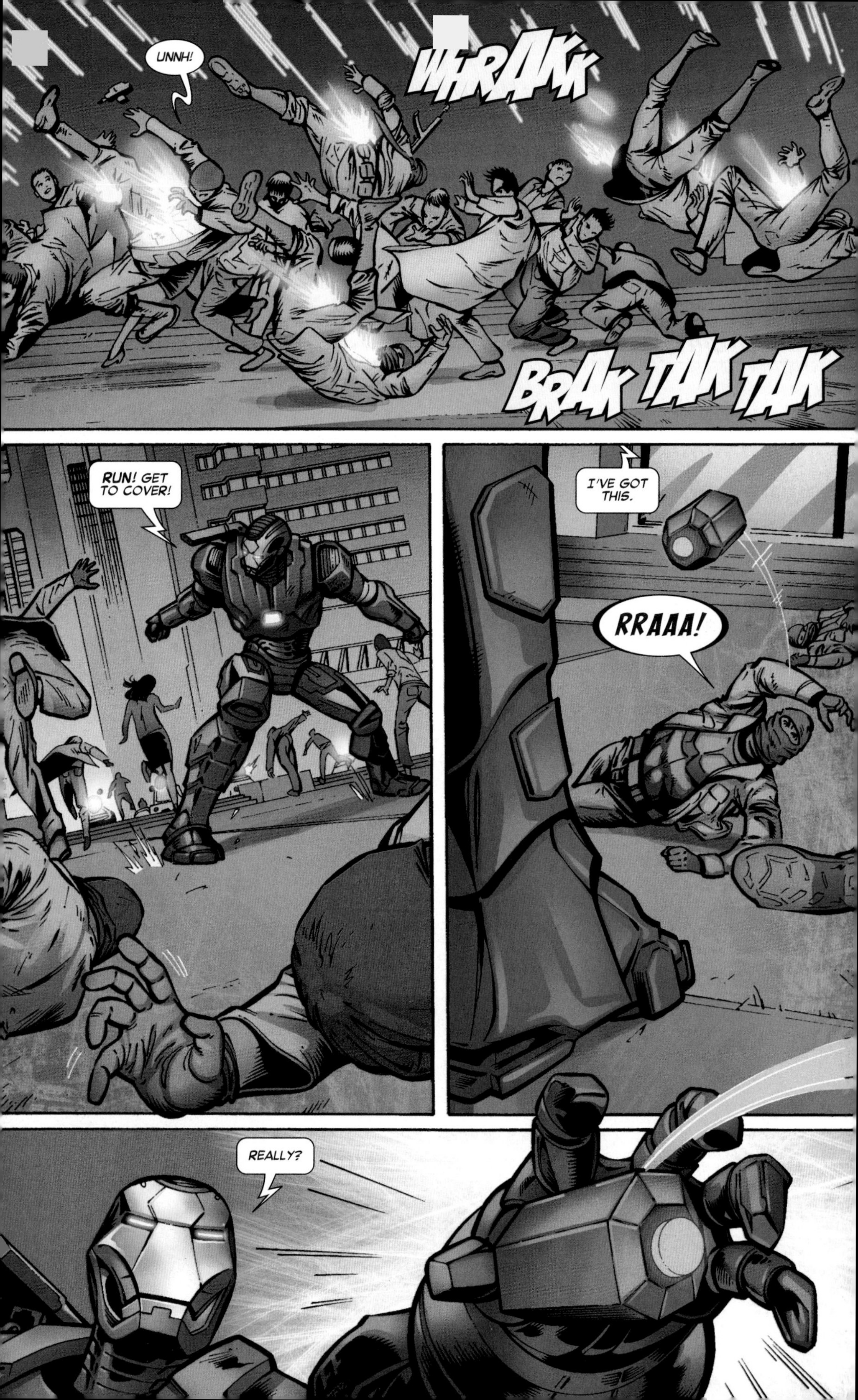
UNNH!
WHRAKK
BRAK TAK TAK
RUN! GET TO COVER!
I'VE GOT THIS.
RRAAA!
REALLY?

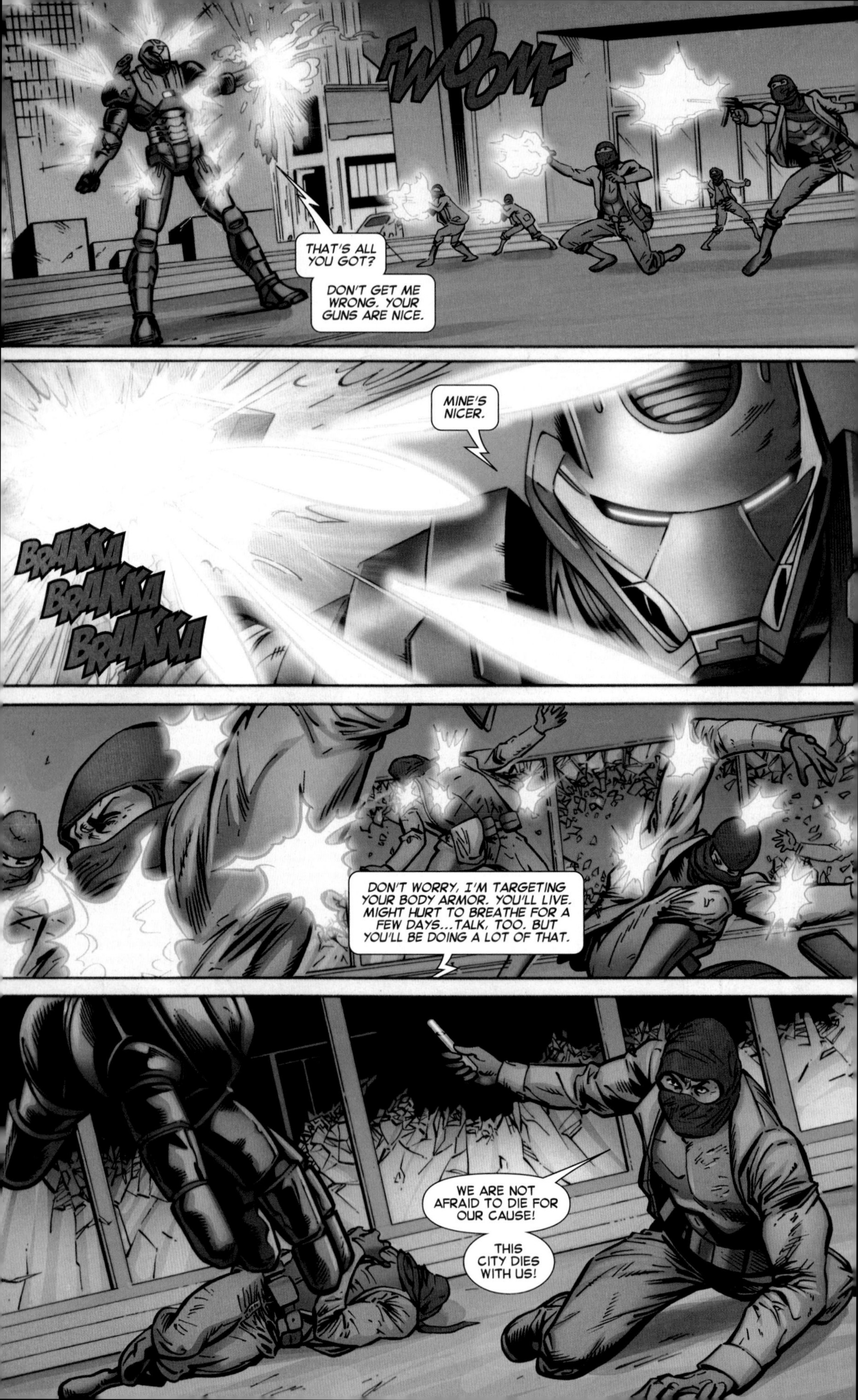
FWOOM
THAT'S ALL YOU GOT?
DON'T GET ME WRONG. YOUR GUNS ARE NICE.
MINE'S NICER.
BRAKKA BRAKKA BRAKKA
DON'T WORRY, I'M TARGETING YOUR BODY ARMOR. YOU'LL LIVE. MIGHT HURT TO BREATHE FOR A FEW DAYS...TALK, TOO. BUT YOU'LL BE DOING A LOT OF THAT.
WE ARE NOT AFRAID TO DIE FOR OUR CAUSE!
THIS CITY DIES WITH US!

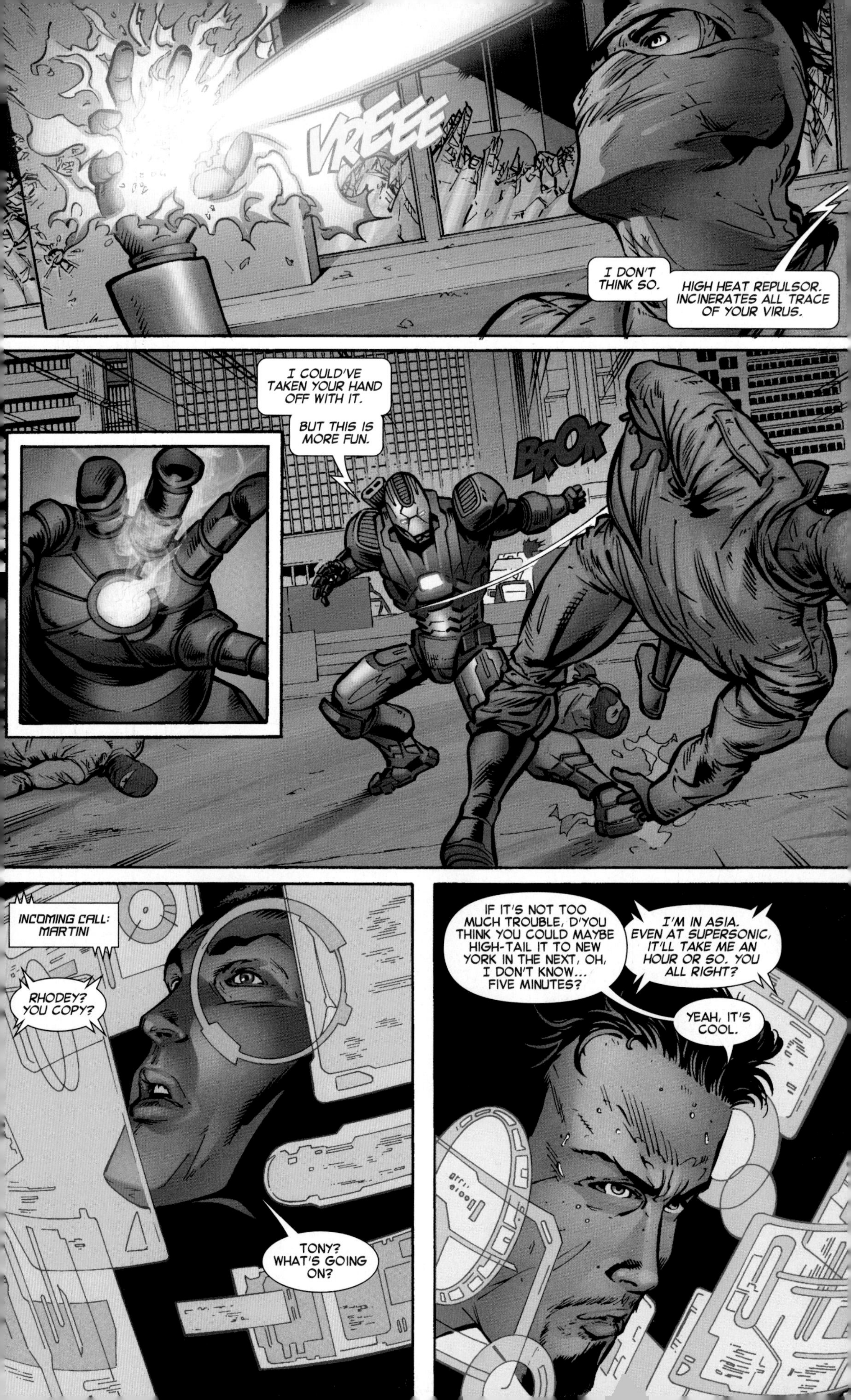
VREEE
I DON'T THINK SO.
HIGH HEAT REPULSOR. INCINERATES ALL TRACE OF YOUR VIRUS.
I COULD'VE TAKEN YOUR HAND OFF WITH IT.
BUT THIS IS MORE FUN.
BROK
INCOMING CALL: MARTINI
RHODEY? YOU COPY?
TONY? WHAT'S GOING ON?
IF IT'S NOT TOO MUCH TROUBLE, D'YOU THINK YOU COULD MAYBE HIGH-TAIL IT TO NEW YORK IN THE NEXT, OH, I DON'T KNOW... FIVE MINUTES?
I'M IN ASIA. EVEN AT SUPERSONIC, IT'LL TAKE ME AN HOUR OR SO. YOU ALL RIGHT?
YEAH, IT'S COOL.

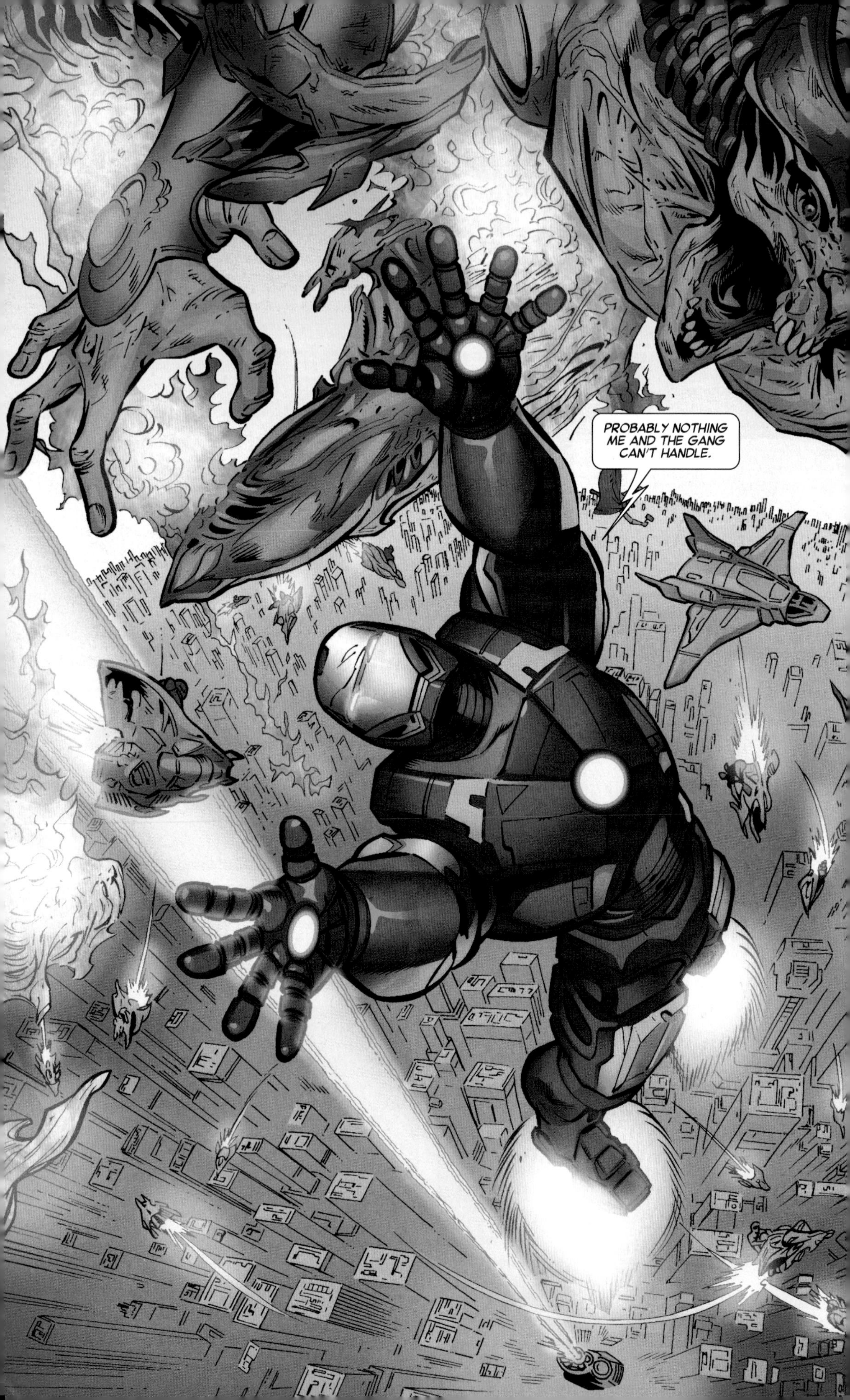
PROBABLY NOTHING ME AND THE GANG CAN'T HANDLE.

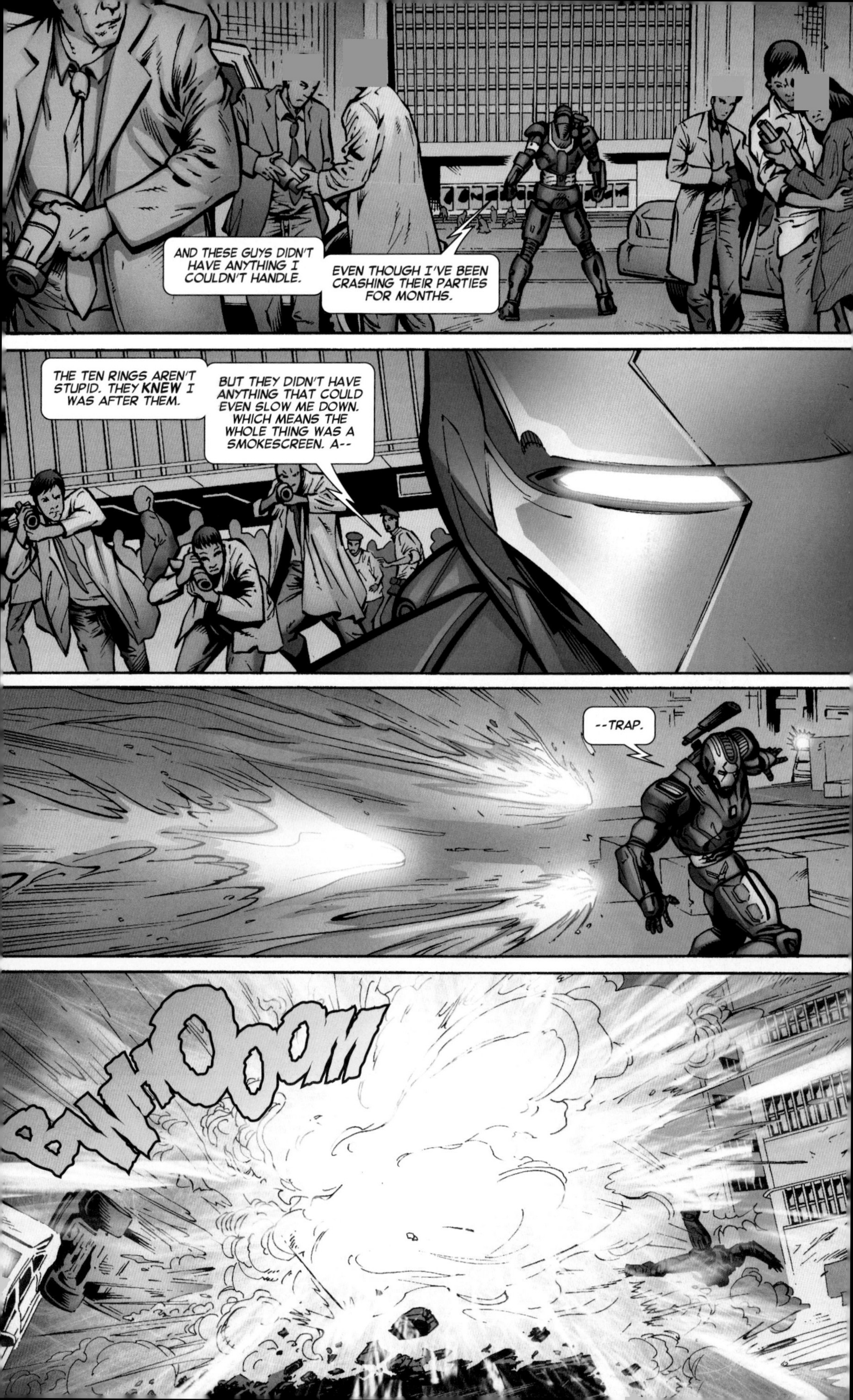
AND THESE GUYS DIDN'T HAVE ANYTHING I COULDN'T HANDLE.
EVEN THOUGH I'VE BEEN CRASHING THEIR PARTIES FOR MONTHS.
THE TEN RINGS AREN'T STUPID. THEY KNEW I WAS AFTER THEM.
BUT THEY DIDN'T HAVE ANYTHING THAT COULD EVEN SLOW ME DOWN. WHICH MEANS THE WHOLE THING WAS A SMOKESCREEN. A--
--TRAP.

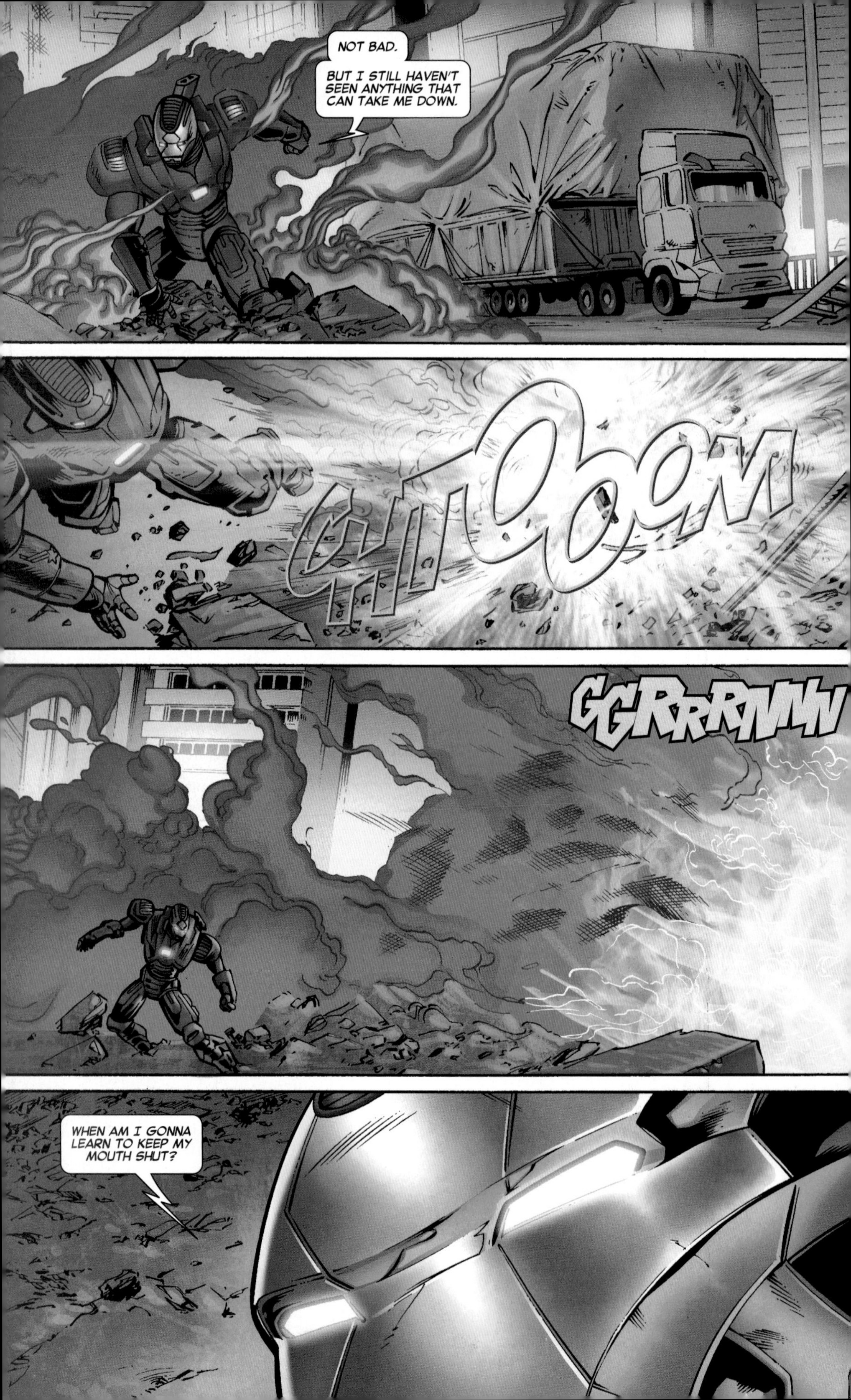
NOT BAD.
BUT I STILL HAVEN'T SEEN ANYTHING THAT CAN TAKE ME DOWN.
CHUOOOM
GGRRRRMMN
WHEN AM I GONNA LEARN TO KEEP MY MOUTH SHUT?

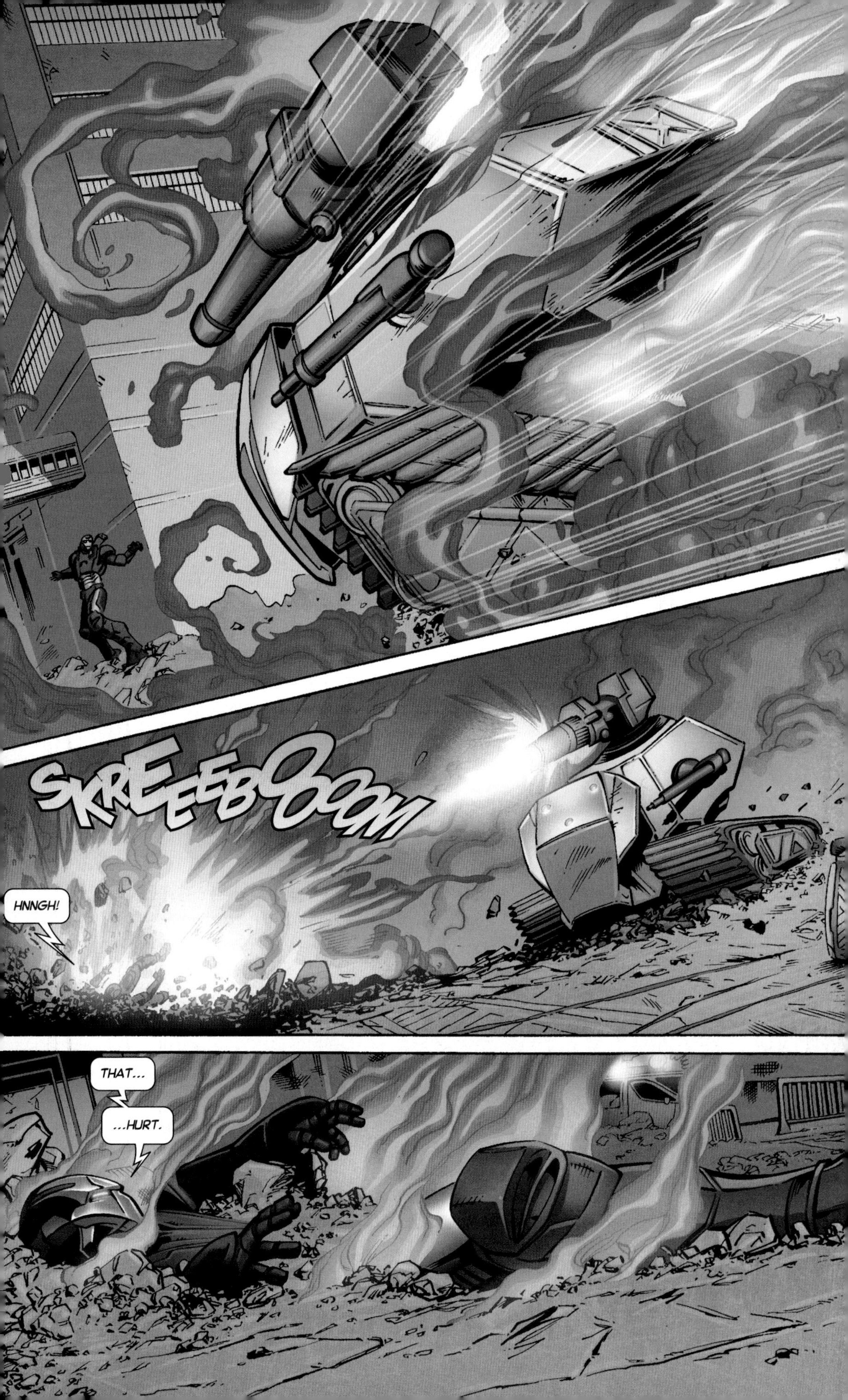
SKREEEBOOOOM
HNNGH!
THAT...
...HURT.

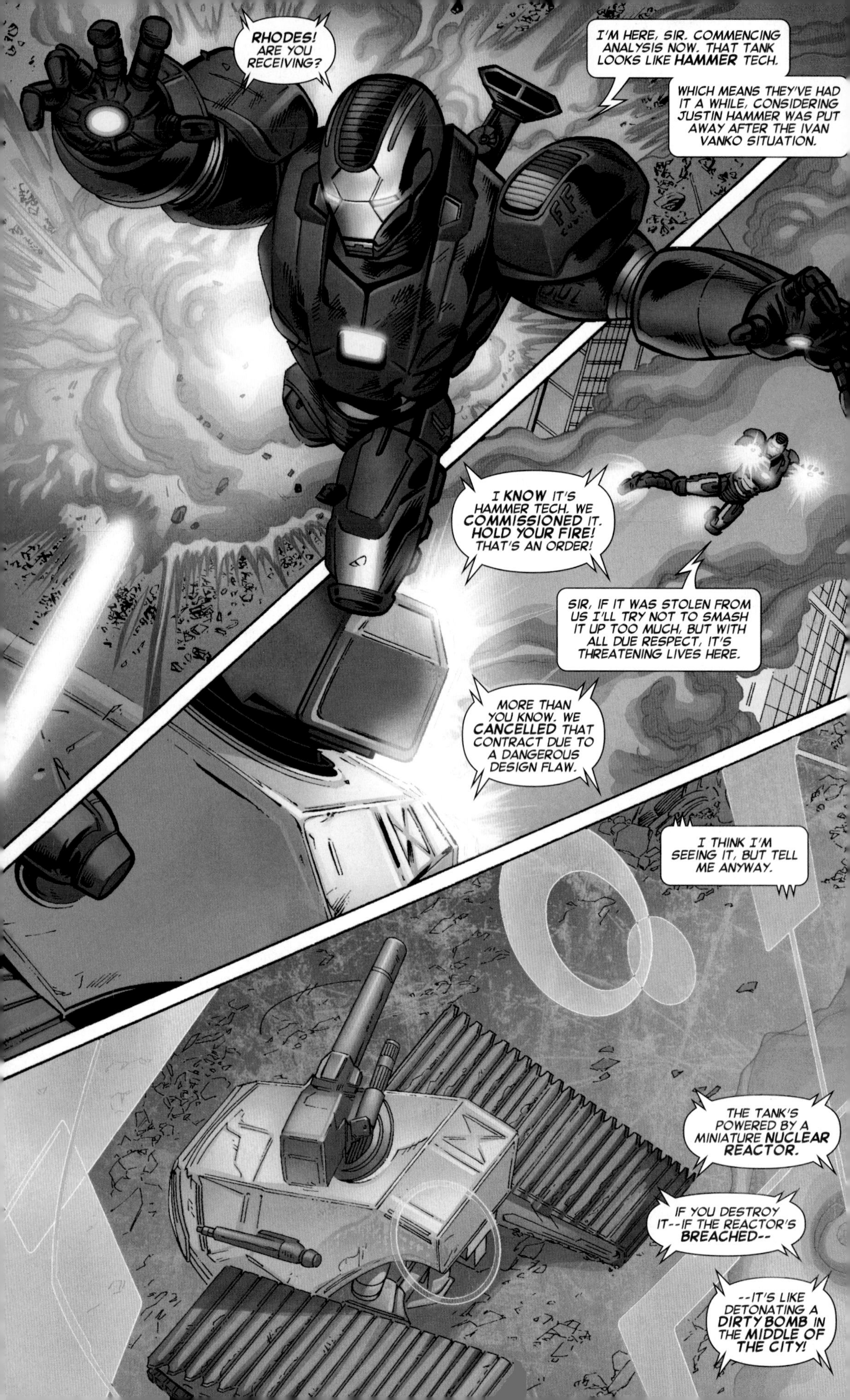
RHODES! ARE YOU RECEIVING?
I'M HERE, SIR. COMMENCING ANALYSIS NOW. THAT TANK LOOKS LIKE HAMMER TECH.
WHICH MEANS THEY'VE HAD IT A WHILE, CONSIDERING JUSTIN HAMMER WAS PUT AWAY AFTER THE IVAN VANKO SITUATION.
I KNOW IT'S HAMMER TECH. WE COMMISSIONED IT. HOLD YOUR FIRE! THAT'S AN ORDER!
SIR, IF IT WAS STOLEN FROM US I'LL TRY NOT TO SMASH IT UP TOO MUCH, BUT WITH ALL DUE RESPECT, IT'S THREATENING LIVES HERE.
MORE THAN YOU KNOW. WE CANCELLED THAT CONTRACT DUE TO A DANGEROUS DESIGN FLAW.
I THINK I'M SEEING IT, BUT TELL ME ANYWAY.
THE TANK'S POWERED BY A MINIATURE NUCLEAR REACTOR.
IF YOU DESTROY IT--IF THE REACTOR'S BREACHED--
--IT'S LIKE DETONATING A DIRTY BOMB IN THE MIDDLE OF THE CITY!

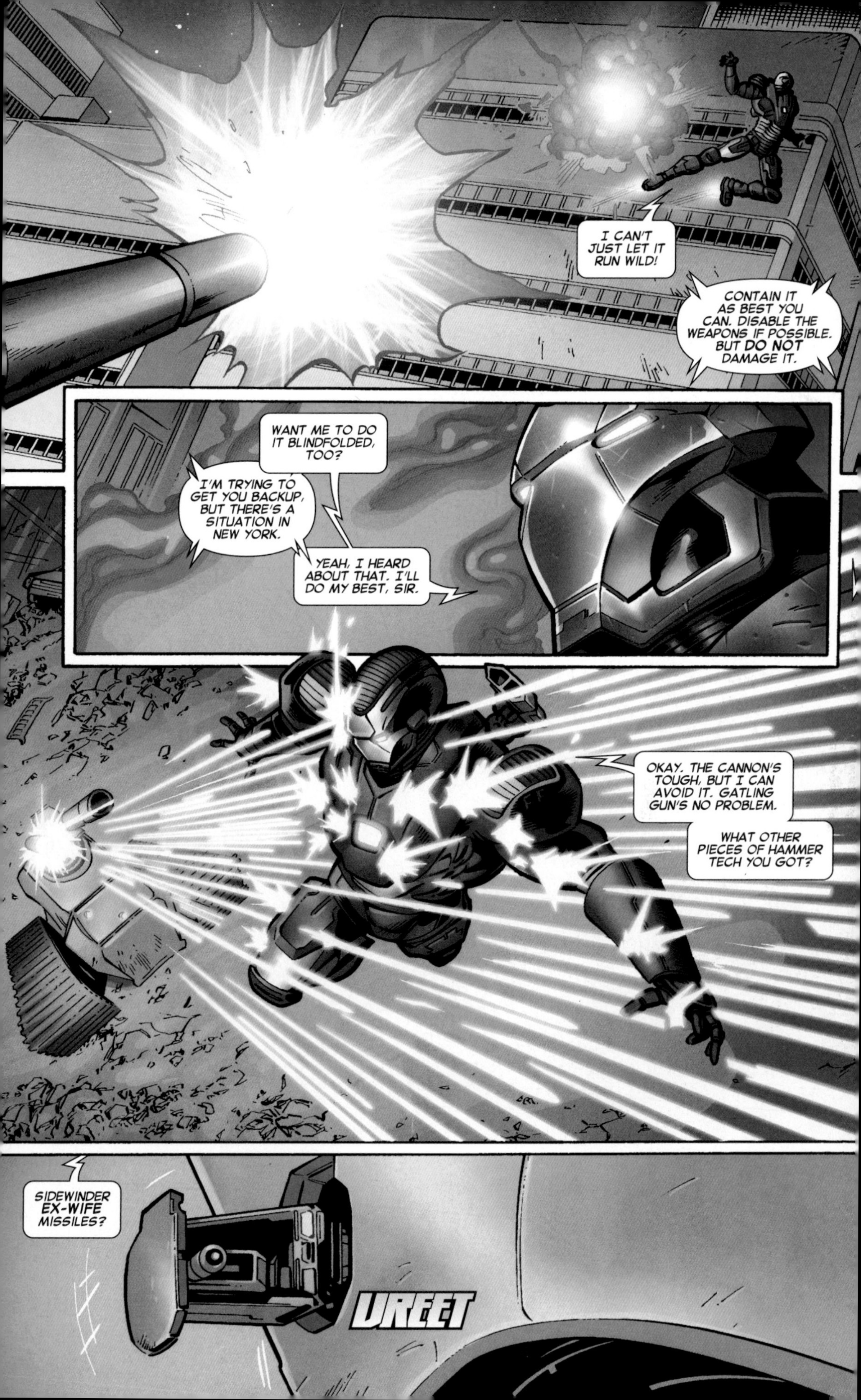
I CAN'T JUST LET IT RUN WILD!
CONTAIN IT AS BEST YOU CAN. DISABLE THE WEAPONS IF POSSIBLE. BUT **DO NOT** DAMAGE IT.
WANT ME TO DO IT BLINDFOLDED, TOO?
I'M TRYING TO GET YOU BACKUP, BUT THERE'S A SITUATION IN NEW YORK.
YEAH, I HEARD ABOUT THAT. I'LL DO MY BEST, SIR.
OKAY. THE CANNON'S TOUGH, BUT I CAN AVOID IT. GATLING GUN'S NO PROBLEM.
WHAT OTHER PIECES OF HAMMER TECH YOU GOT?
SIDEWINDER **EX-WIFE** MISSILES?
UREET

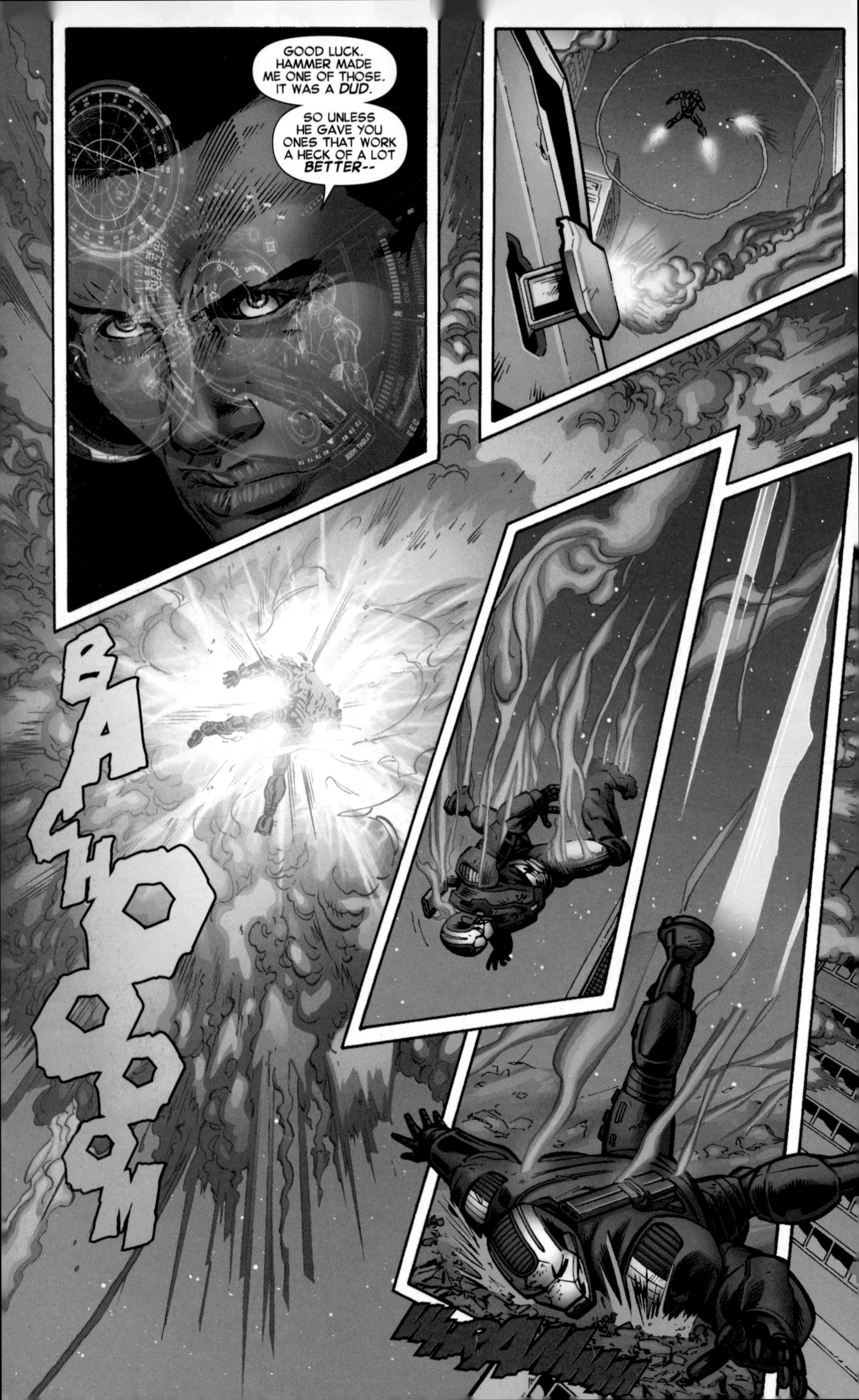
GOOD LUCK. HAMMER MADE ME ONE OF THOSE. IT WAS A DUD.
SO UNLESS HE GAVE YOU ONES THAT WORK A HECK OF A LOT BETTER--
BAKOOOM

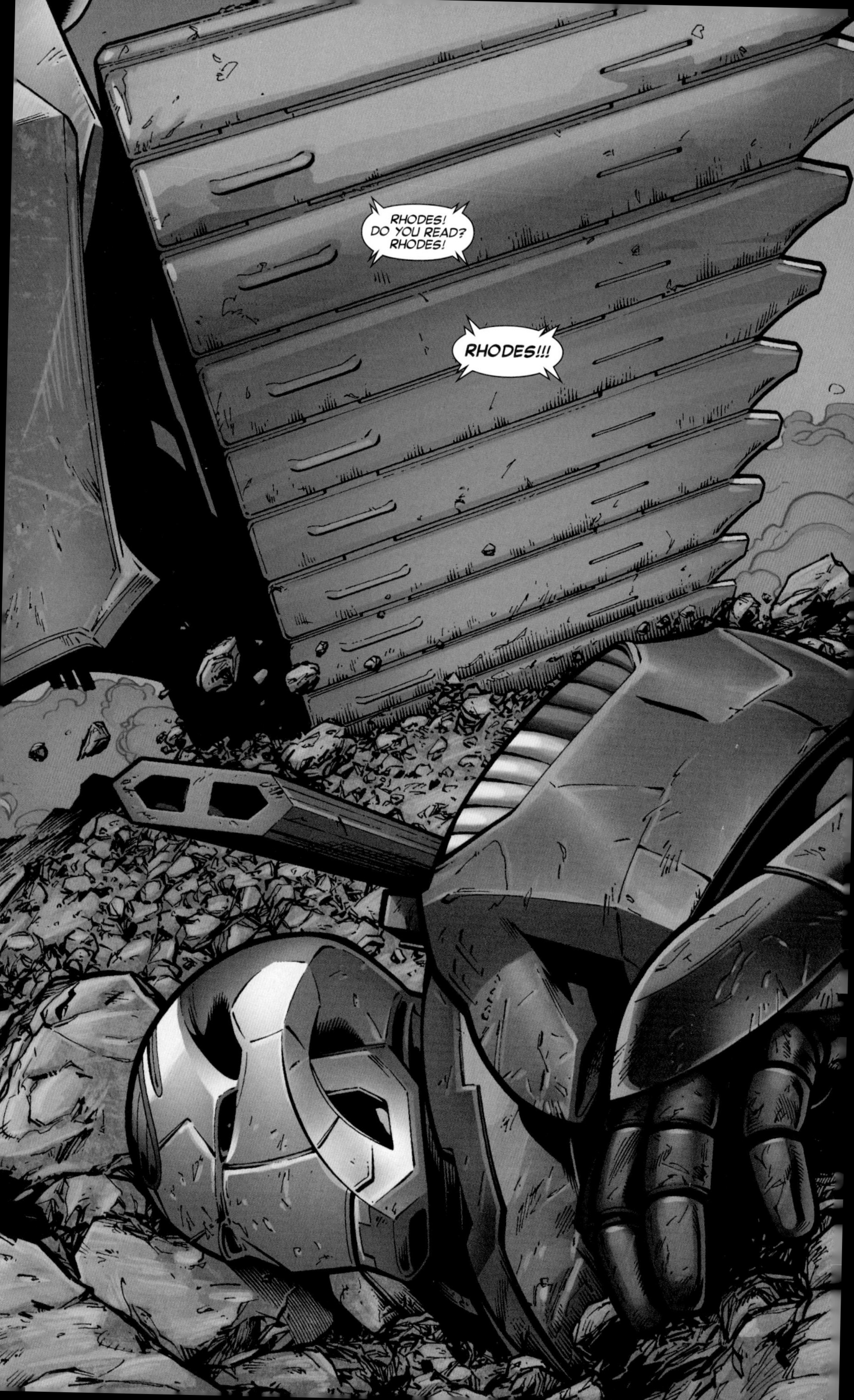
RHODES! DO YOU READ? RHODES!
RHODES!!!

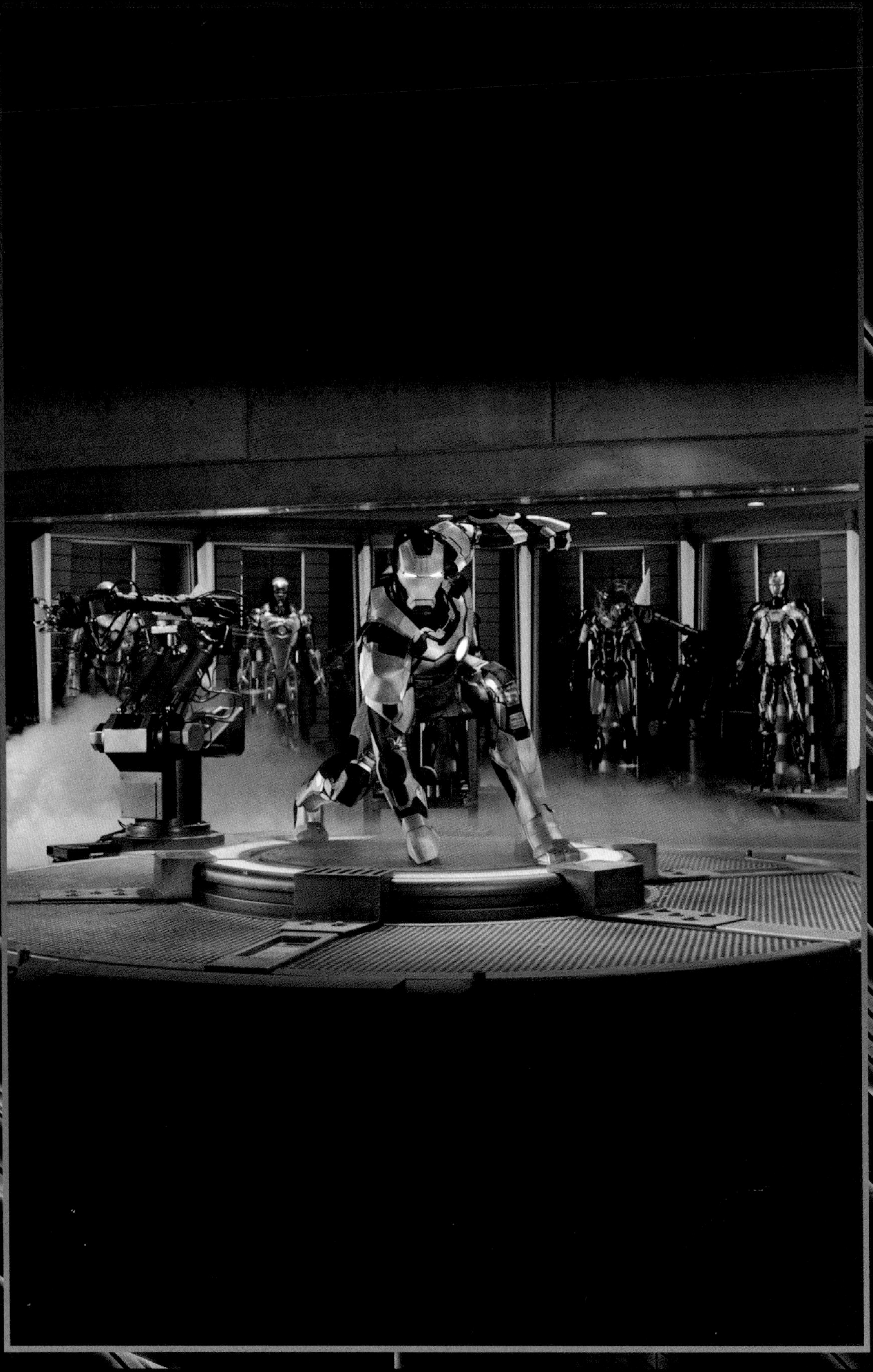

MARVEL'S IRON MAN 3 PRELUDE #2

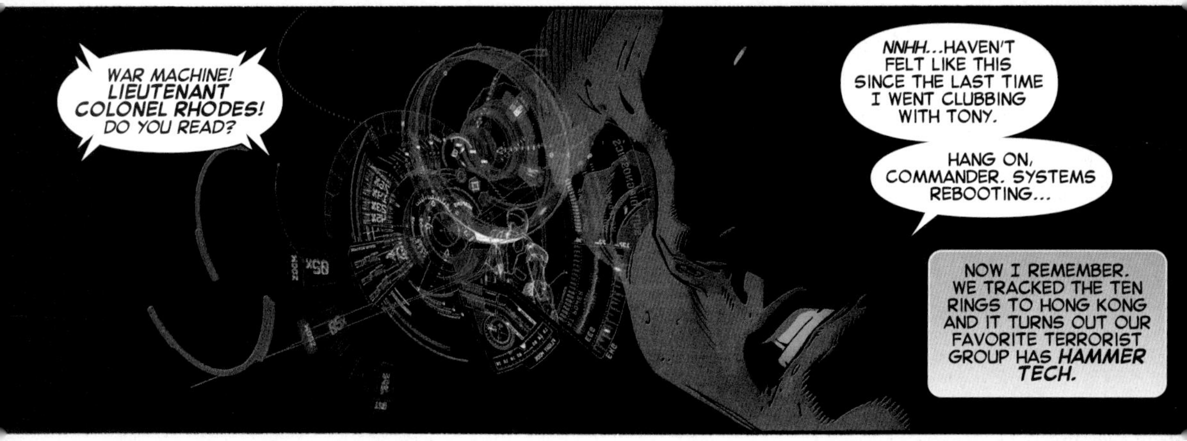
WAR MACHINE! LIEUTENANT COLONEL RHODES! DO YOU READ?
NNHH...HAVEN'T FELT LIKE THIS SINCE THE LAST TIME I WENT CLUBBING WITH TONY.
HANG ON, COMMANDER. SYSTEMS REBOOTING...
NOW I REMEMBER. WE TRACKED THE TEN RINGS TO HONG KONG AND IT TURNS OUT OUR FAVORITE TERRORIST GROUP HAS HAMMER TECH.

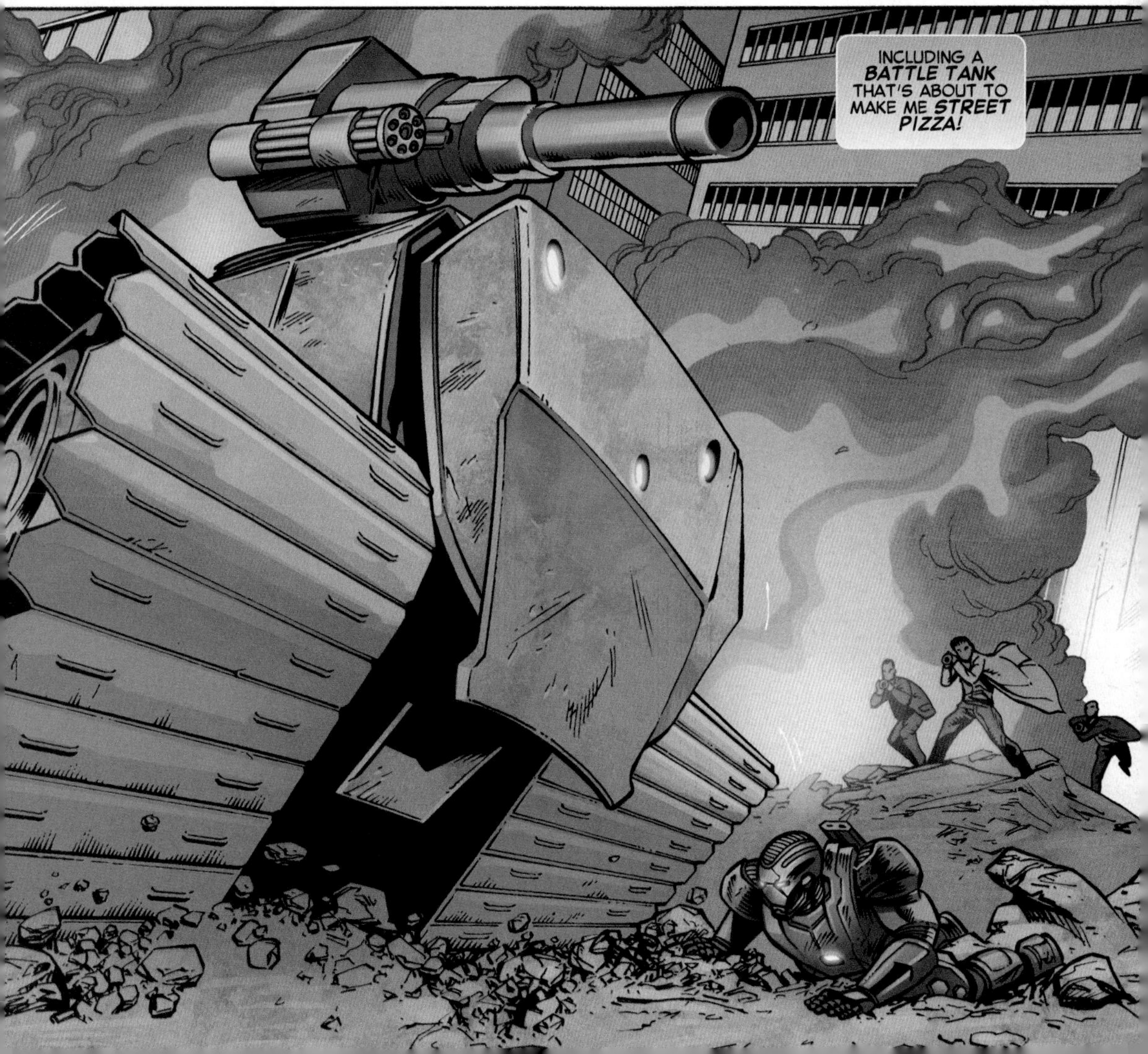
INCLUDING A BATTLE TANK THAT'S ABOUT TO MAKE ME STREET PIZZA!

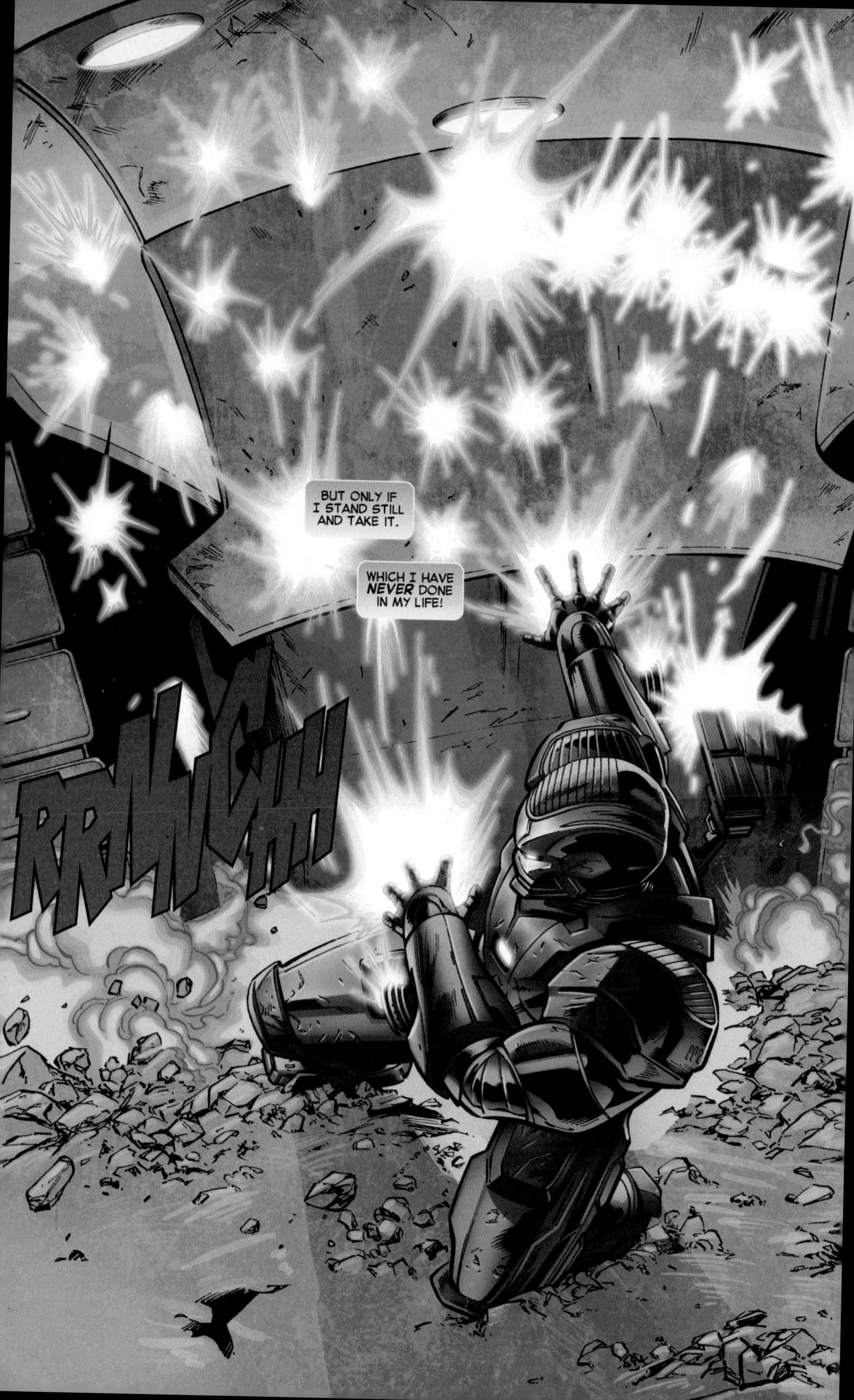
BUT ONLY IF I STAND STILL AND TAKE IT.
WHICH I HAVE *NEVER* DONE IN MY LIFE!
RRMMCHH

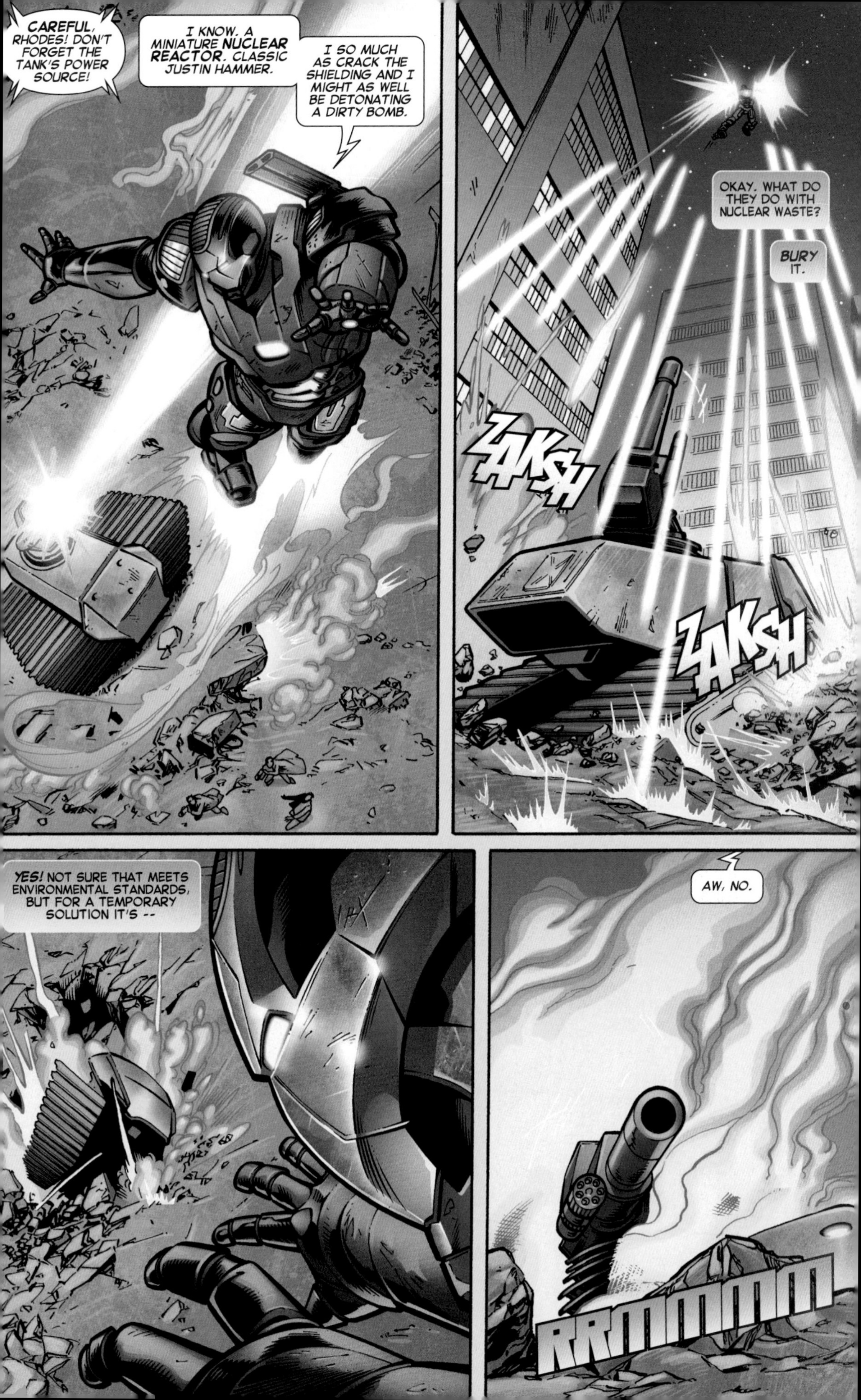
CAREFUL, RHODES! DON'T FORGET THE TANK'S POWER SOURCE!
I KNOW. A MINIATURE NUCLEAR REACTOR. CLASSIC JUSTIN HAMMER.
I SO MUCH AS CRACK THE SHIELDING AND I MIGHT AS WELL BE DETONATING A DIRTY BOMB.
OKAY. WHAT DO THEY DO WITH NUCLEAR WASTE?
BURY IT.
ZAKSH
ZAKSH
YES! NOT SURE THAT MEETS ENVIRONMENTAL STANDARDS, BUT FOR A TEMPORARY SOLUTION IT'S --
AW, NO.
RRMMMM

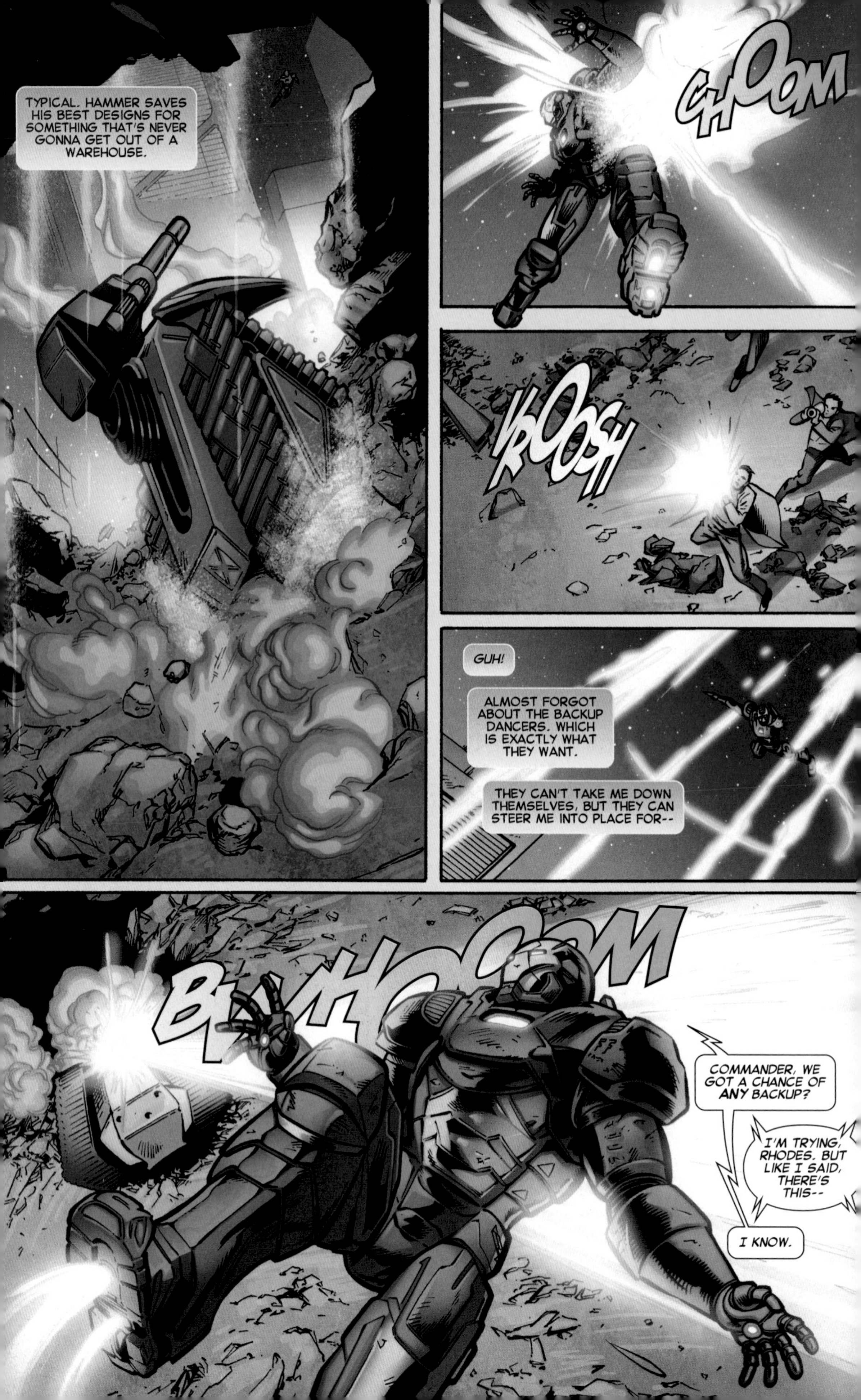
TYPICAL. HAMMER SAVES HIS BEST DESIGNS FOR SOMETHING THAT'S NEVER GONNA GET OUT OF A WAREHOUSE.
CHOOOM
VROOSH
GUH!
ALMOST FORGOT ABOUT THE BACKUP DANCERS. WHICH IS EXACTLY WHAT THEY WANT.
THEY CAN'T TAKE ME DOWN THEMSELVES, BUT THEY CAN STEER ME INTO PLACE FOR--
COMMANDER, WE GOT A CHANCE OF ANY BACKUP?
I'M TRYING, RHODES. BUT LIKE I SAID, THERE'S THIS--
I KNOW.

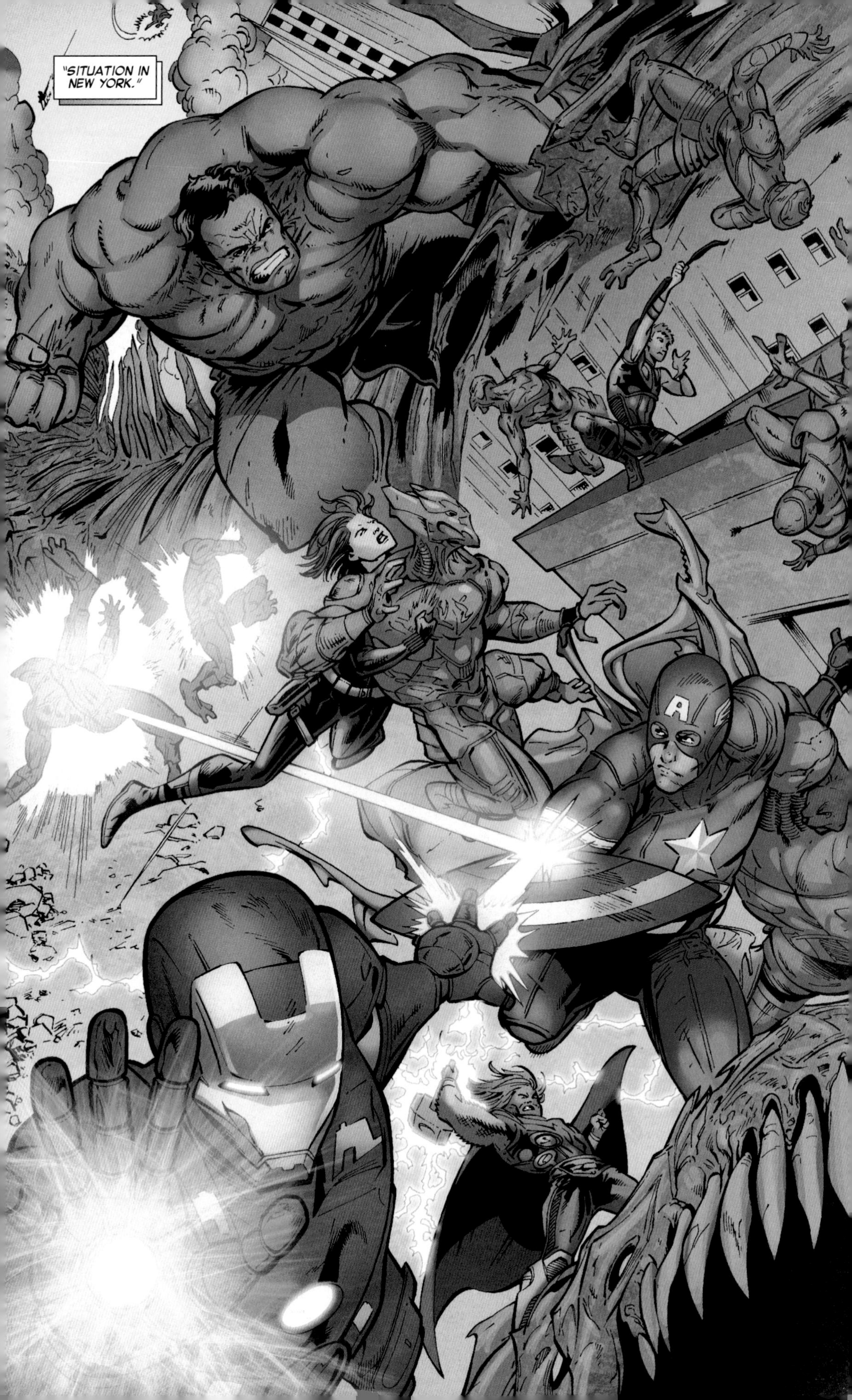
"SITUATION IN NEW YORK."

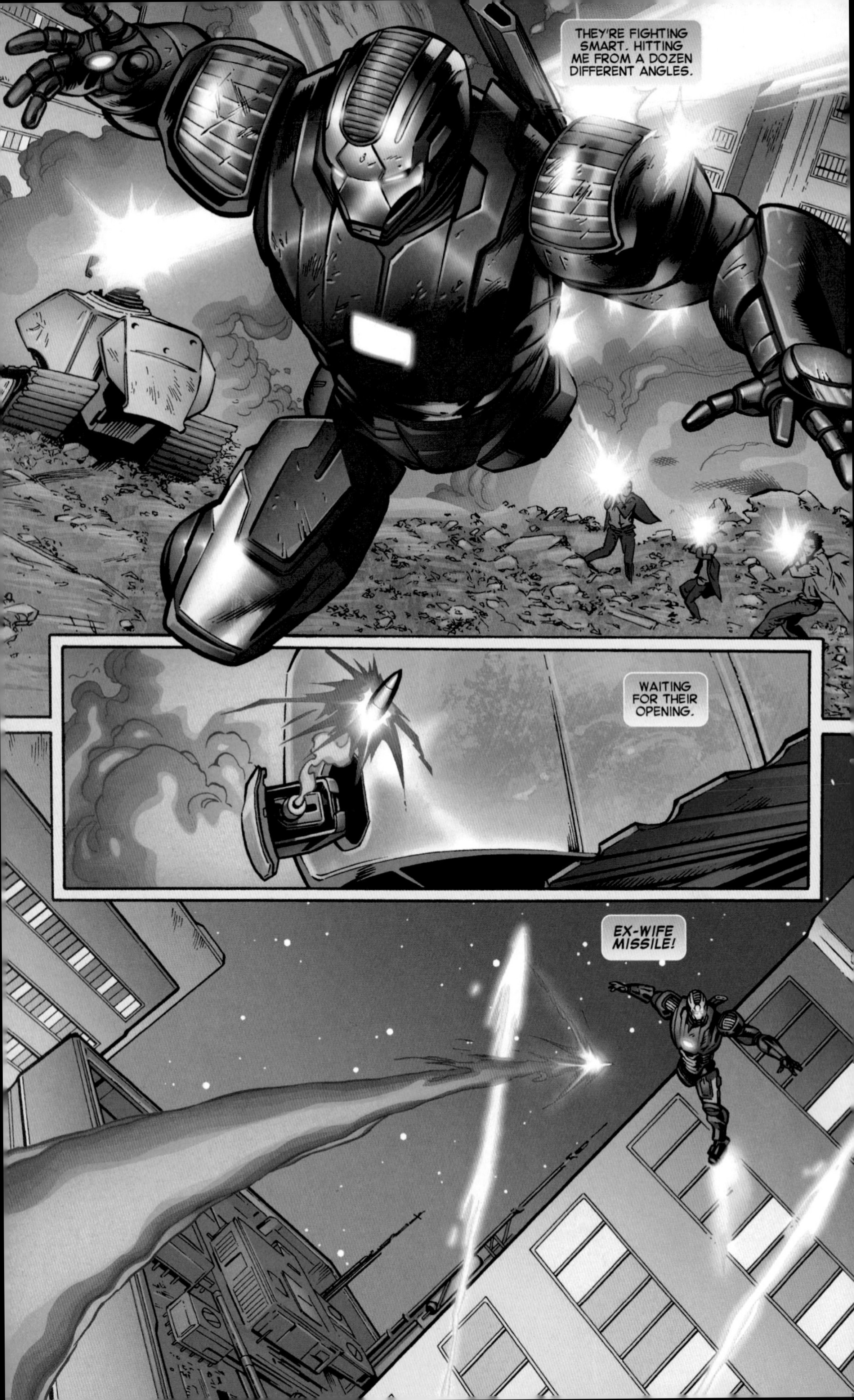
THEY'RE FIGHTING SMART. HITTING ME FROM A DOZEN DIFFERENT ANGLES.
WAITING FOR THEIR OPENING.
EX-WIFE MISSILE!

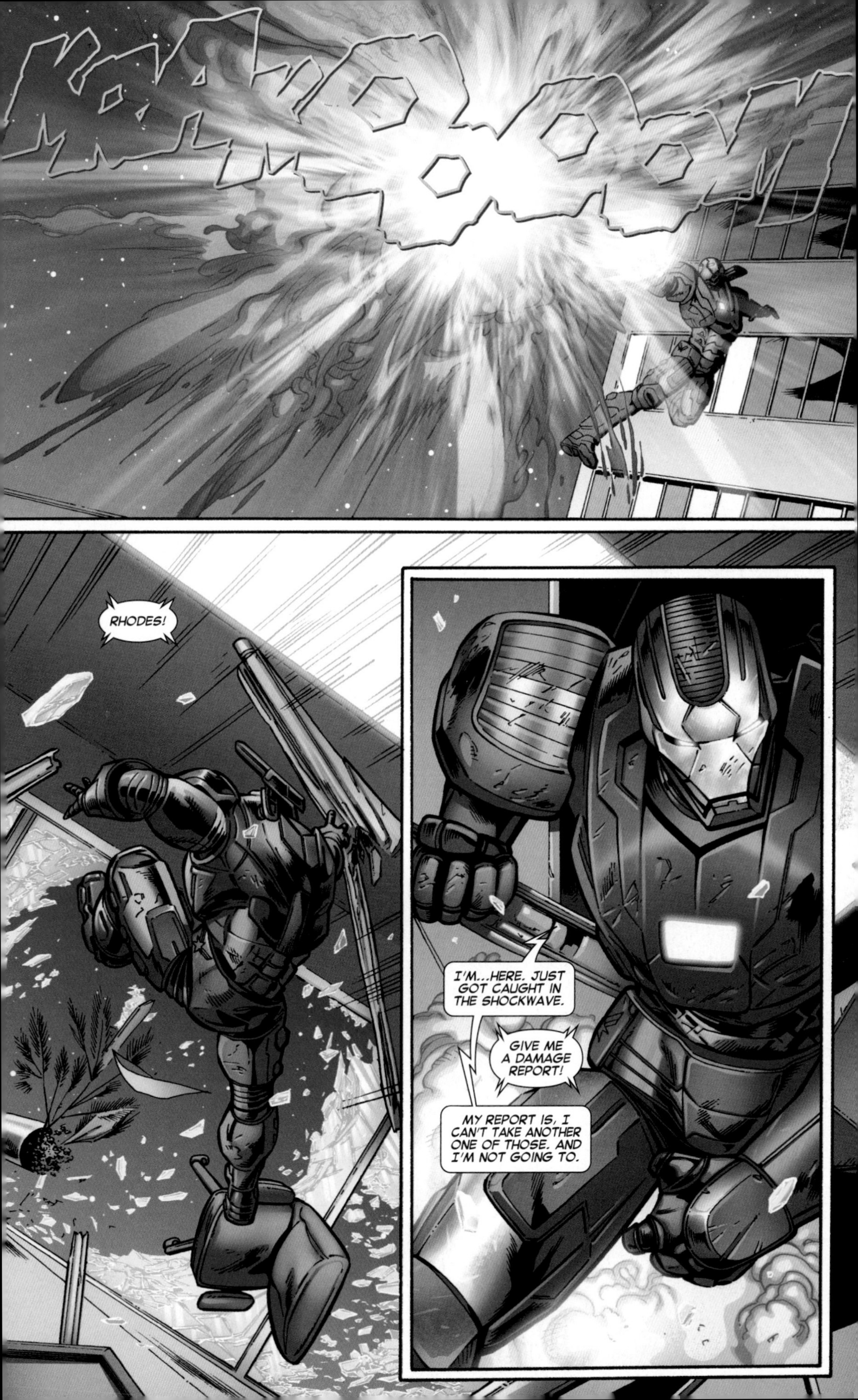
KA-WOOOOOM!
RHODES!
I'M...HERE. JUST GOT CAUGHT IN THE SHOCKWAVE.
GIVE ME A DAMAGE REPORT!
MY REPORT IS, I CAN'T TAKE ANOTHER ONE OF THOSE. AND I'M NOT GOING TO.

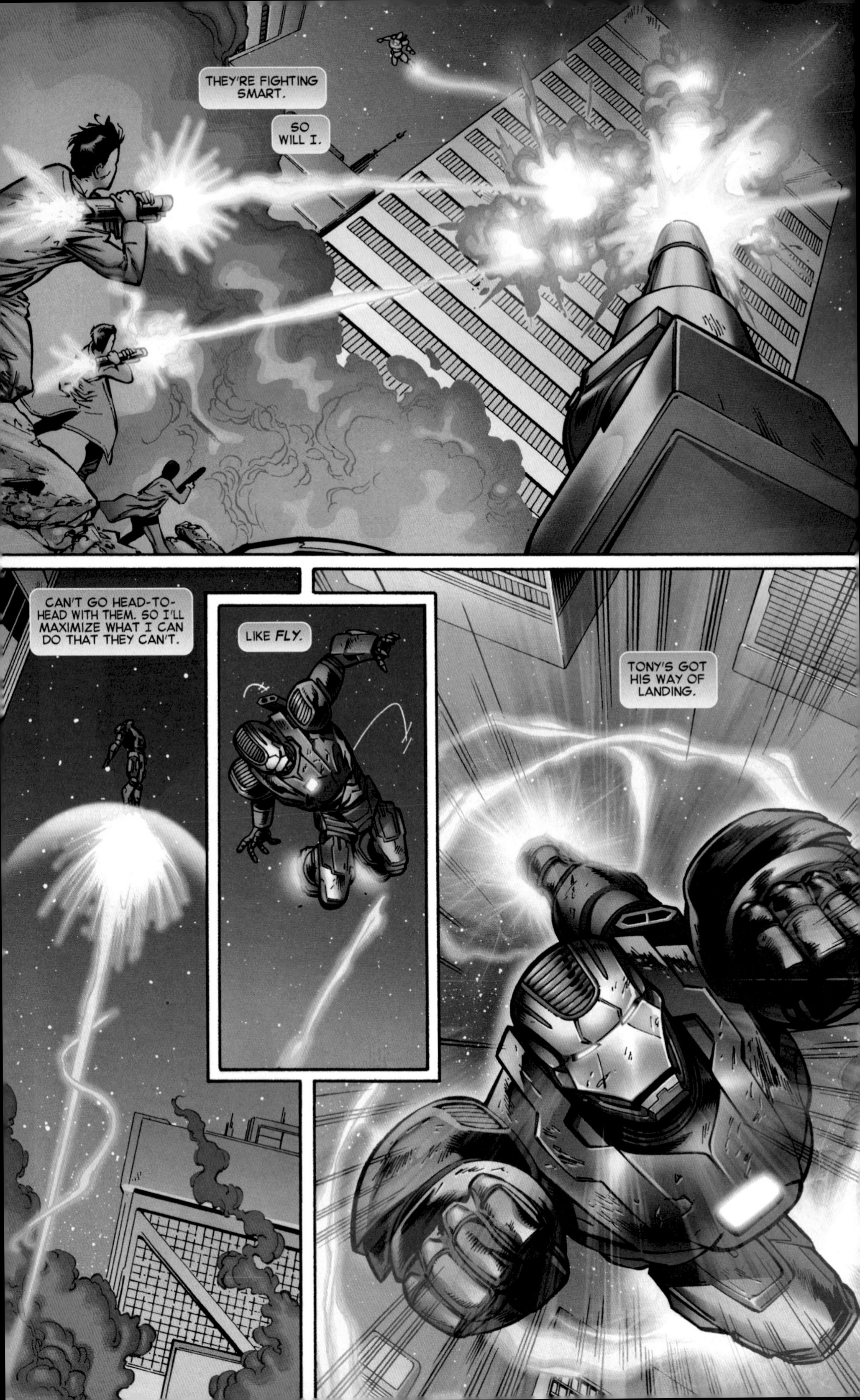
THEY'RE FIGHTING SMART.
SO WILL I.
CAN'T GO HEAD-TO-HEAD WITH THEM. SO I'LL MAXIMIZE WHAT I CAN DO THAT THEY CAN'T.
LIKE FLY.
TONY'S GOT HIS WAY OF LANDING.

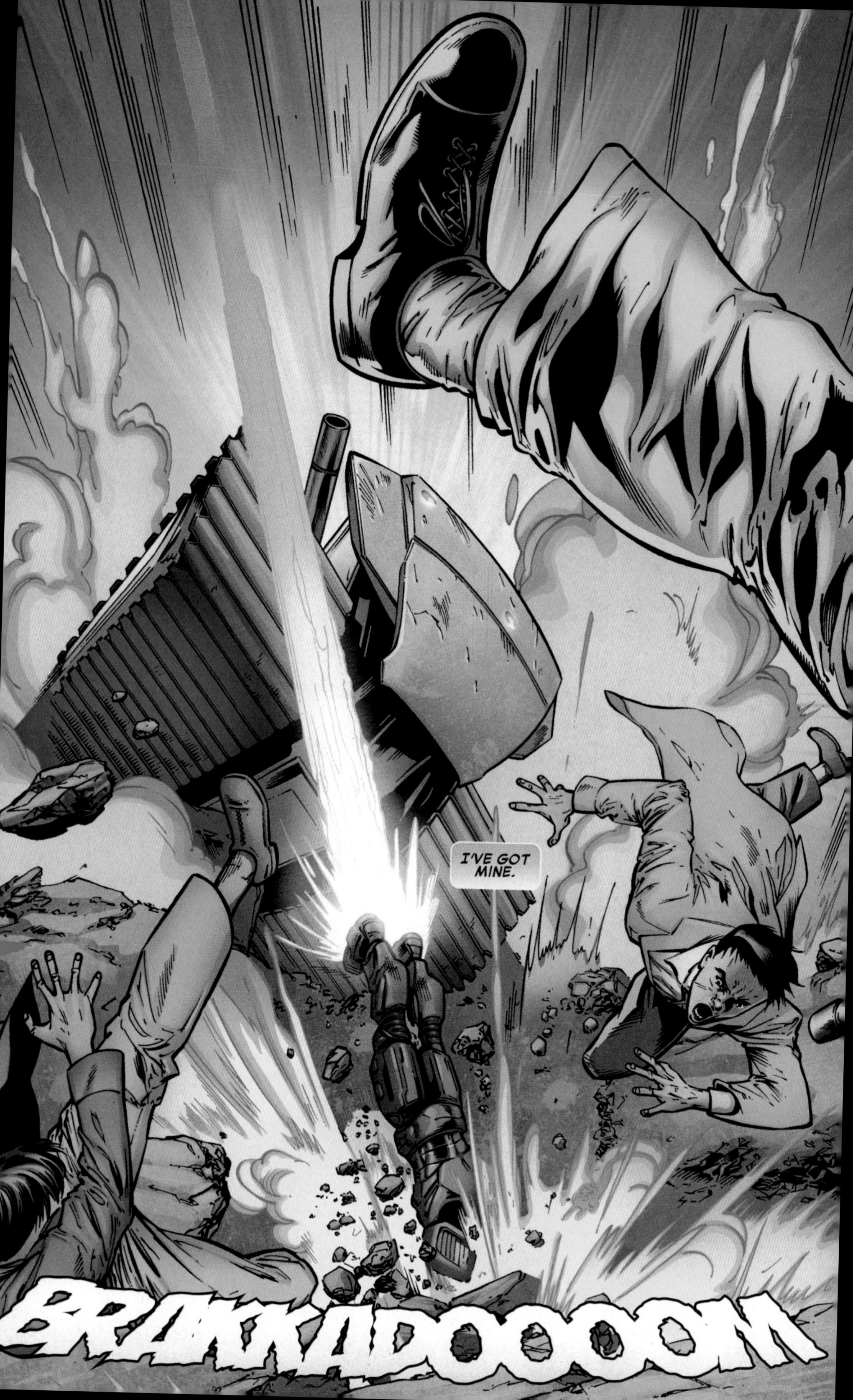
I'VE GOT MINE.
BRAKADOOOOOM

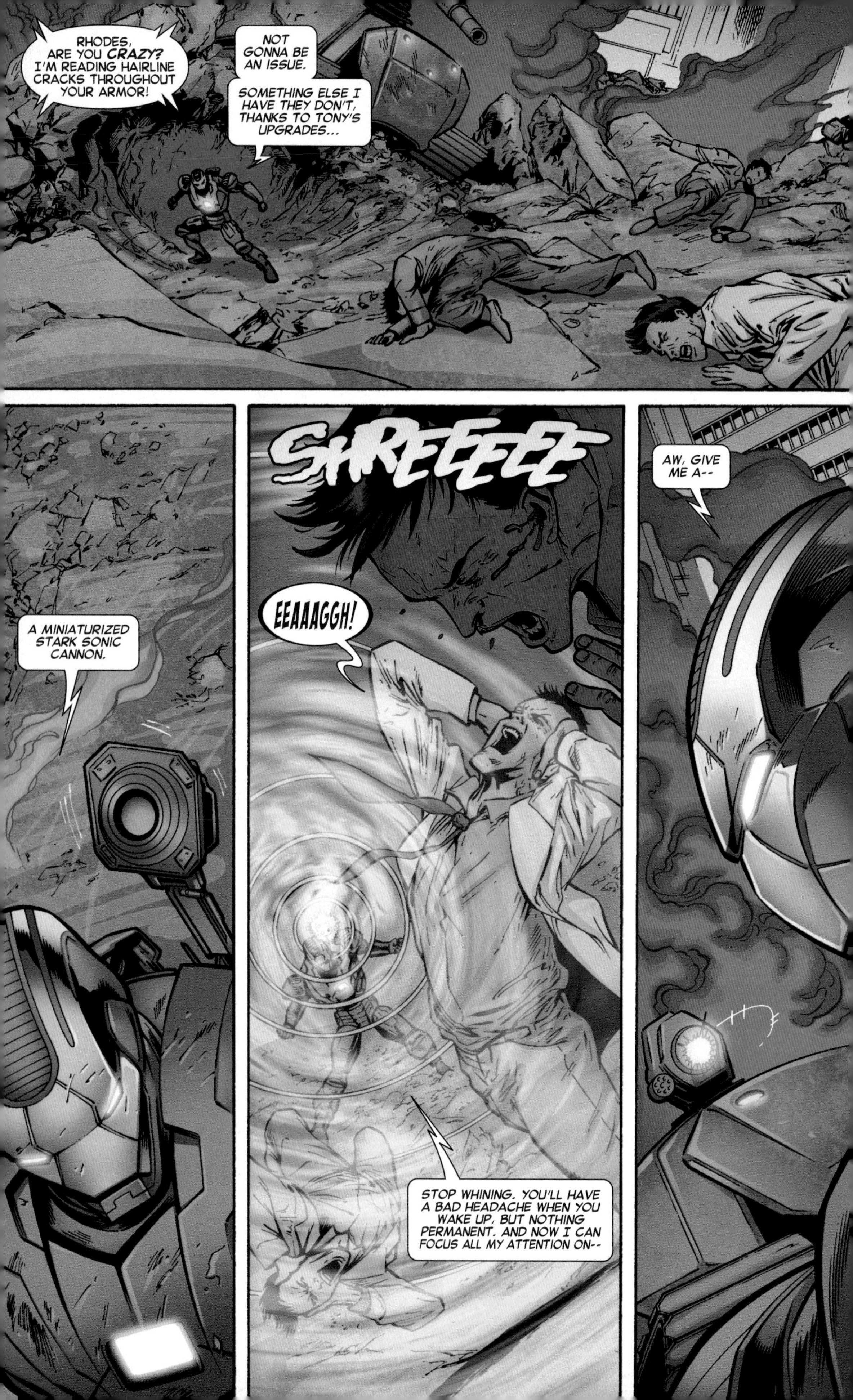
RHODES, ARE YOU CRAZY? I'M READING HAIRLINE CRACKS THROUGHOUT YOUR ARMOR!
NOT GONNA BE AN ISSUE.
SOMETHING ELSE I HAVE THEY DON'T, THANKS TO TONY'S UPGRADES...
A MINIATURIZED STARK SONIC CANNON.
SHREEEEE
EEAAAAGGH!
STOP WHINING. YOU'LL HAVE A BAD HEADACHE WHEN YOU WAKE UP, BUT NOTHING PERMANENT. AND NOW I CAN FOCUS ALL MY ATTENTION ON--
AW, GIVE ME A--

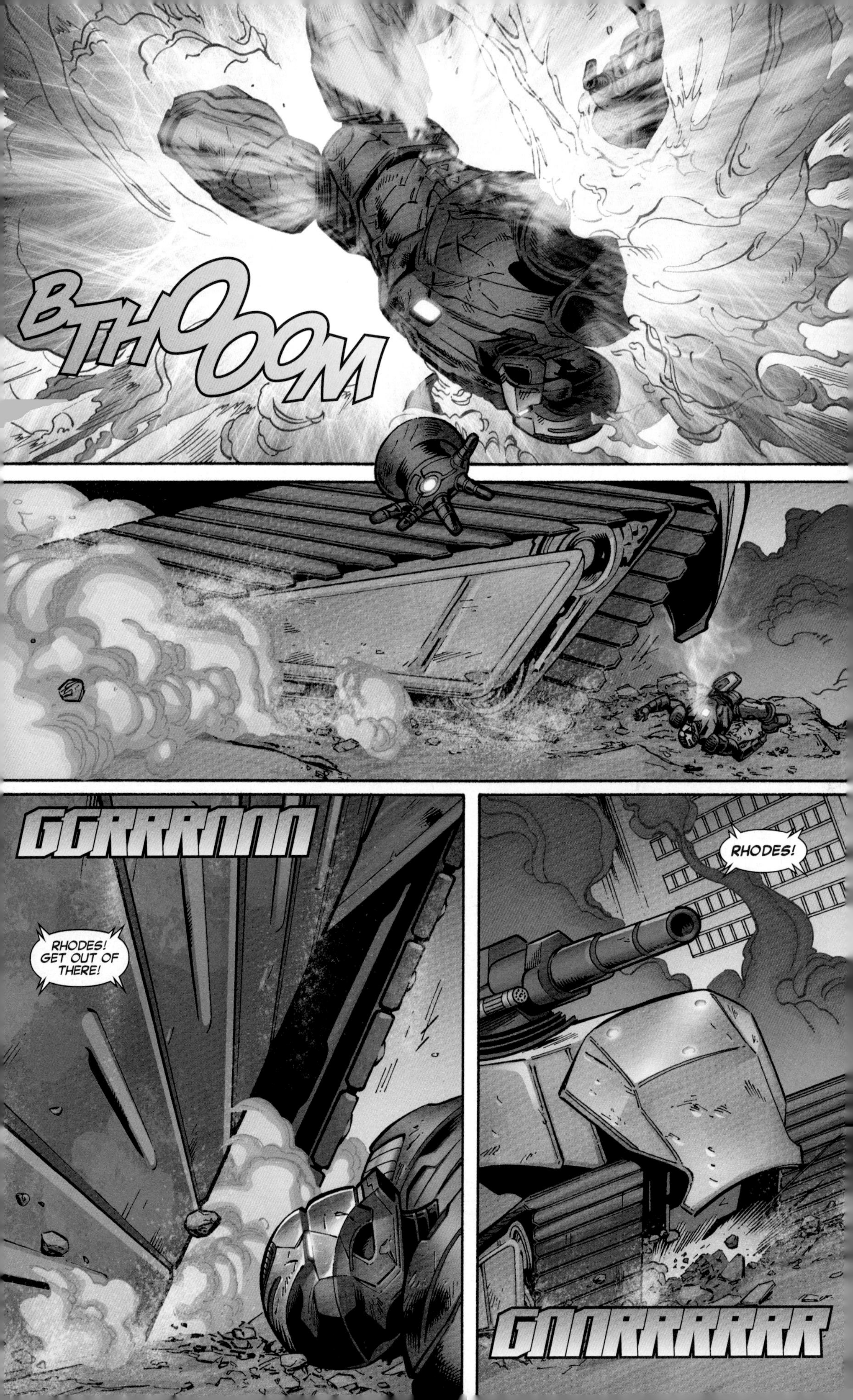
BTHOOOOM
GGRRRNNN
RHODES! GET OUT OF THERE!
RHODES!
GNNRRRRRRR

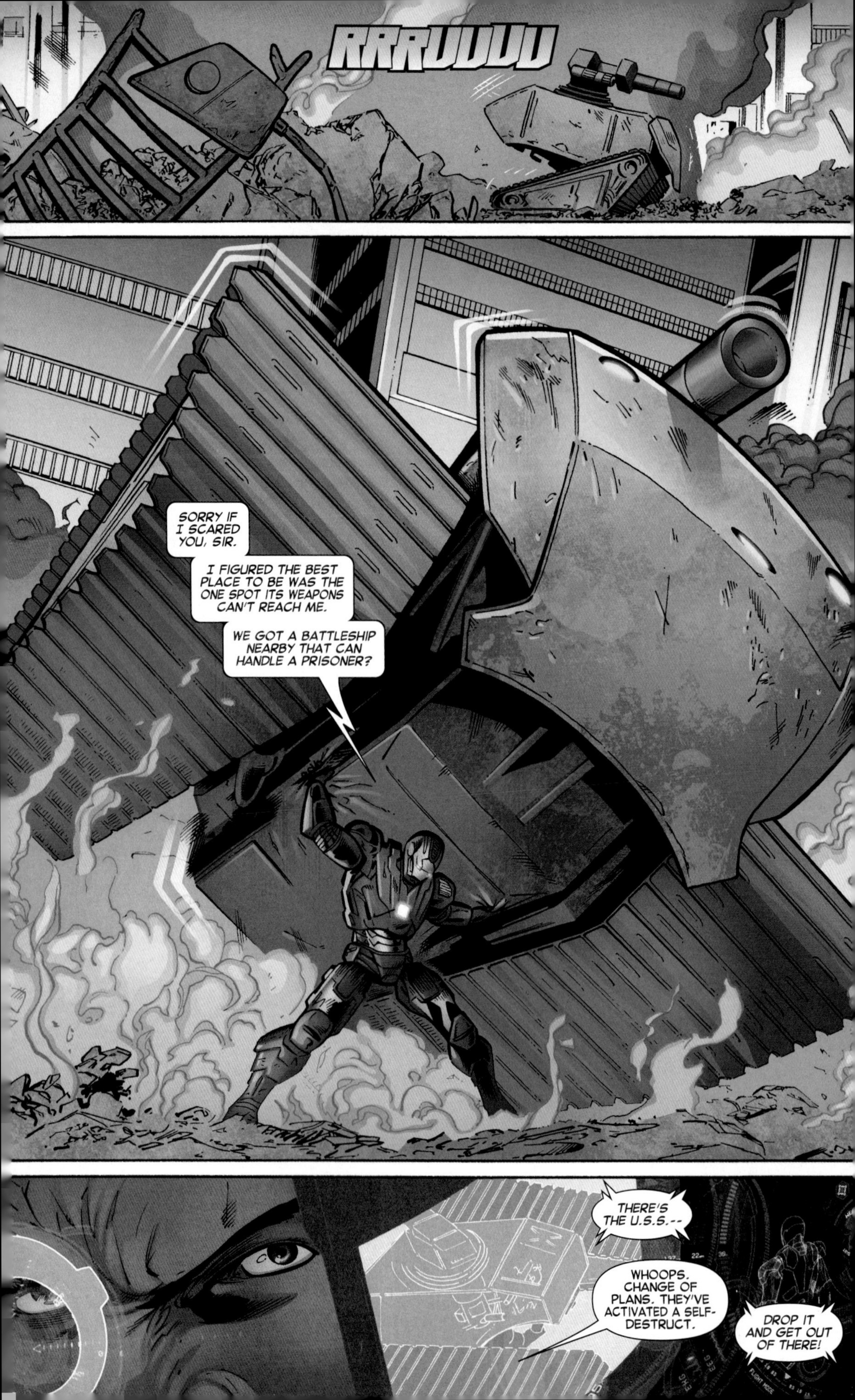
RRRUUUU
SORRY IF I SCARED YOU, SIR.
I FIGURED THE BEST PLACE TO BE WAS THE ONE SPOT ITS WEAPONS CAN'T REACH ME.
WE GOT A BATTLESHIP NEARBY THAT CAN HANDLE A PRISONER?
THERE'S THE U.S.S.--
WHOOPS. CHANGE OF PLANS. THEY'VE ACTIVATED A SELF-DESTRUCT.
DROP IT AND GET OUT OF THERE!

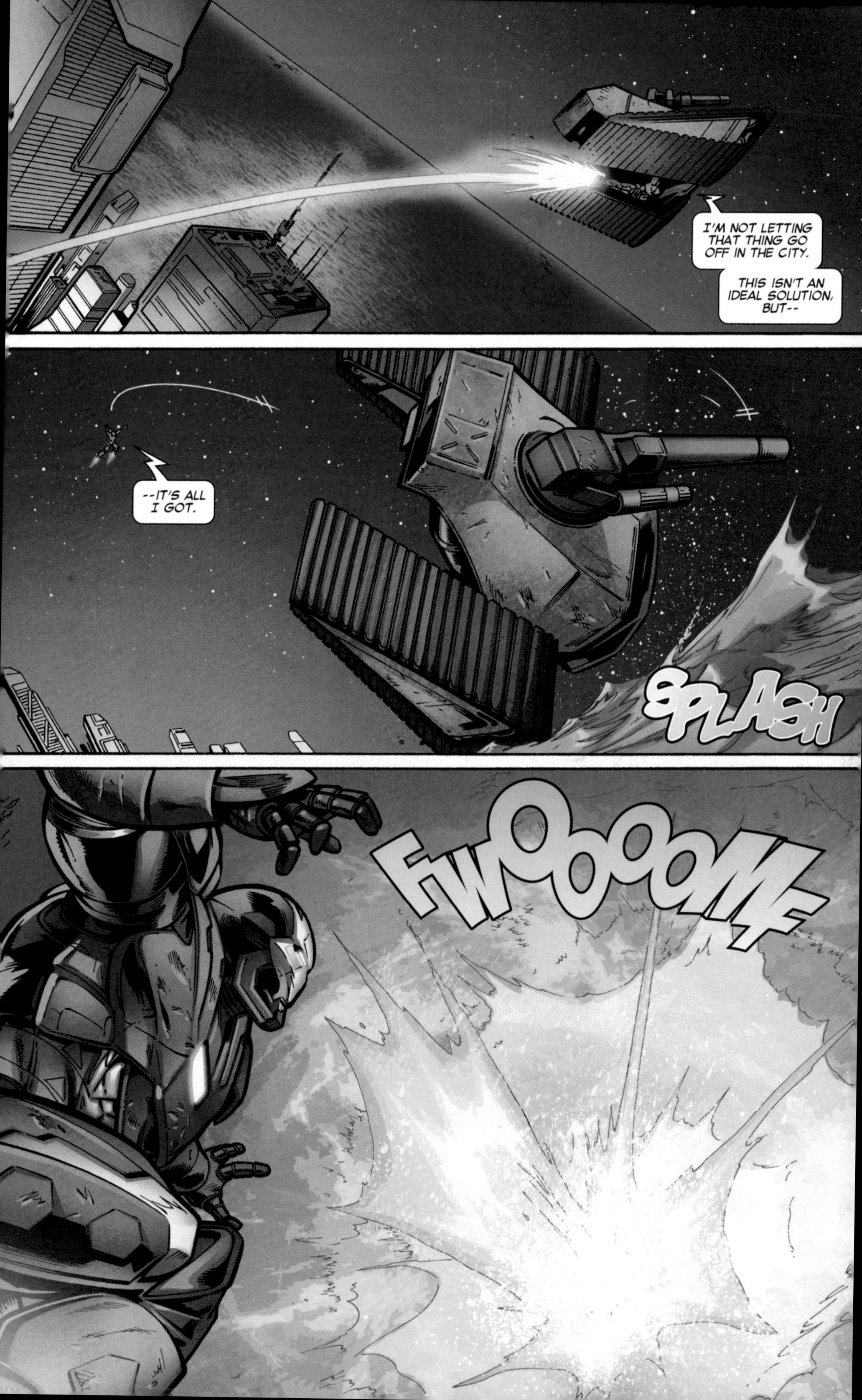
I'M NOT LETTING THAT THING GO OFF IN THE CITY.
THIS ISN'T AN IDEAL SOLUTION, BUT--
--IT'S ALL I GOT.
SPLASH
FWOOOOMF

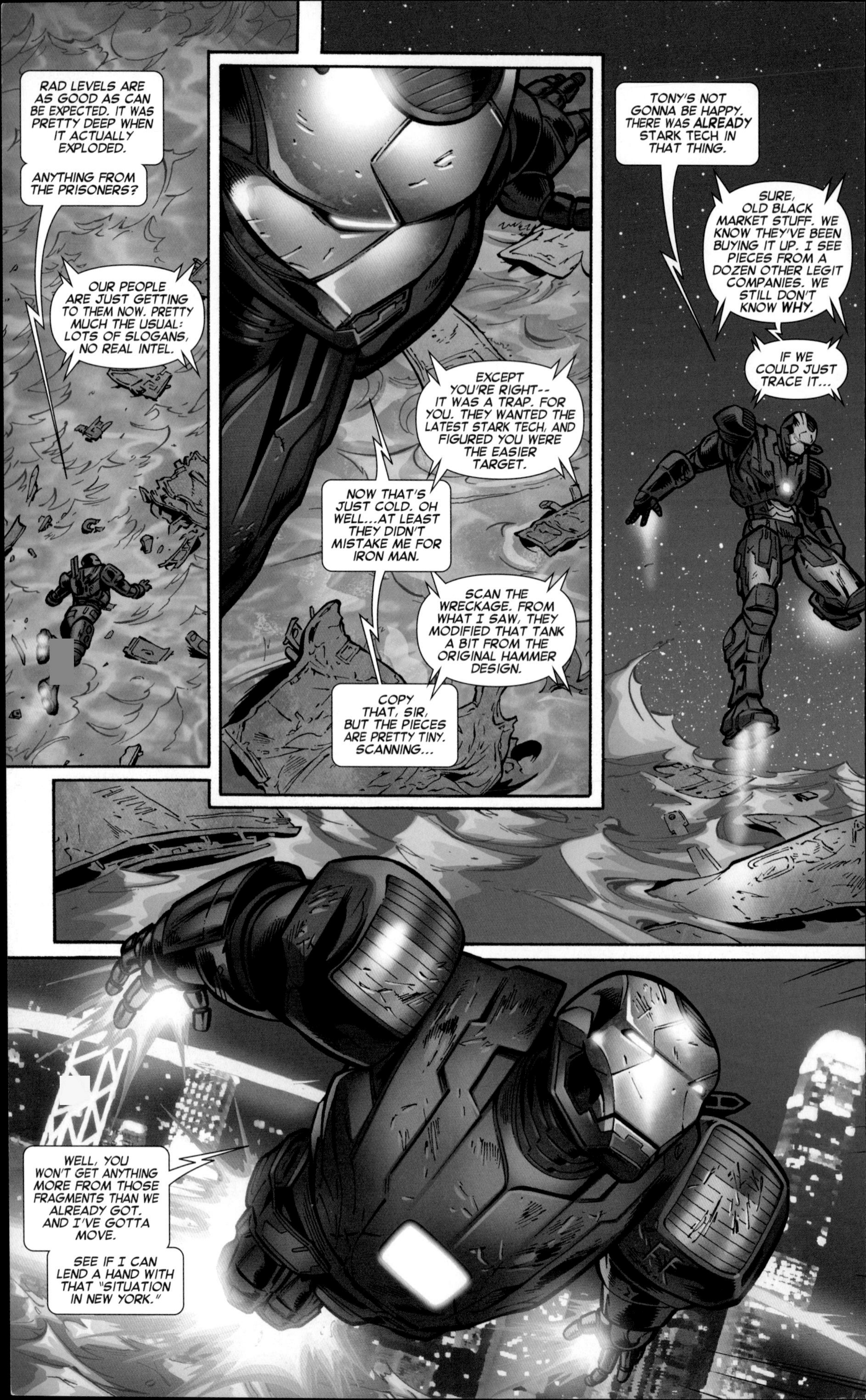

RAD LEVELS ARE AS GOOD AS CAN BE EXPECTED. IT WAS PRETTY DEEP WHEN IT ACTUALLY EXPLODED.
ANYTHING FROM THE PRISONERS?
OUR PEOPLE ARE JUST GETTING TO THEM NOW. PRETTY MUCH THE USUAL: LOTS OF SLOGANS, NO REAL INTEL.
EXCEPT YOU'RE RIGHT-- IT WAS A TRAP. FOR YOU. THEY WANTED THE LATEST STARK TECH, AND FIGURED YOU WERE THE EASIER TARGET.
NOW THAT'S JUST COLD. OH WELL...AT LEAST THEY DIDN'T MISTAKE ME FOR IRON MAN.
SCAN THE WRECKAGE. FROM WHAT I SAW, THEY MODIFIED THAT TANK A BIT FROM THE ORIGINAL HAMMER DESIGN.
COPY THAT, SIR, BUT THE PIECES ARE PRETTY TINY. SCANNING...
TONY'S NOT GONNA BE HAPPY. THERE WAS ALREADY STARK TECH IN THAT THING.
SURE, OLD BLACK MARKET STUFF. WE KNOW THEY'VE BEEN BUYING IT UP. I SEE PIECES FROM A DOZEN OTHER LEGIT COMPANIES. WE STILL DON'T KNOW WHY.
IF WE COULD JUST TRACE IT...
WELL, YOU WON'T GET ANYTHING MORE FROM THOSE FRAGMENTS THAN WE ALREADY GOT. AND I'VE GOTTA MOVE.
SEE IF I CAN LEND A HAND WITH THAT "SITUATION IN NEW YORK."

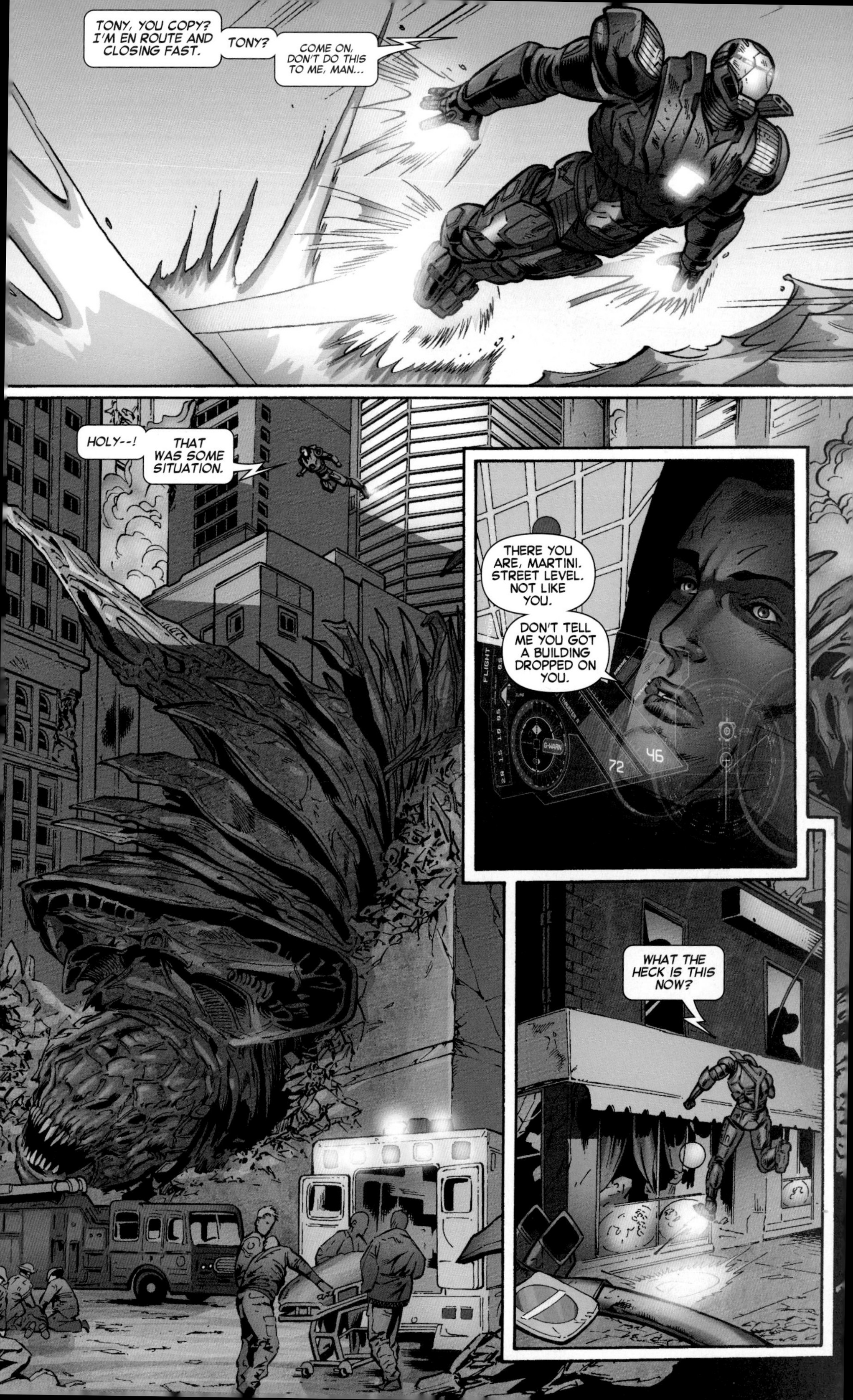
TONY, YOU COPY? I'M EN ROUTE AND CLOSING FAST.
TONY?
COME ON, DON'T DO THIS TO ME, MAN...
HOLY--!
THAT WAS SOME SITUATION.
THERE YOU ARE, MARTINI. STREET LEVEL. NOT LIKE YOU.
DON'T TELL ME YOU GOT A BUILDING DROPPED ON YOU.
FLIGHT
G-WARN
72
46
WHAT THE HECK IS THIS NOW?

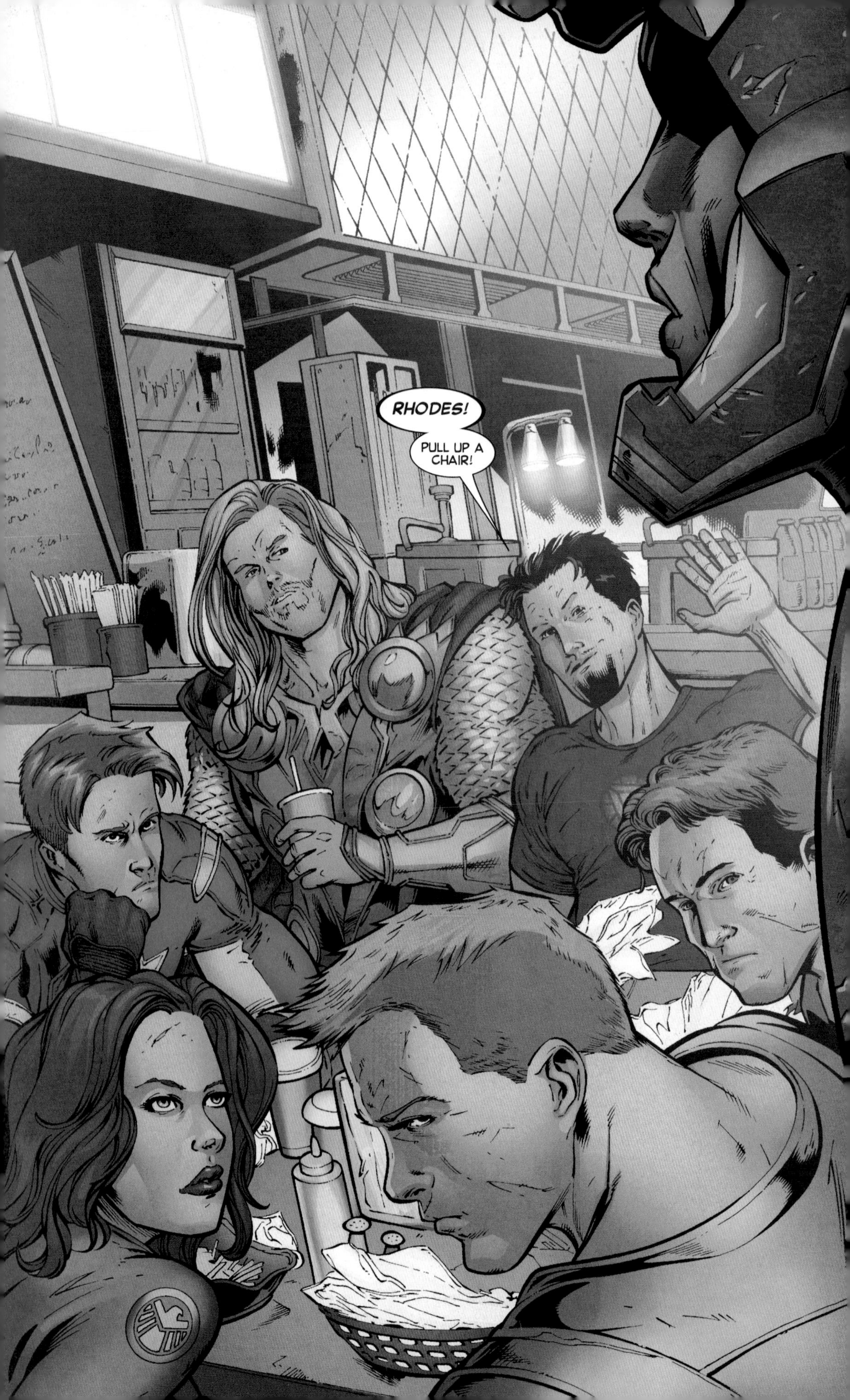
RHODES!
PULL UP A CHAIR!

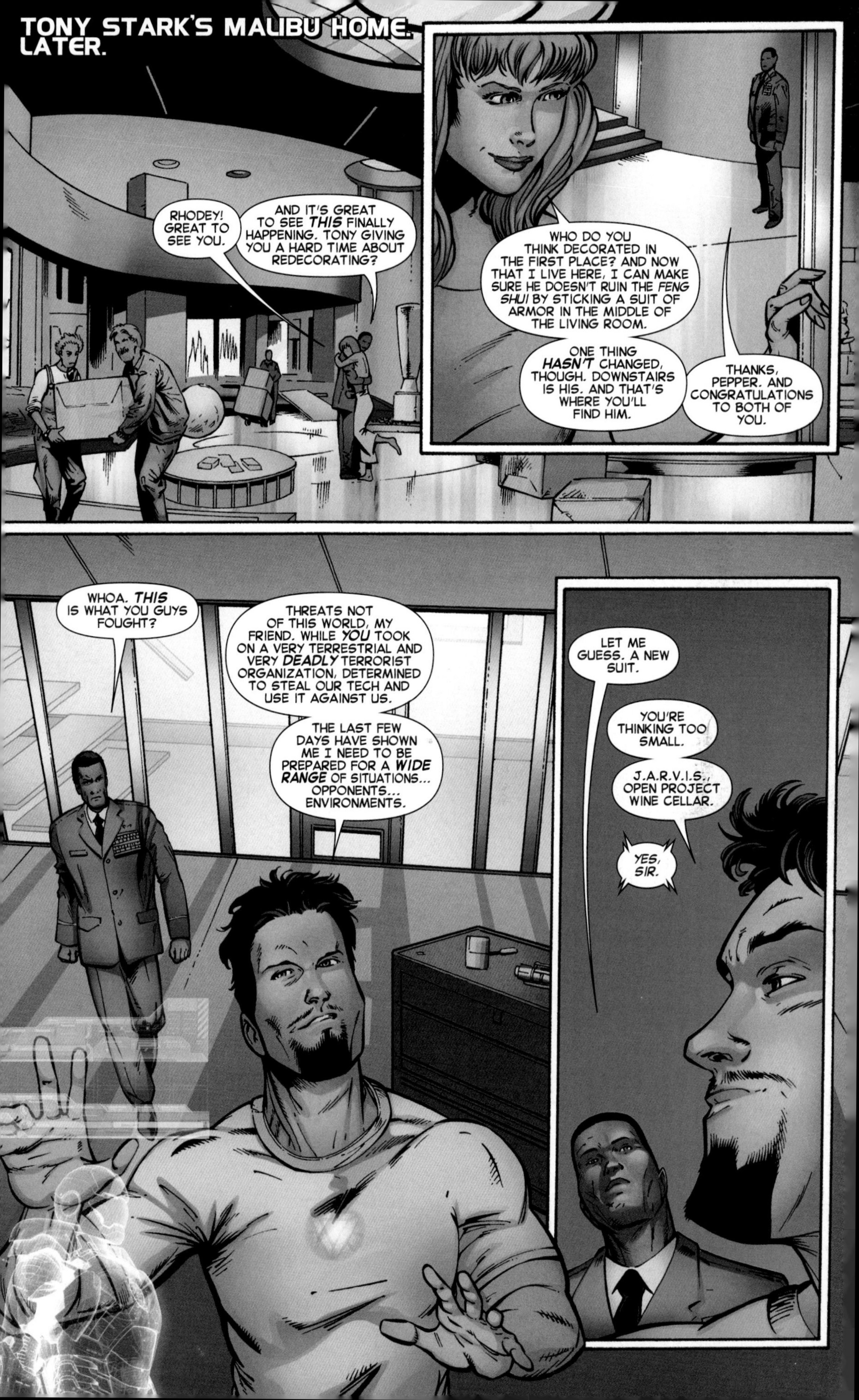
TONY STARK'S MALIBU HOME. LATER.
RHODEY! GREAT TO SEE YOU.
AND IT'S GREAT TO SEE THIS FINALLY HAPPENING. TONY GIVING YOU A HARD TIME ABOUT REDECORATING?
WHO DO YOU THINK DECORATED IN THE FIRST PLACE? AND NOW THAT I LIVE HERE, I CAN MAKE SURE HE DOESN'T RUIN THE FENG SHUI BY STICKING A SUIT OF ARMOR IN THE MIDDLE OF THE LIVING ROOM.
ONE THING HASN'T CHANGED, THOUGH. DOWNSTAIRS IS HIS. AND THAT'S WHERE YOU'LL FIND HIM.
THANKS, PEPPER. AND CONGRATULATIONS TO BOTH OF YOU.
WHOA. THIS IS WHAT YOU GUYS FOUGHT?
THREATS NOT OF THIS WORLD, MY FRIEND. WHILE YOU TOOK ON A VERY TERRESTRIAL AND VERY DEADLY TERRORIST ORGANIZATION, DETERMINED TO STEAL OUR TECH AND USE IT AGAINST US.
THE LAST FEW DAYS HAVE SHOWN ME I NEED TO BE PREPARED FOR A WIDE RANGE OF SITUATIONS... OPPONENTS... ENVIRONMENTS.
LET ME GUESS. A NEW SUIT.
YOU'RE THINKING TOO SMALL.
J.A.R.V.I.S., OPEN PROJECT WINE CELLAR.
YES, SIR.

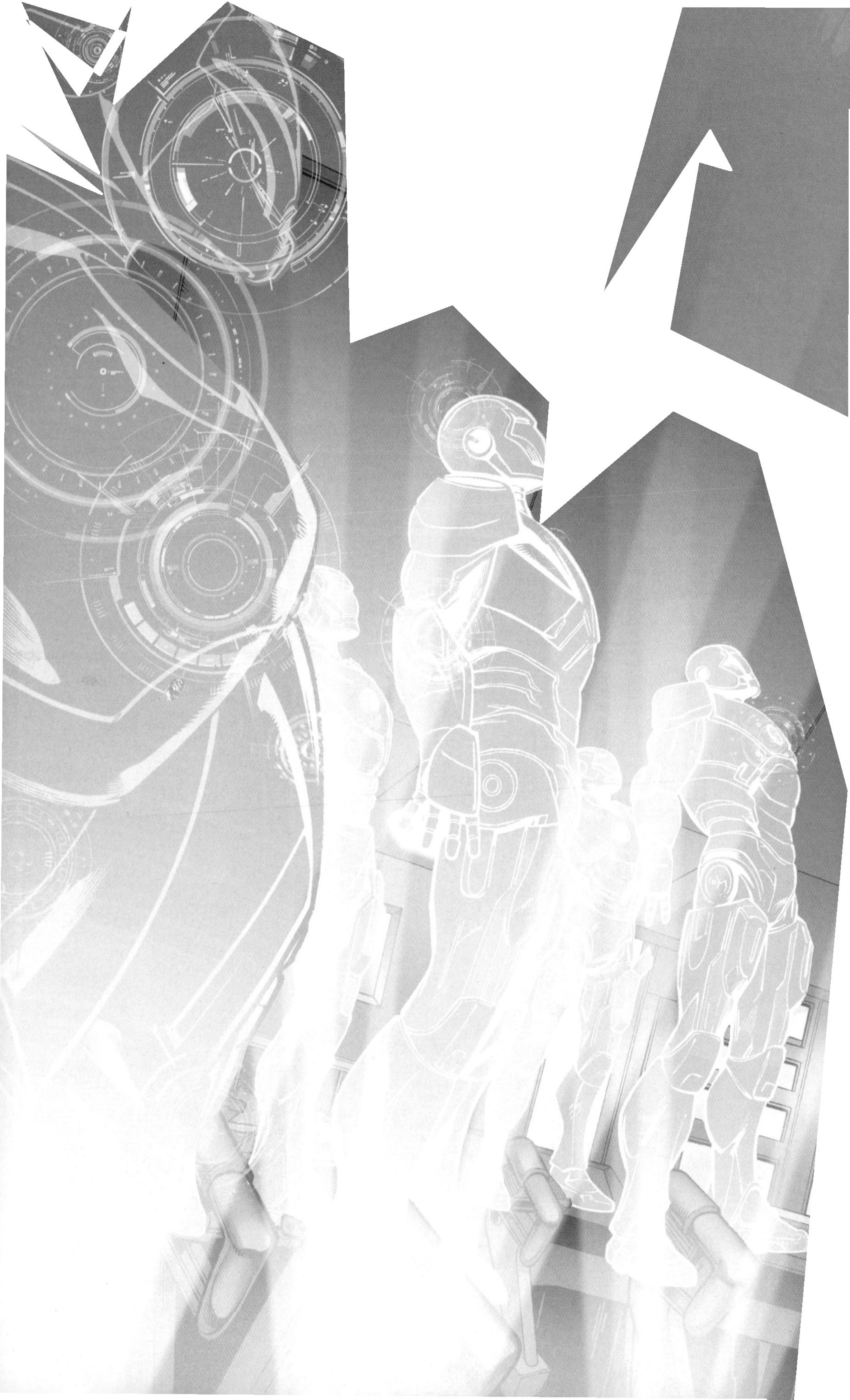

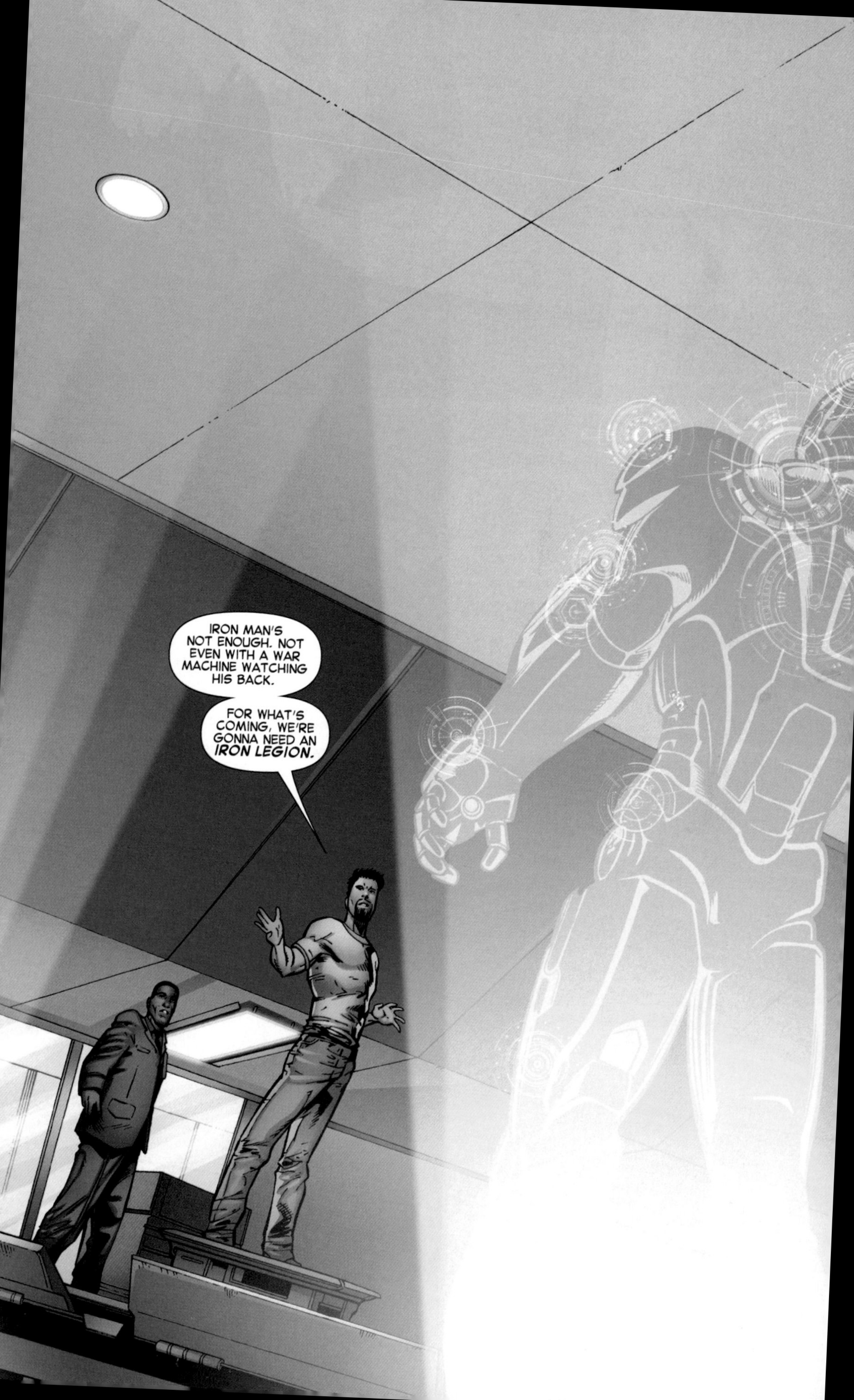
IRON MAN'S NOT ENOUGH. NOT EVEN WITH A WAR MACHINE WATCHING HIS BACK.
FOR WHAT'S COMING, WE'RE GONNA NEED AN ***IRON LEGION.***

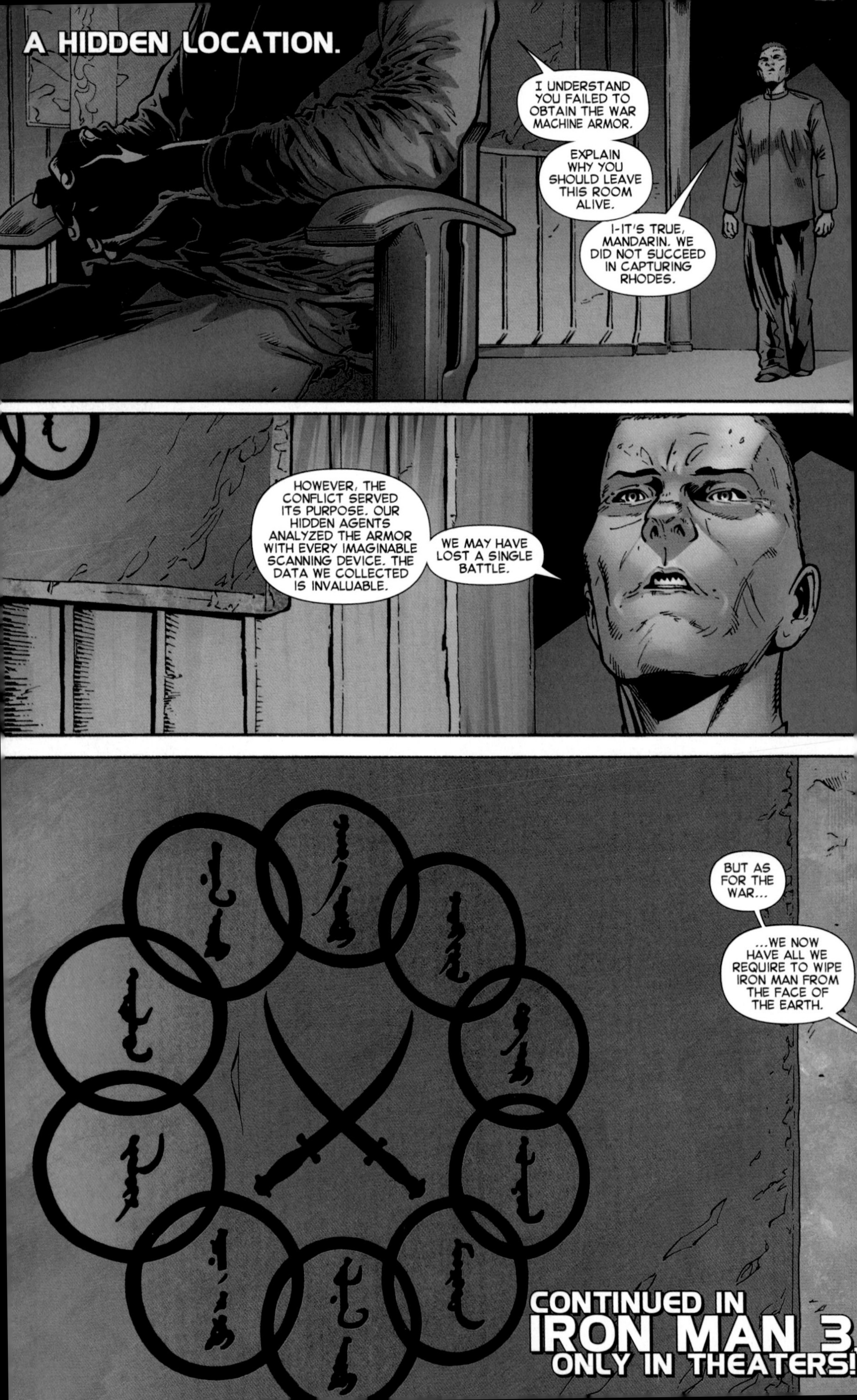
A HIDDEN LOCATION.
I UNDERSTAND YOU FAILED TO OBTAIN THE WAR MACHINE ARMOR.
EXPLAIN WHY YOU SHOULD LEAVE THIS ROOM ALIVE.
I-IT'S TRUE, MANDARIN. WE DID NOT SUCCEED IN CAPTURING RHODES.
WE MAY HAVE LOST A SINGLE BATTLE.
HOWEVER, THE CONFLICT SERVED ITS PURPOSE. OUR HIDDEN AGENTS ANALYZED THE ARMOR WITH EVERY IMAGINABLE SCANNING DEVICE. THE DATA WE COLLECTED IS INVALUABLE.
BUT AS FOR THE WAR...
...WE NOW HAVE ALL WE REQUIRE TO WIPE IRON MAN FROM THE FACE OF THE EARTH.
CONTINUED IN IRON MAN 3 ONLY IN THEATERS!

NEXT:

5/3/13

Facebook.com/IronMan

MARVEL

IN THEATERS MAY 3, 2013

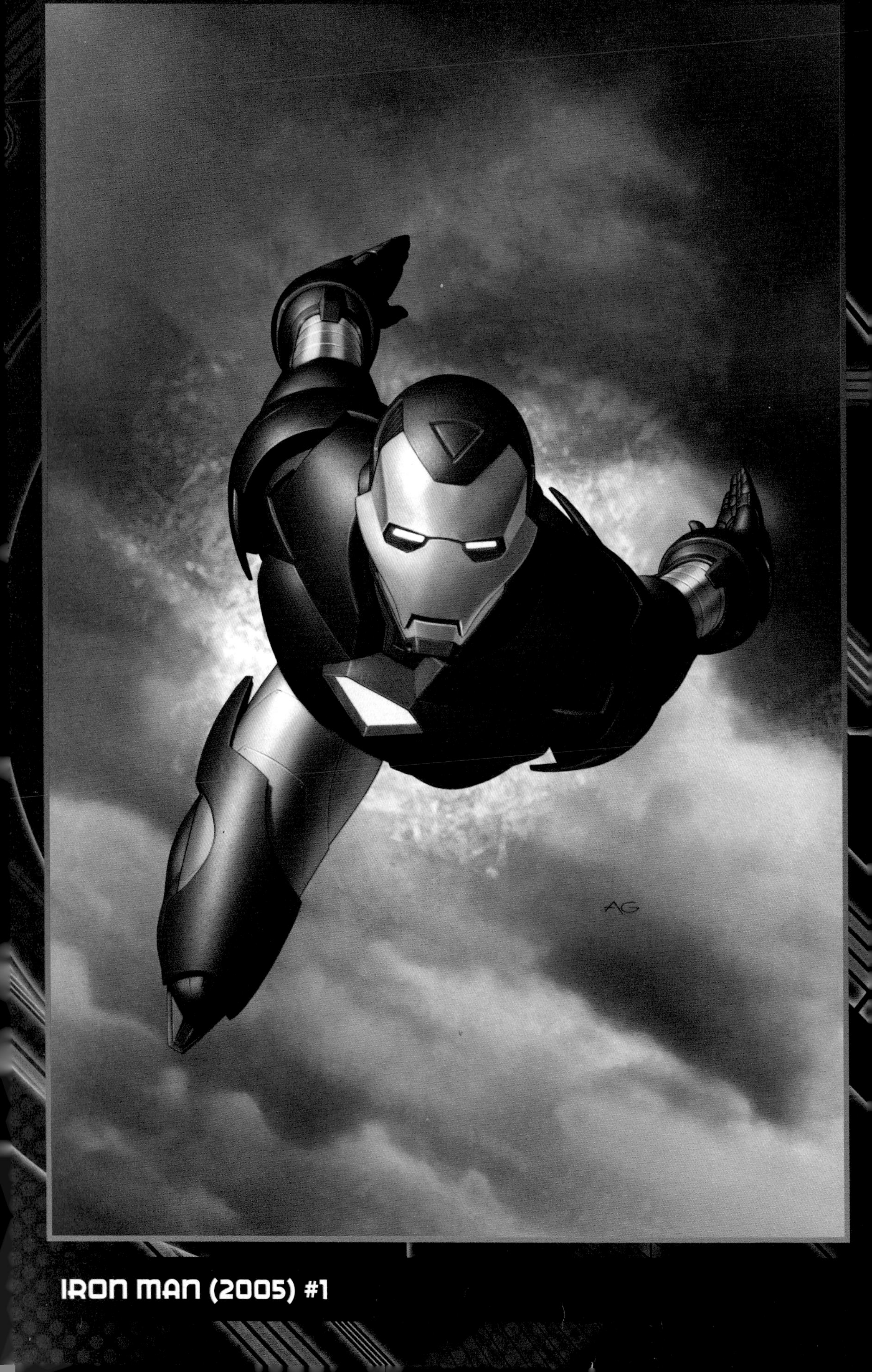
AG

IRON MAN (2005) #1

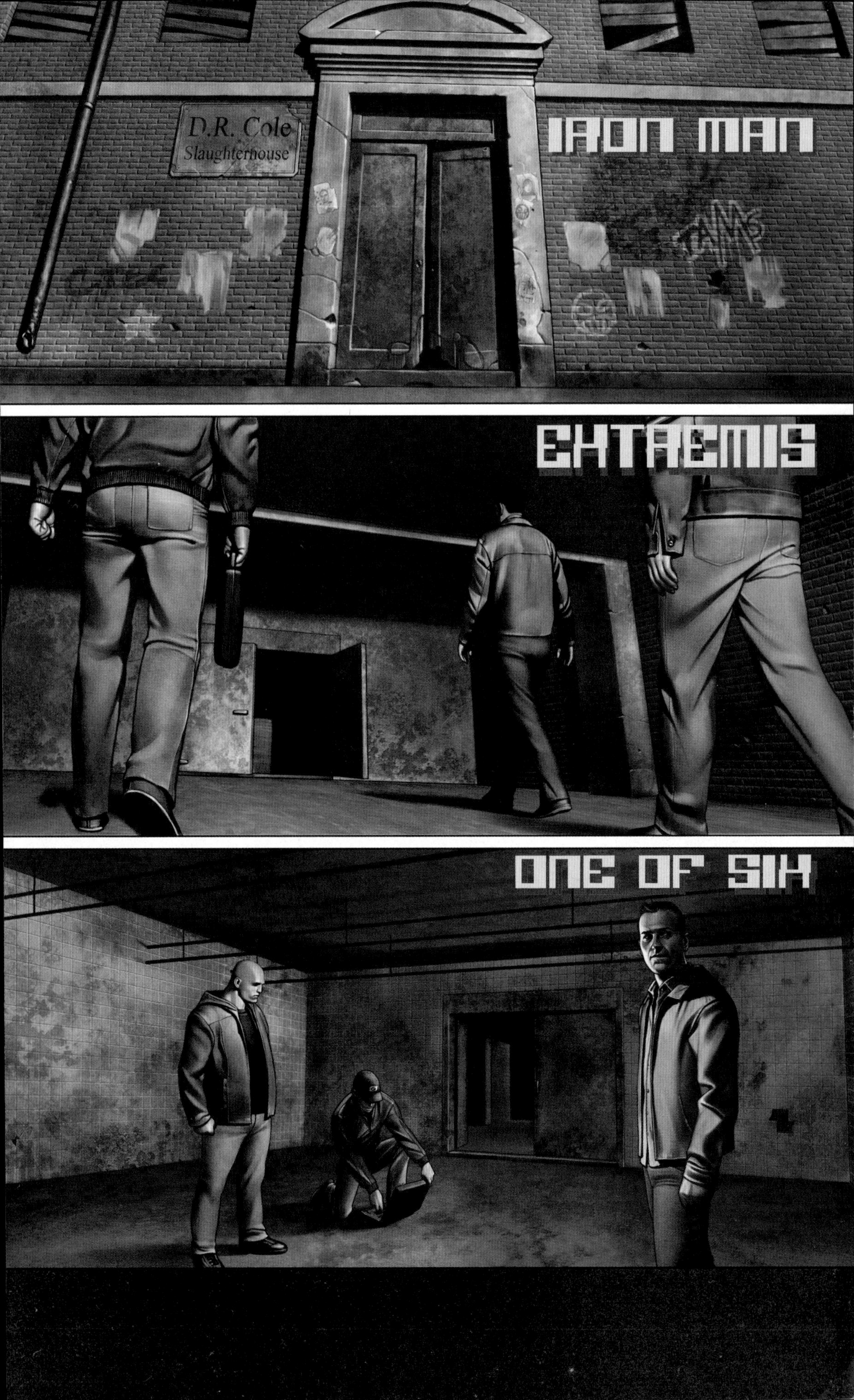
D.R. Cole
Slaughterhouse
IRON MAN
EXTREMIS
ONE OF SIX

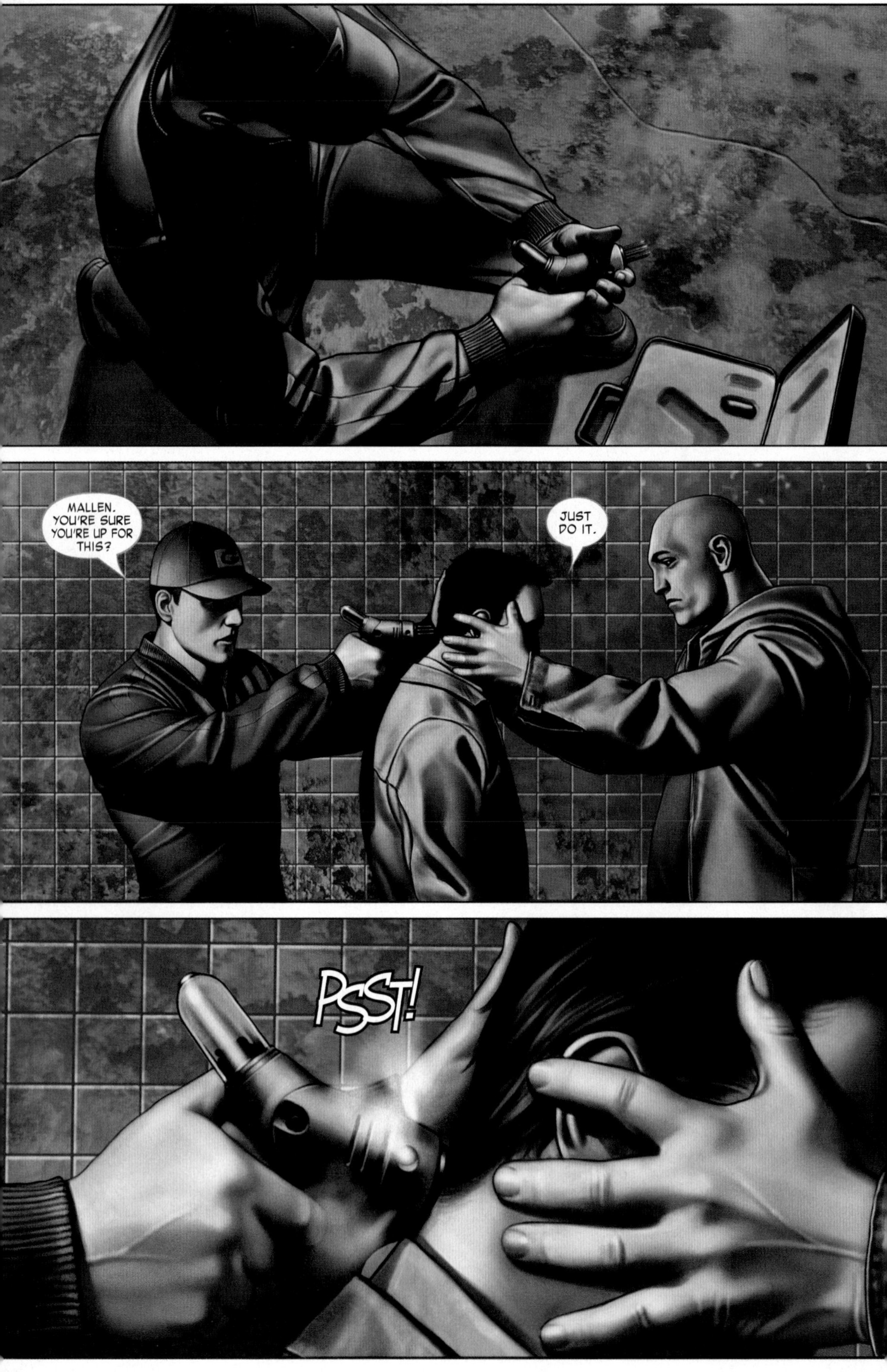
MALLEN. YOU'RE SURE YOU'RE UP FOR THIS?
JUST DO IT.
PSST!

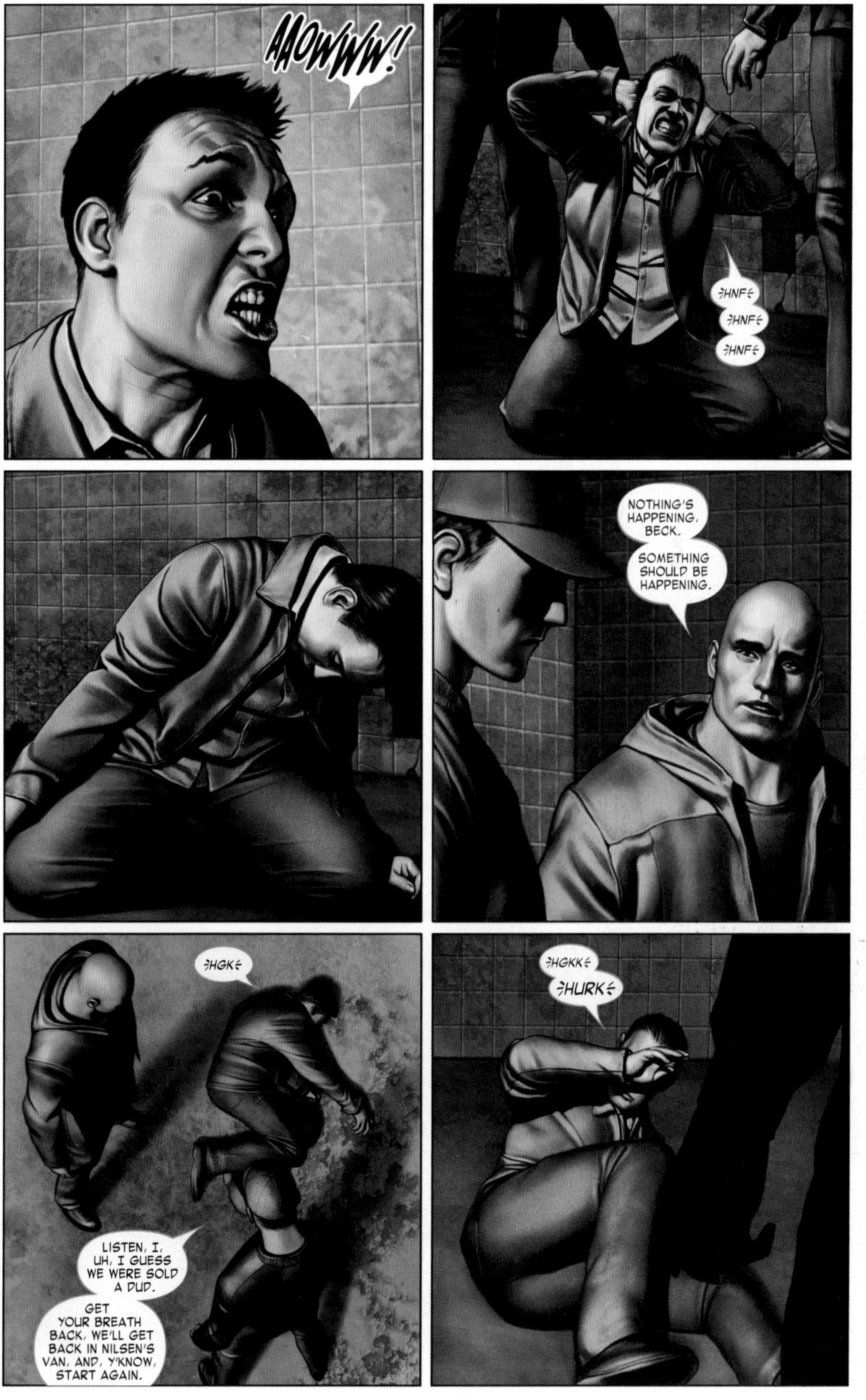
AAOWWW!
HNF
HNF
HNF
NOTHING'S HAPPENING, BECK.
SOMETHING SHOULD BE HAPPENING.
HGK
LISTEN, I, UH, I GUESS WE WERE SOLD A DUD.
GET YOUR BREATH BACK, WE'LL GET BACK IN NILSEN'S VAN, AND, Y'KNOW, START AGAIN.
HGKK
HURK

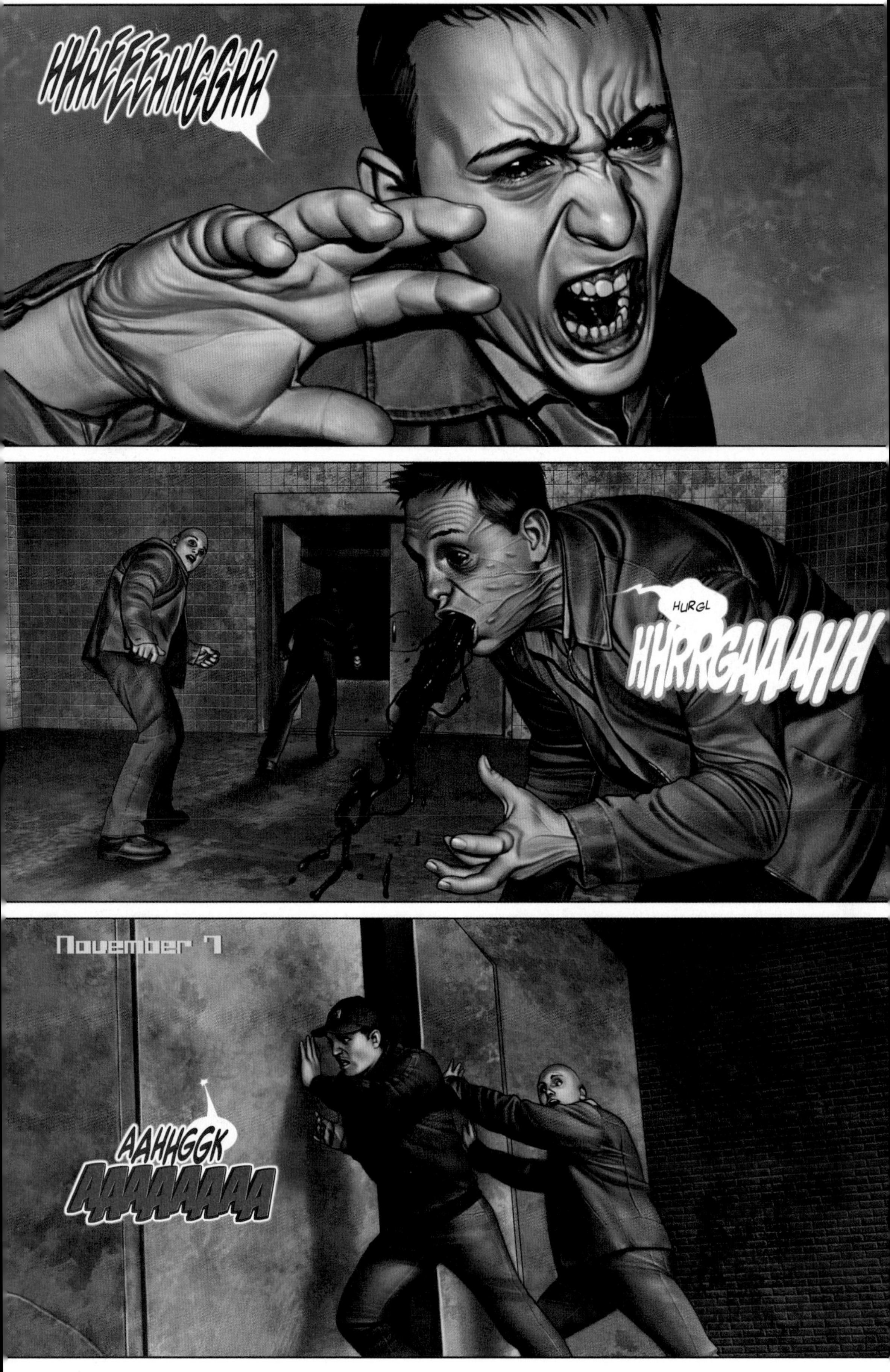
HHHEEEHHGGHH
HURGL
HHRRGAAAAHH
November 7
AAHHGGK
AAAAAAAA

BZZT!
BZZT!

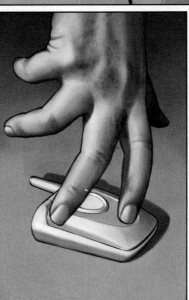

YEAH.

MR. STARK?

YEAH.

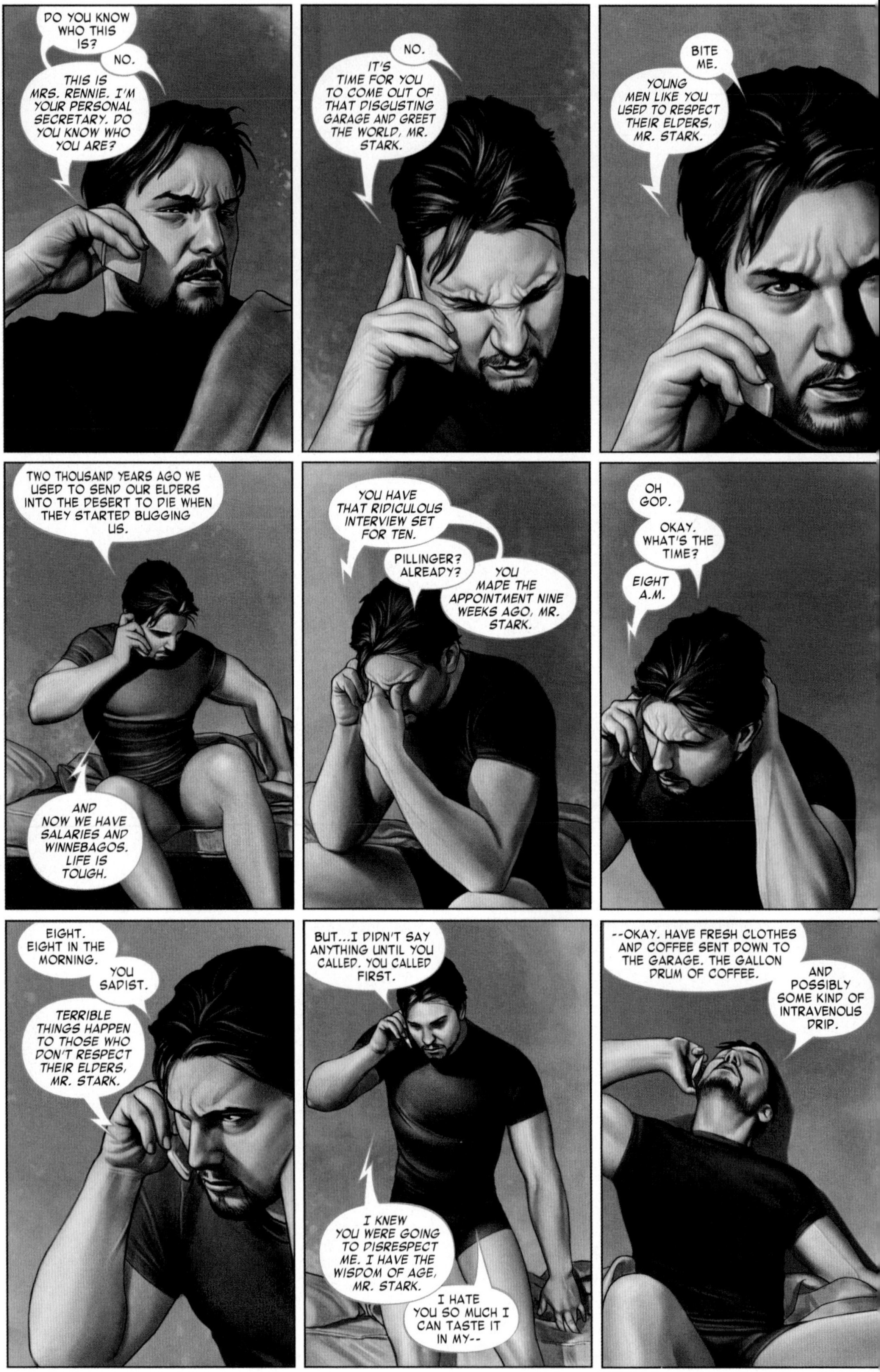
DO YOU KNOW WHO THIS IS?
NO.
THIS IS MRS. RENNIE. I'M YOUR PERSONAL SECRETARY. DO YOU KNOW WHO YOU ARE?
NO.
IT'S TIME FOR YOU TO COME OUT OF THAT DISGUSTING GARAGE AND GREET THE WORLD, MR. STARK.
BITE ME.
YOUNG MEN LIKE YOU USED TO RESPECT THEIR ELDERS, MR. STARK.
TWO THOUSAND YEARS AGO WE USED TO SEND OUR ELDERS INTO THE DESERT TO DIE WHEN THEY STARTED BUGGING US.
AND NOW WE HAVE SALARIES AND WINNEBAGOS. LIFE IS TOUGH.
YOU HAVE THAT RIDICULOUS INTERVIEW SET FOR TEN.
PILLINGER? ALREADY?
YOU MADE THE APPOINTMENT NINE WEEKS AGO, MR. STARK.
OH GOD.
OKAY. WHAT'S THE TIME?
EIGHT A.M.
EIGHT. EIGHT IN THE MORNING.
YOU SADIST.
TERRIBLE THINGS HAPPEN TO THOSE WHO DON'T RESPECT THEIR ELDERS, MR. STARK.
BUT...I DIDN'T SAY ANYTHING UNTIL YOU CALLED. YOU CALLED FIRST.
I KNEW YOU WERE GOING TO DISRESPECT ME. I HAVE THE WISDOM OF AGE, MR. STARK.
I HATE YOU SO MUCH I CAN TASTE IT IN MY--
--OKAY. HAVE FRESH CLOTHES AND COFFEE SENT DOWN TO THE GARAGE. THE GALLON DRUM OF COFFEE.
AND POSSIBLY SOME KIND OF INTRAVENOUS DRIP.

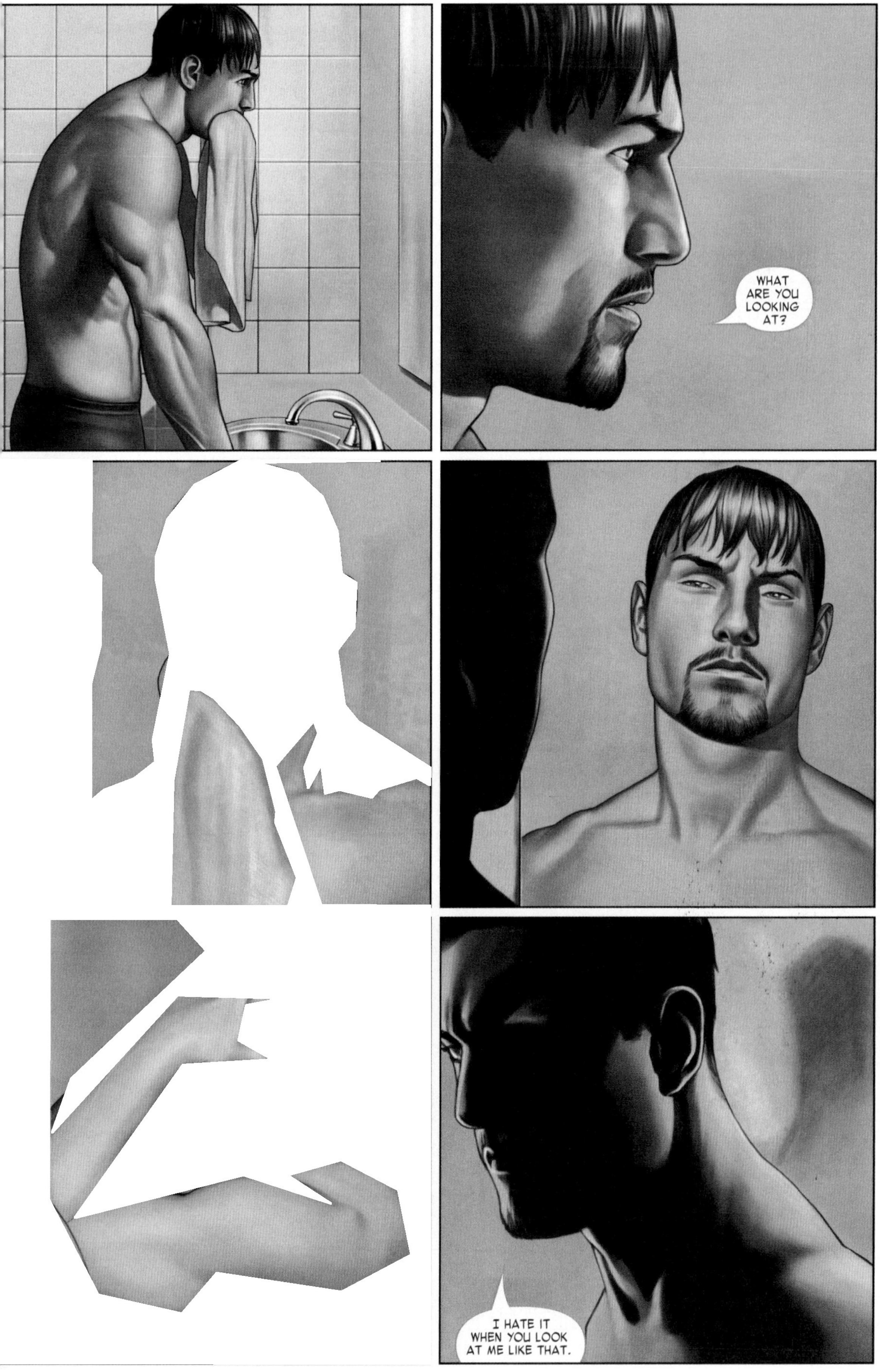
WHAT ARE YOU LOOKING AT?
I HATE IT WHEN YOU LOOK AT ME LIKE THAT.

Austin, TH

YES, THE SPECIAL PROJECTS VAULT HAS BEEN COMPROMISED.

YES, WE'RE WORKING ON THAT NOW, BUT I HAVE TO REFER YOU TO GENERAL FISHER--

--NO, DR. KILLIAN IS GUIDING THE EFFORT FROM THIS END.

Dr ALDRICH KILLIAN

They know Extremis has been extracted from the vault. It's chaos, outside my blessed door.

This place is so badly organized: no one seems to be qualified to know what has been stolen or what to do about it.

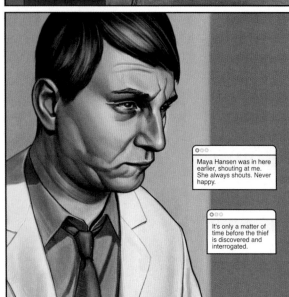

Maya Hansen was in here earlier, shouting at me. She always shouts. Never happy.

It's only a matter of time before the thief is discovered and interrogated.

I won't get through an interrogation.

I know that I've loosed something terrible. Knowing that it had to be done: it doesn't ease the burden.

All the e-mails are on this machine, if you can find them. I can do that much.
But understand. This had to be done.
I'm shaking. Getting hard to type. Goodbye.
End
Print
I'VE NEVER BEEN IN LOVE.
NEVER.
NO ONE'S EVER LOVED ME.

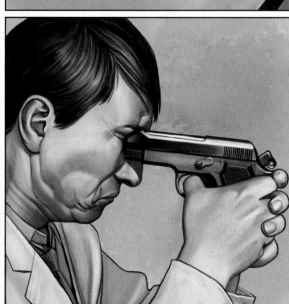

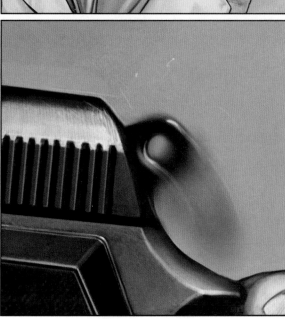

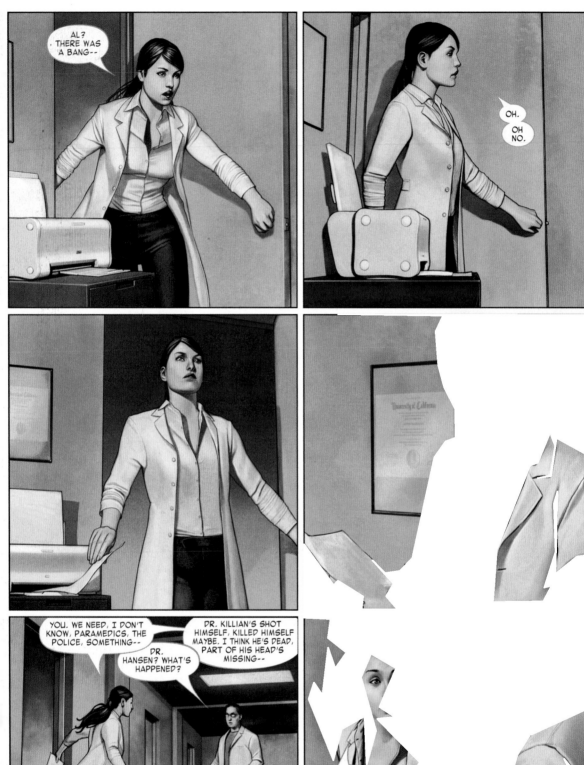

AL? THERE WAS A BANG--

OH. OH NO.

YOU. WE NEED, I DON'T KNOW, PARAMEDICS, THE POLICE, SOMETHING--

DR. HANSEN? WHAT'S HAPPENED?

DR. KILLIAN'S SHOT HIMSELF, KILLED HIMSELF MAYBE. I THINK HE'S DEAD, PART OF HIS HEAD'S MISSING--

HE'S SHOT HIMSELF IN THE HEAD AND IT WAS HIM.

HE STOLE THE EXTREMIS DOSE. THIS IS HIS, I DON'T KNOW, HIS CONFESSION.

HE STOLE THE EXTREMIS DOSE AND GAVE IT TO SOMEONE.

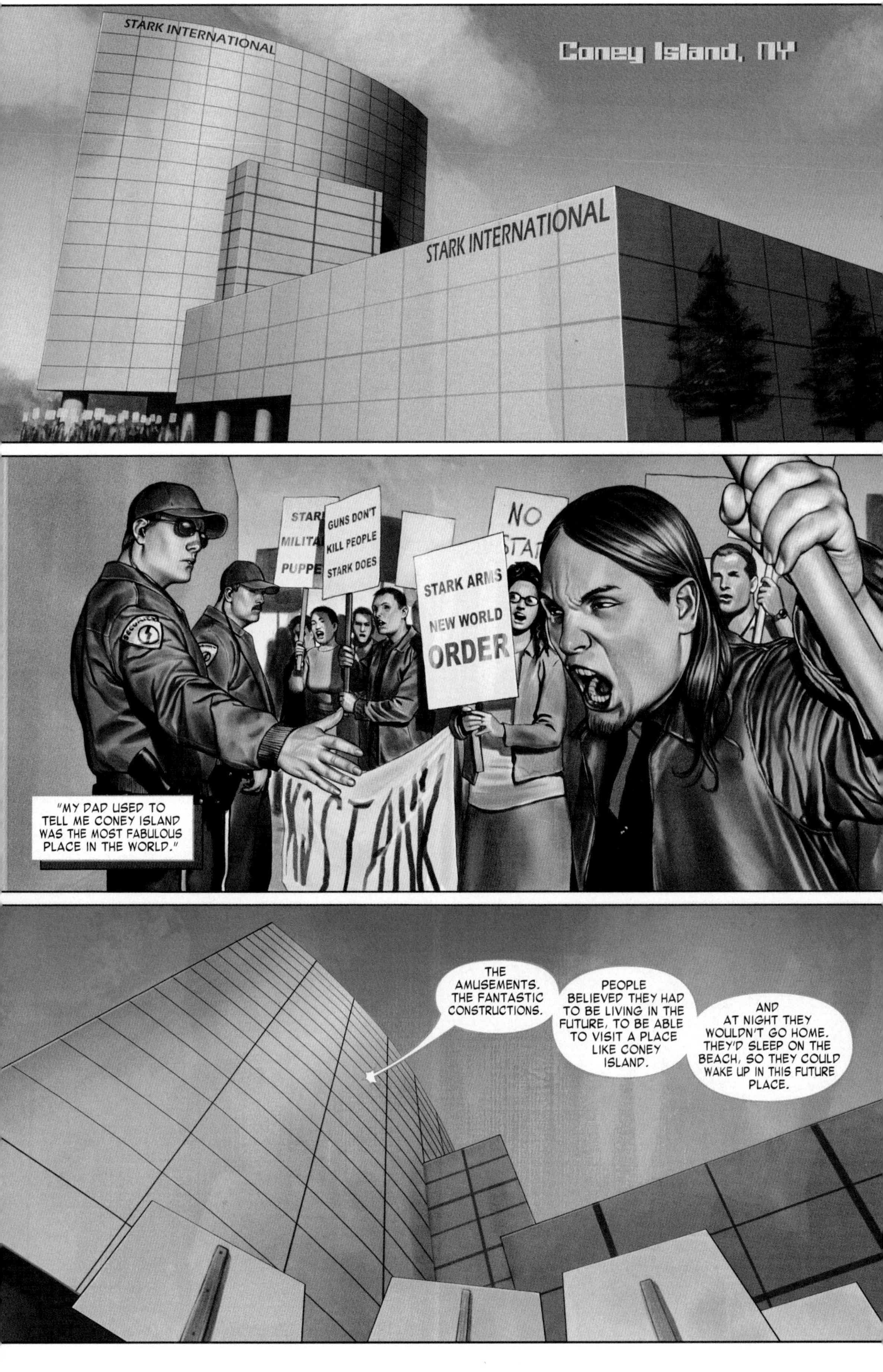
STARK INTERNATIONAL
Coney Island, NY
STARK INTERNATIONAL
GUNS DON'T KILL PEOPLE STARK DOES
STARK ARMS NEW WORLD ORDER
"MY DAD USED TO TELL ME CONEY ISLAND WAS THE MOST FABULOUS PLACE IN THE WORLD."
THE AMUSEMENTS. THE FANTASTIC CONSTRUCTIONS.
PEOPLE BELIEVED THEY HAD TO BE LIVING IN THE FUTURE, TO BE ABLE TO VISIT A PLACE LIKE CONEY ISLAND.
AND AT NIGHT THEY WOULDN'T GO HOME. THEY'D SLEEP ON THE BEACH, SO THEY COULD WAKE UP IN THIS FUTURE PLACE.

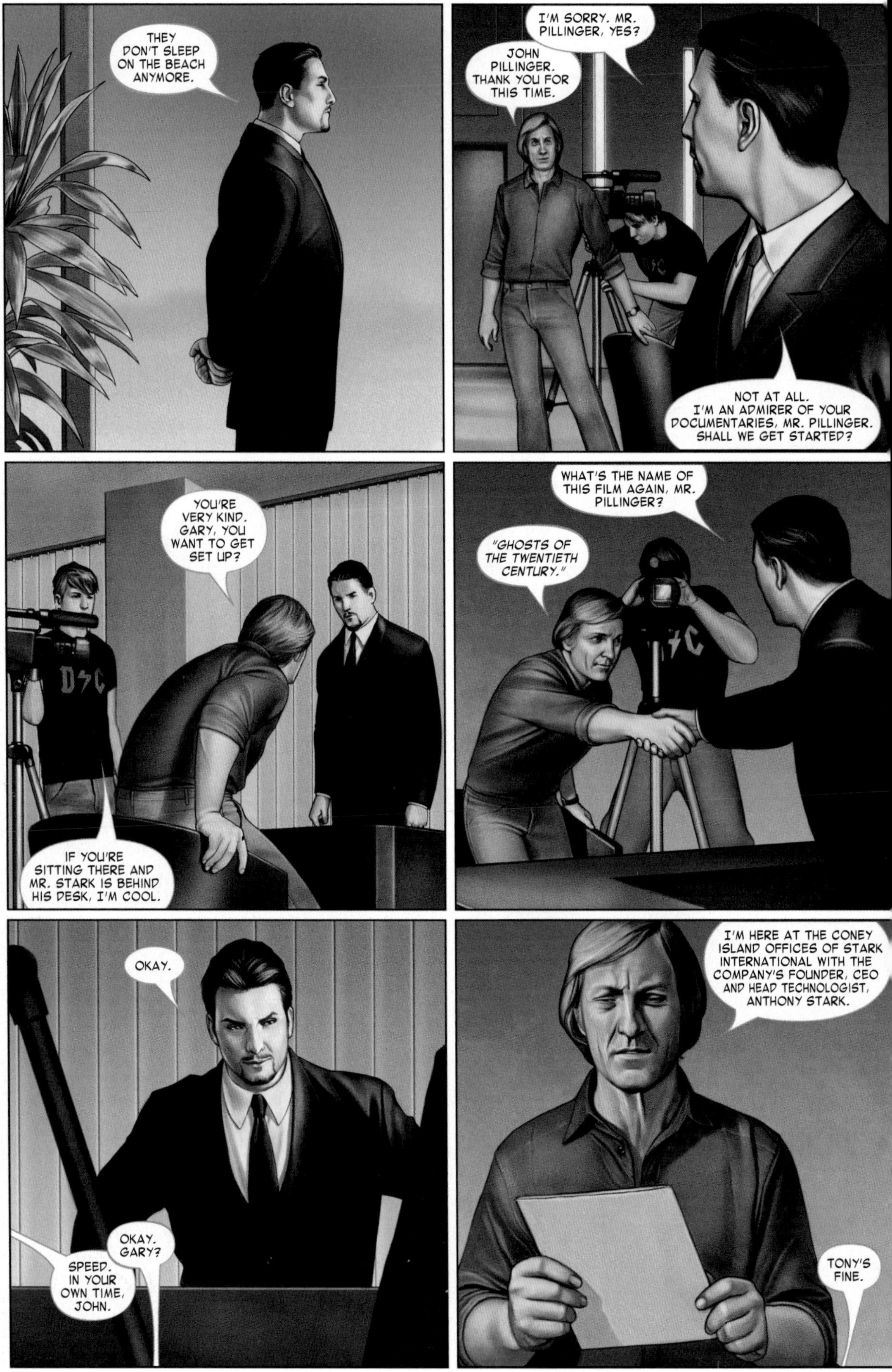
THEY DON'T SLEEP ON THE BEACH ANYMORE.
I'M SORRY. MR. PILLINGER, YES?
JOHN PILLINGER. THANK YOU FOR THIS TIME.
NOT AT ALL. I'M AN ADMIRER OF YOUR DOCUMENTARIES, MR. PILLINGER. SHALL WE GET STARTED?
YOU'RE VERY KIND. GARY, YOU WANT TO GET SET UP?
IF YOU'RE SITTING THERE AND MR. STARK IS BEHIND HIS DESK, I'M COOL.
WHAT'S THE NAME OF THIS FILM AGAIN, MR. PILLINGER?
"GHOSTS OF THE TWENTIETH CENTURY."
OKAY.
OKAY. GARY?
SPEED. IN YOUR OWN TIME, JOHN.
I'M HERE AT THE CONEY ISLAND OFFICES OF STARK INTERNATIONAL WITH THE COMPANY'S FOUNDER, CEO AND HEAD TECHNOLOGIST, ANTHONY STARK.
TONY'S FINE.

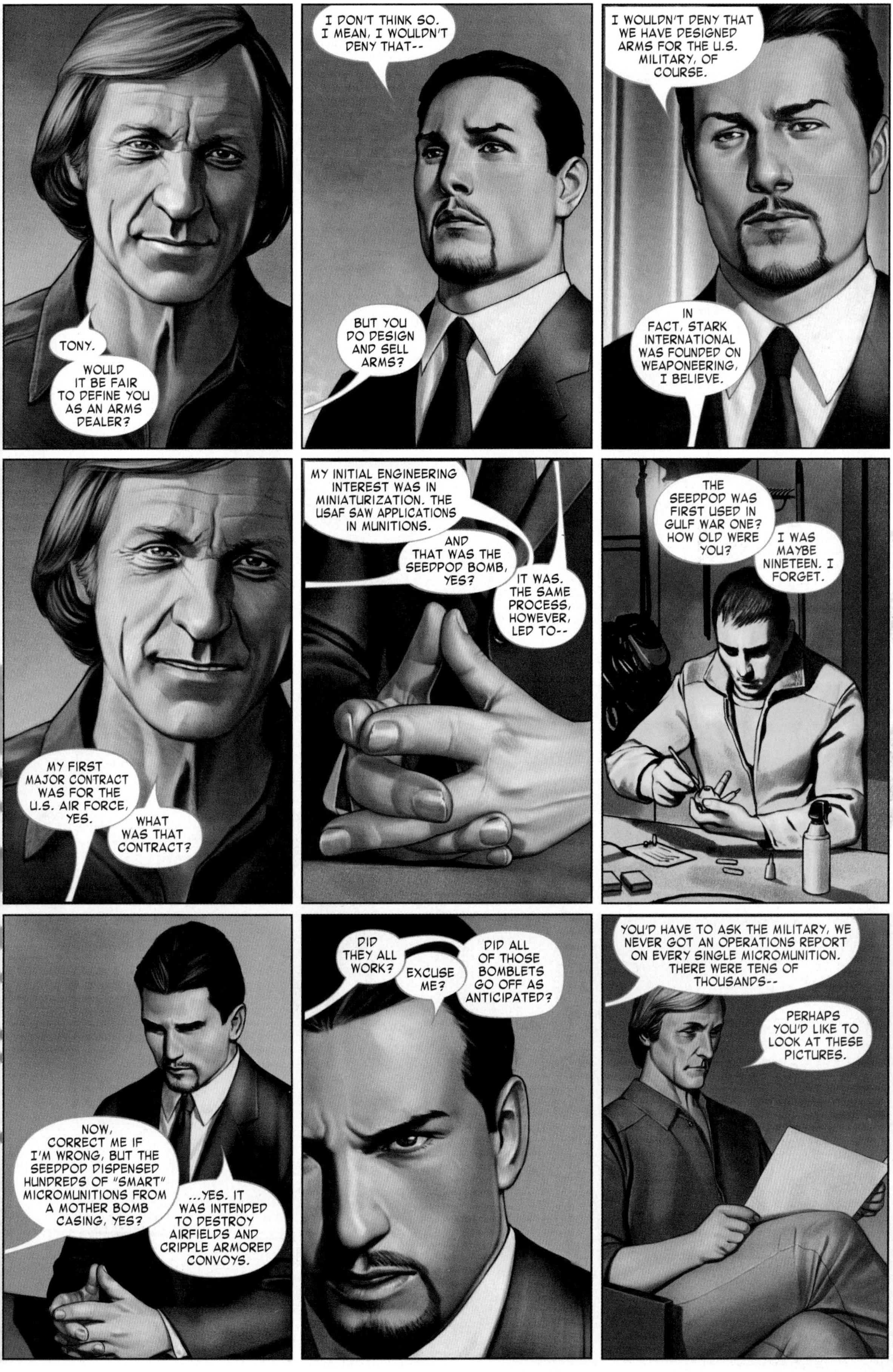
TONY.
WOULD IT BE FAIR TO DEFINE YOU AS AN ARMS DEALER?
I DON'T THINK SO. I MEAN, I WOULDN'T DENY THAT--
BUT YOU DO DESIGN AND SELL ARMS?
I WOULDN'T DENY THAT WE HAVE DESIGNED ARMS FOR THE U.S. MILITARY, OF COURSE.
IN FACT, STARK INTERNATIONAL WAS FOUNDED ON WEAPONEERING, I BELIEVE.
MY FIRST MAJOR CONTRACT WAS FOR THE U.S. AIR FORCE, YES.
WHAT WAS THAT CONTRACT?
MY INITIAL ENGINEERING INTEREST WAS IN MINIATURIZATION. THE USAF SAW APPLICATIONS IN MUNITIONS.
AND THAT WAS THE SEEDPOD BOMB, YES?
IT WAS. THE SAME PROCESS, HOWEVER, LED TO--
THE SEEDPOD WAS FIRST USED IN GULF WAR ONE? HOW OLD WERE YOU?
I WAS MAYBE NINETEEN. I FORGET.
NOW, CORRECT ME IF I'M WRONG, BUT THE SEEDPOD DISPENSED HUNDREDS OF "SMART" MICROMUNITIONS FROM A MOTHER BOMB CASING, YES?
...YES. IT WAS INTENDED TO DESTROY AIRFIELDS AND CRIPPLE ARMORED CONVOYS.
DID THEY ALL WORK?
EXCUSE ME?
DID ALL OF THOSE BOMBLETS GO OFF AS ANTICIPATED?
YOU'D HAVE TO ASK THE MILITARY, WE NEVER GOT AN OPERATIONS REPORT ON EVERY SINGLE MICROMUNITION. THERE WERE TENS OF THOUSANDS--
PERHAPS YOU'D LIKE TO LOOK AT THESE PICTURES.

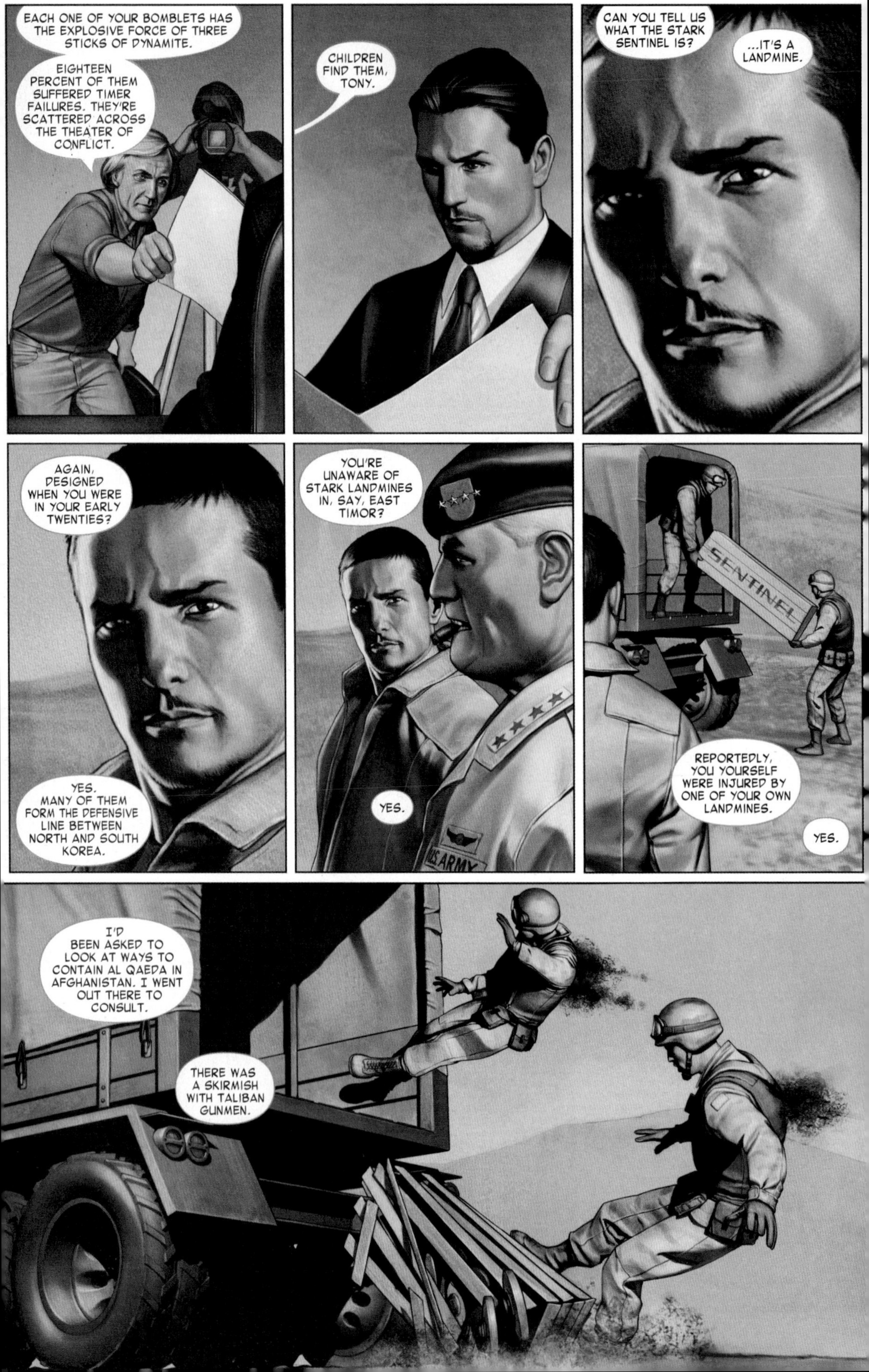
EACH ONE OF YOUR BOMBLETS HAS THE EXPLOSIVE FORCE OF THREE STICKS OF DYNAMITE.
EIGHTEEN PERCENT OF THEM SUFFERED TIMER FAILURES. THEY'RE SCATTERED ACROSS THE THEATER OF CONFLICT.
CHILDREN FIND THEM, TONY.
CAN YOU TELL US WHAT THE STARK SENTINEL IS?
...IT'S A LANDMINE.
AGAIN, DESIGNED WHEN YOU WERE IN YOUR EARLY TWENTIES?
YES. MANY OF THEM FORM THE DEFENSIVE LINE BETWEEN NORTH AND SOUTH KOREA.
YOU'RE UNAWARE OF STARK LANDMINES IN, SAY, EAST TIMOR?
YES.
U.S. ARMY
SENTINEL
REPORTEDLY, YOU YOURSELF WERE INJURED BY ONE OF YOUR OWN LANDMINES.
YES.
I'D BEEN ASKED TO LOOK AT WAYS TO CONTAIN AL QAEDA IN AFGHANISTAN. I WENT OUT THERE TO CONSULT.
THERE WAS A SKIRMISH WITH TALIBAN GUNMEN.

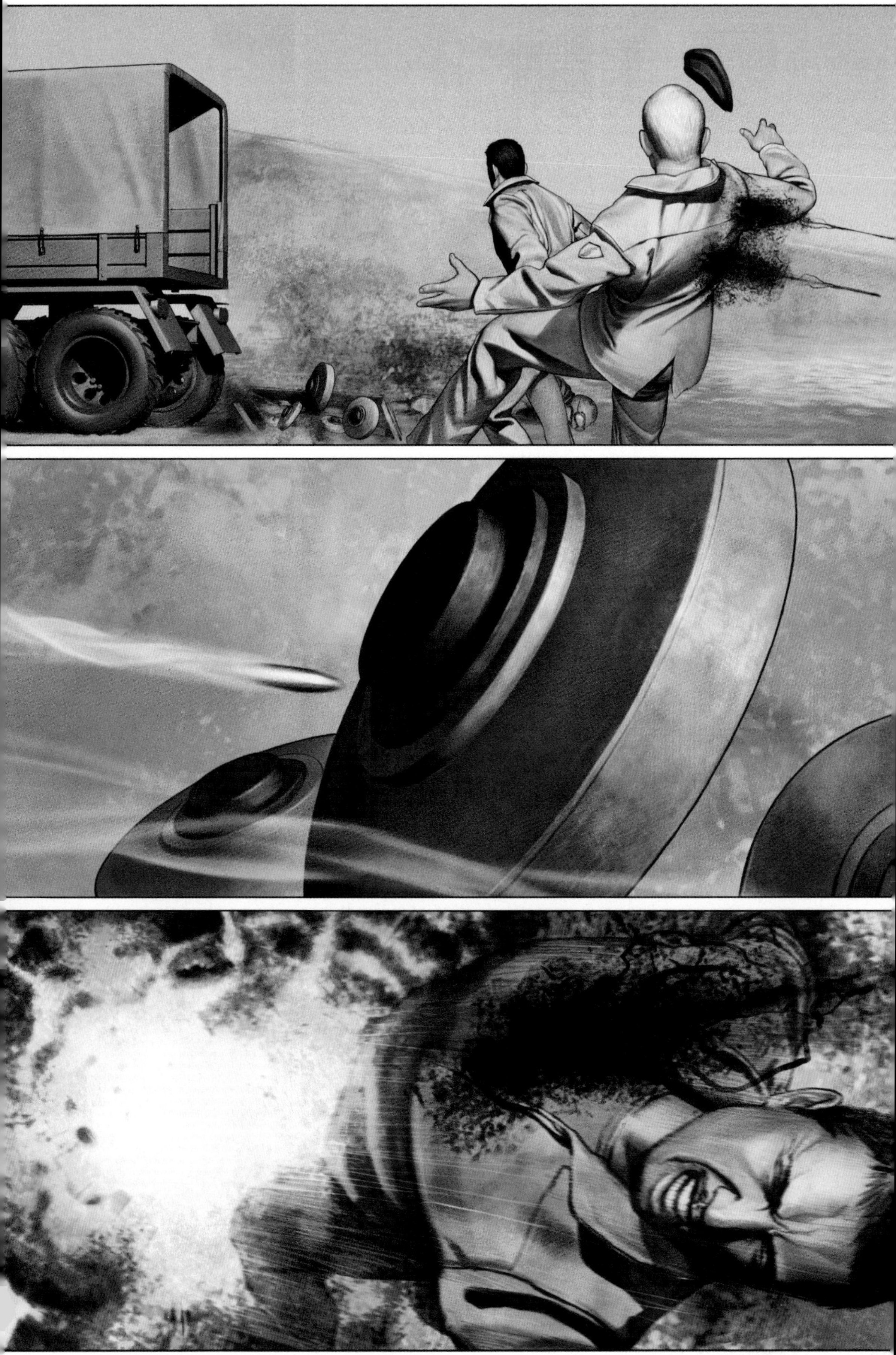

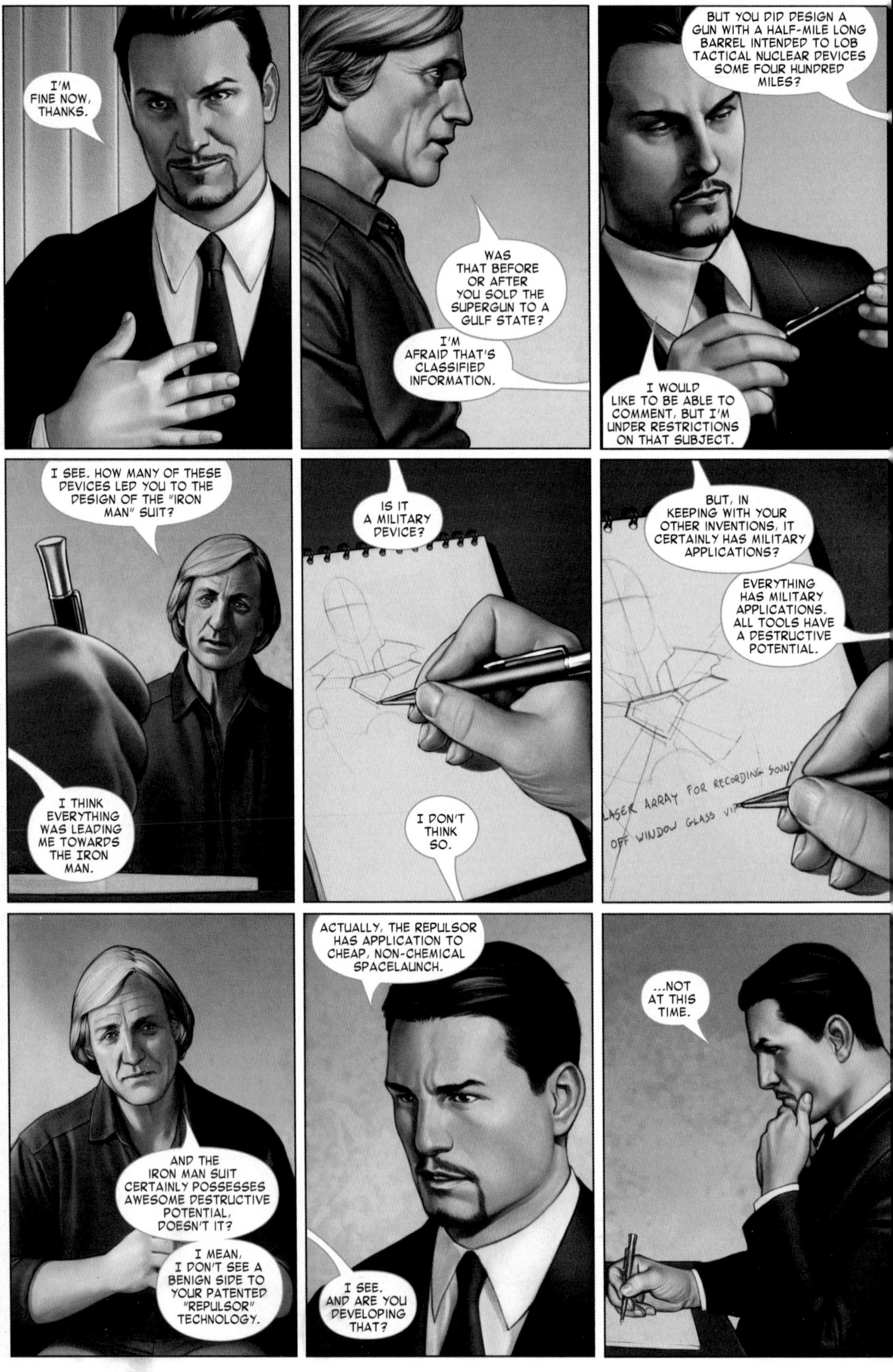
I'M FINE NOW, THANKS.
WAS THAT BEFORE OR AFTER YOU SOLD THE SUPERGUN TO A GULF STATE?
I'M AFRAID THAT'S CLASSIFIED INFORMATION.
BUT YOU DID DESIGN A GUN WITH A HALF-MILE LONG BARREL INTENDED TO LOB TACTICAL NUCLEAR DEVICES SOME FOUR HUNDRED MILES?
I WOULD LIKE TO BE ABLE TO COMMENT, BUT I'M UNDER RESTRICTIONS ON THAT SUBJECT.
I SEE. HOW MANY OF THESE DEVICES LED YOU TO THE DESIGN OF THE "IRON MAN" SUIT?
I THINK EVERYTHING WAS LEADING ME TOWARDS THE IRON MAN.
IS IT A MILITARY DEVICE?
I DON'T THINK SO.
BUT, IN KEEPING WITH YOUR OTHER INVENTIONS, IT CERTAINLY HAS MILITARY APPLICATIONS?
EVERYTHING HAS MILITARY APPLICATIONS. ALL TOOLS HAVE A DESTRUCTIVE POTENTIAL.
LASER ARRAY FOR RECORDING SOUN
OFF WINDOW GLASS VI
AND THE IRON MAN SUIT CERTAINLY POSSESSES AWESOME DESTRUCTIVE POTENTIAL, DOESN'T IT?
I MEAN, I DON'T SEE A BENIGN SIDE TO YOUR PATENTED "REPULSOR" TECHNOLOGY.
ACTUALLY, THE REPULSOR HAS APPLICATION TO CHEAP, NON-CHEMICAL SPACELAUNCH.
I SEE. AND ARE YOU DEVELOPING THAT?
...NOT AT THIS TIME.

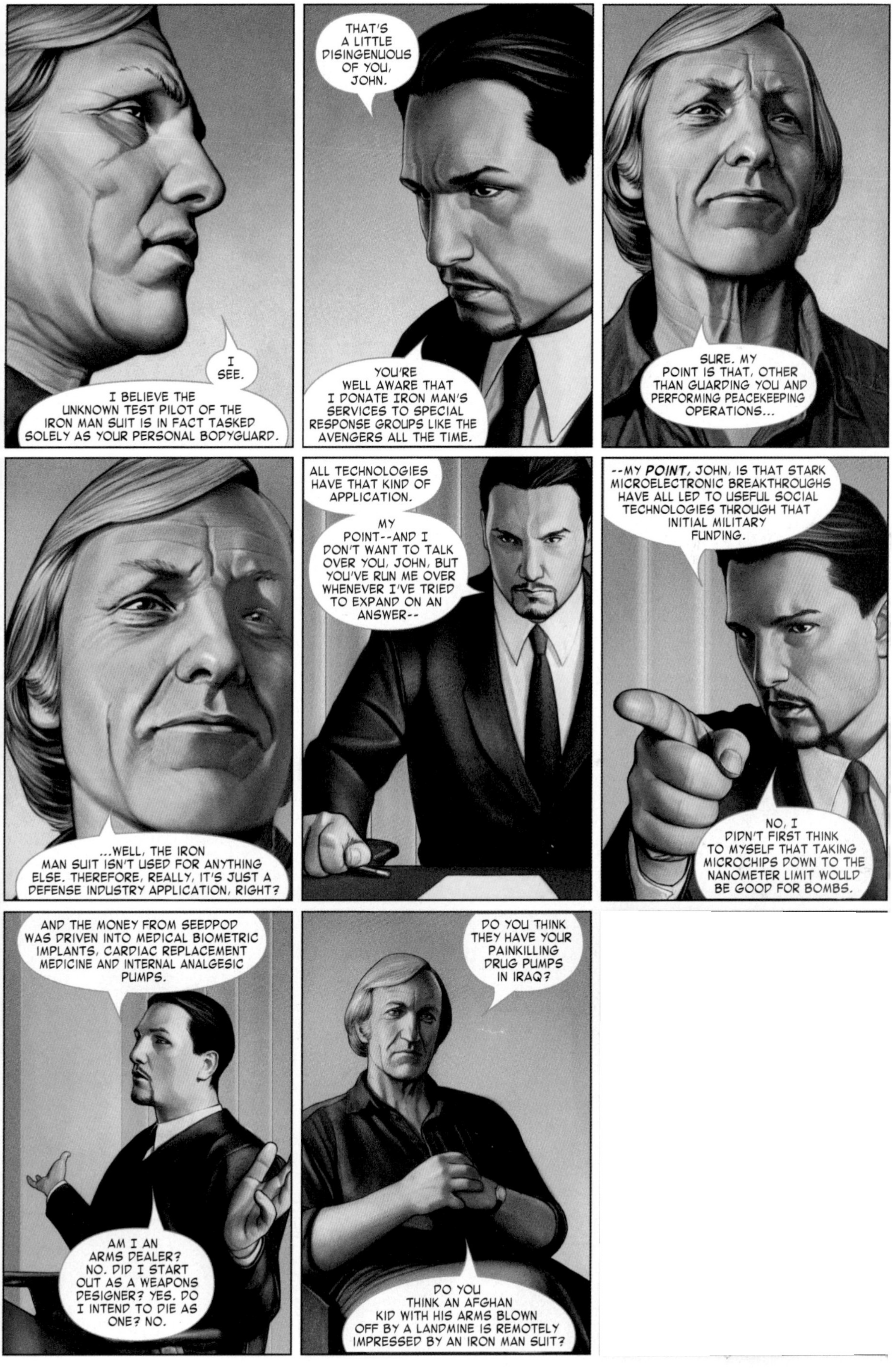
I SEE.
I BELIEVE THE UNKNOWN TEST PILOT OF THE IRON MAN SUIT IS IN FACT TASKED SOLELY AS YOUR PERSONAL BODYGUARD.
THAT'S A LITTLE DISINGENUOUS OF YOU, JOHN.
YOU'RE WELL AWARE THAT I DONATE IRON MAN'S SERVICES TO SPECIAL RESPONSE GROUPS LIKE THE AVENGERS ALL THE TIME.
SURE. MY POINT IS THAT, OTHER THAN GUARDING YOU AND PERFORMING PEACEKEEPING OPERATIONS...
...WELL, THE IRON MAN SUIT ISN'T USED FOR ANYTHING ELSE. THEREFORE, REALLY, IT'S JUST A DEFENSE INDUSTRY APPLICATION, RIGHT?
ALL TECHNOLOGIES HAVE THAT KIND OF APPLICATION.
MY POINT--AND I DON'T WANT TO TALK OVER YOU, JOHN, BUT YOU'VE RUN ME OVER WHENEVER I'VE TRIED TO EXPAND ON AN ANSWER--
--MY ***POINT,*** JOHN, IS THAT STARK MICROELECTRONIC BREAKTHROUGHS HAVE ALL LED TO USEFUL SOCIAL TECHNOLOGIES THROUGH THAT INITIAL MILITARY FUNDING.
NO, I DIDN'T FIRST THINK TO MYSELF THAT TAKING MICROCHIPS DOWN TO THE NANOMETER LIMIT WOULD BE GOOD FOR BOMBS.
AND THE MONEY FROM SEEDPOD WAS DRIVEN INTO MEDICAL BIOMETRIC IMPLANTS, CARDIAC REPLACEMENT MEDICINE AND INTERNAL ANALGESIC PUMPS.
AM I AN ARMS DEALER? NO. DID I START OUT AS A WEAPONS DESIGNER? YES. DO I INTEND TO DIE AS ONE? NO.
DO YOU THINK THEY HAVE YOUR PAINKILLING DRUG PUMPS IN IRAQ?
DO YOU THINK AN AFGHAN KID WITH HIS ARMS BLOWN OFF BY A LANDMINE IS REMOTELY IMPRESSED BY AN IRON MAN SUIT?

I NEVER CLAIMED TO BE PERFECT. I ALWAYS KNEW THERE WOULD BE BLOOD ON MY HANDS. I'M TRYING...

...I'M TRYING TO IMPROVE THE WORLD.

IMPROVE THE WORLD. THANKS FOR YOUR TIME.

I'M CURIOUS, ACTUALLY. IF YOU KNOW MY WORK, WHY DID YOU AGREE TO THIS INTERVIEW?

ME FIRST. WHY AM I A GHOST OF THE TWENTIETH CENTURY?

BECAUSE YOUR ARMS WORK OF THE NINETIES STILL HAUNTS THE POVERTY- AND WAR-STRICKEN COUNTRIES THEY WERE DEPLOYED IN.

I WANTED TO MEET YOU.

YOU'VE BEEN MAKING YOUR INVESTIGATIVE FILMS FOR WHAT, TWENTY YEARS NOW? I WANTED TO ASK:

HAVE YOU CHANGED ANYTHING?

YOU'VE BEEN UNCOVERING DISTURBING THINGS ALL OVER THE WORLD FOR TWENTY YEARS NOW. HAVE YOU CHANGED ANYTHING?

YOU'VE WORKED VERY HARD. MOST PEOPLE HAVE NO IDEA OF THE KIND OF WORK YOU'VE DONE.

INTELLECTUALS, CRITICS AND ACTIVISTS FOLLOW YOUR FILMS CLOSELY, BUT CULTURALLY YOU'RE ALMOST INVISIBLE, MR. PILLINGER.

HAVE YOU CHANGED ANYTHING?

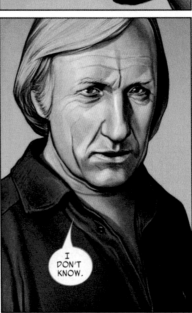

I DON'T KNOW.

ME NEITHER. IT'S BEEN AN HONOR TO MEET YOU, MR. PILLINGER.

...YES. THANK YOU FOR YOUR TIME, MR. STARK.

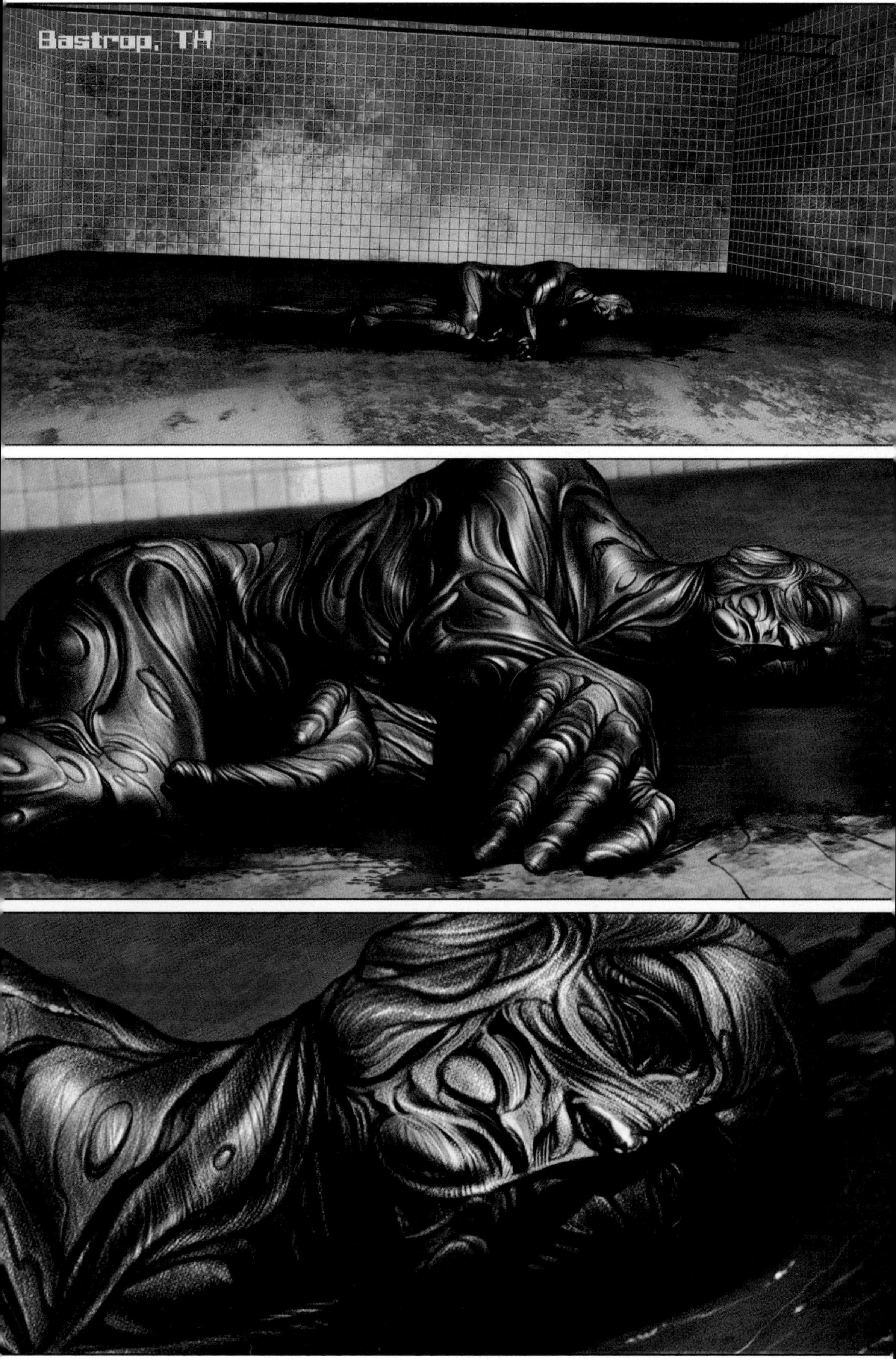
Bastrop, TX

MR. STARK, SINCE YOU'VE REJOINED THE LIVING, I'VE SCHEDULED A SENIOR STAFF MEETING FOR--

CANCEL IT.

I'M GOING BACK DOWN TO THE GARAGE.

--NO, GEOFF, WE'LL TALK ABOUT THE INTERVIEW LATER.

I'M WELL AWARE THAT BILL STEPPED DOWN AS CEO OF MICROSOFT AND TOOK A *"CHIEF TECHNOLOGIST"* TITLE--

--ALL RIGHT. SENIOR STAFF AT FOUR. BUT NOW I NEED TO BE IN THE GARAGE.

STARK VOICELOG: RECORD: DATESTAMP.

JOHN PILLINGER SAYS THE IRON MAN SUIT IS A MILITARY APPLICATION.

I TOLD HIM HE WAS WRONG. I'M TRYING TO DECIDE IF I WAS LYING.

I'VE NEVER SOLD ANY ELEMENT OF THE IRON MAN TO THE MILITARY.

IT'S USED FOR EXTRAORDINARY RESCUE AND RESPONSE SITUATIONS.

IRON MAN SAVES LIVES.

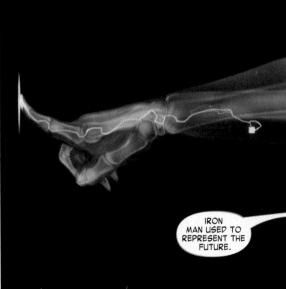

IRON MAN USED TO REPRESENT THE FUTURE.

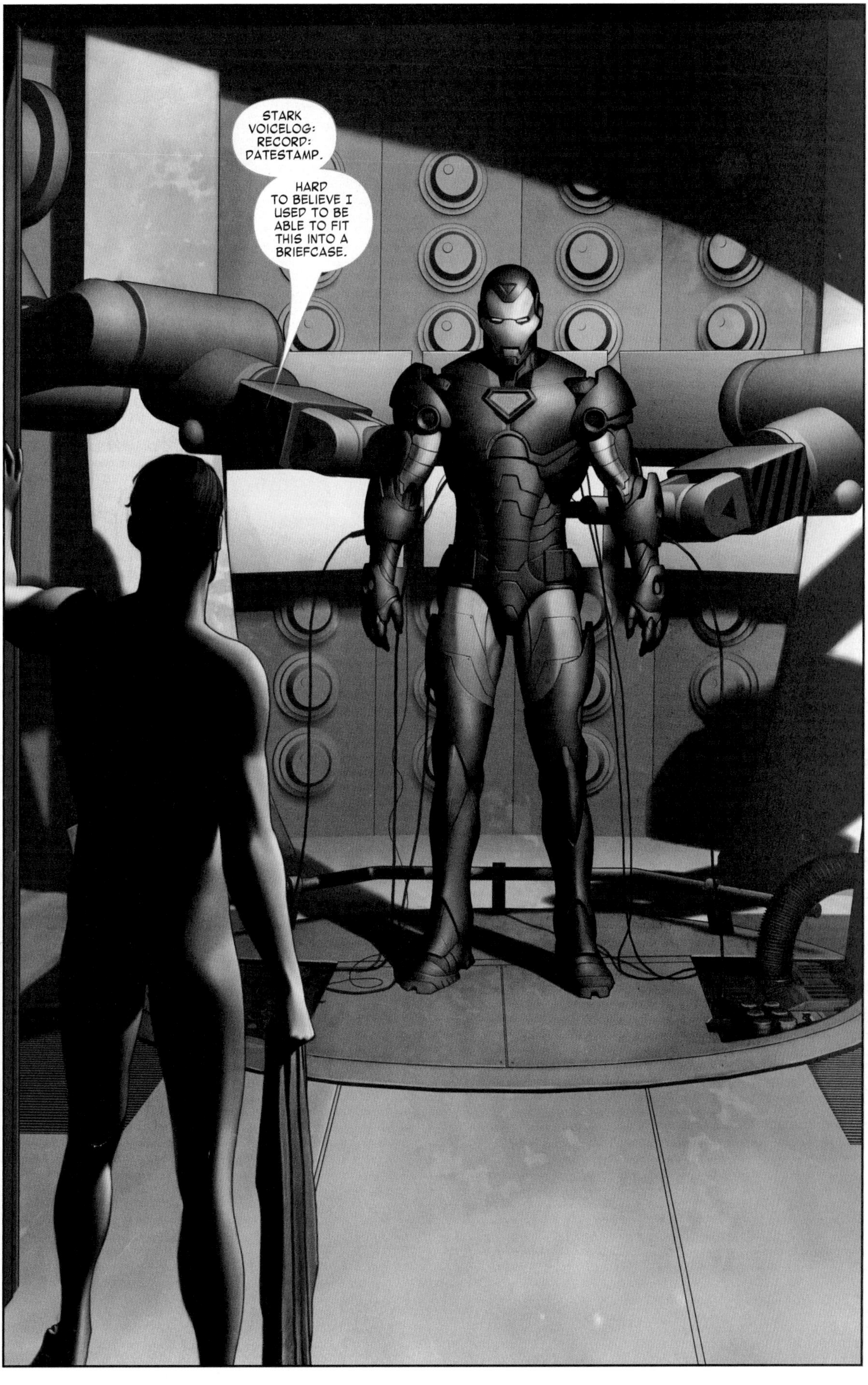
STARK VOICELOG: RECORD: DATESTAMP.
HARD TO BELIEVE I USED TO BE ABLE TO FIT THIS INTO A BRIEFCASE.

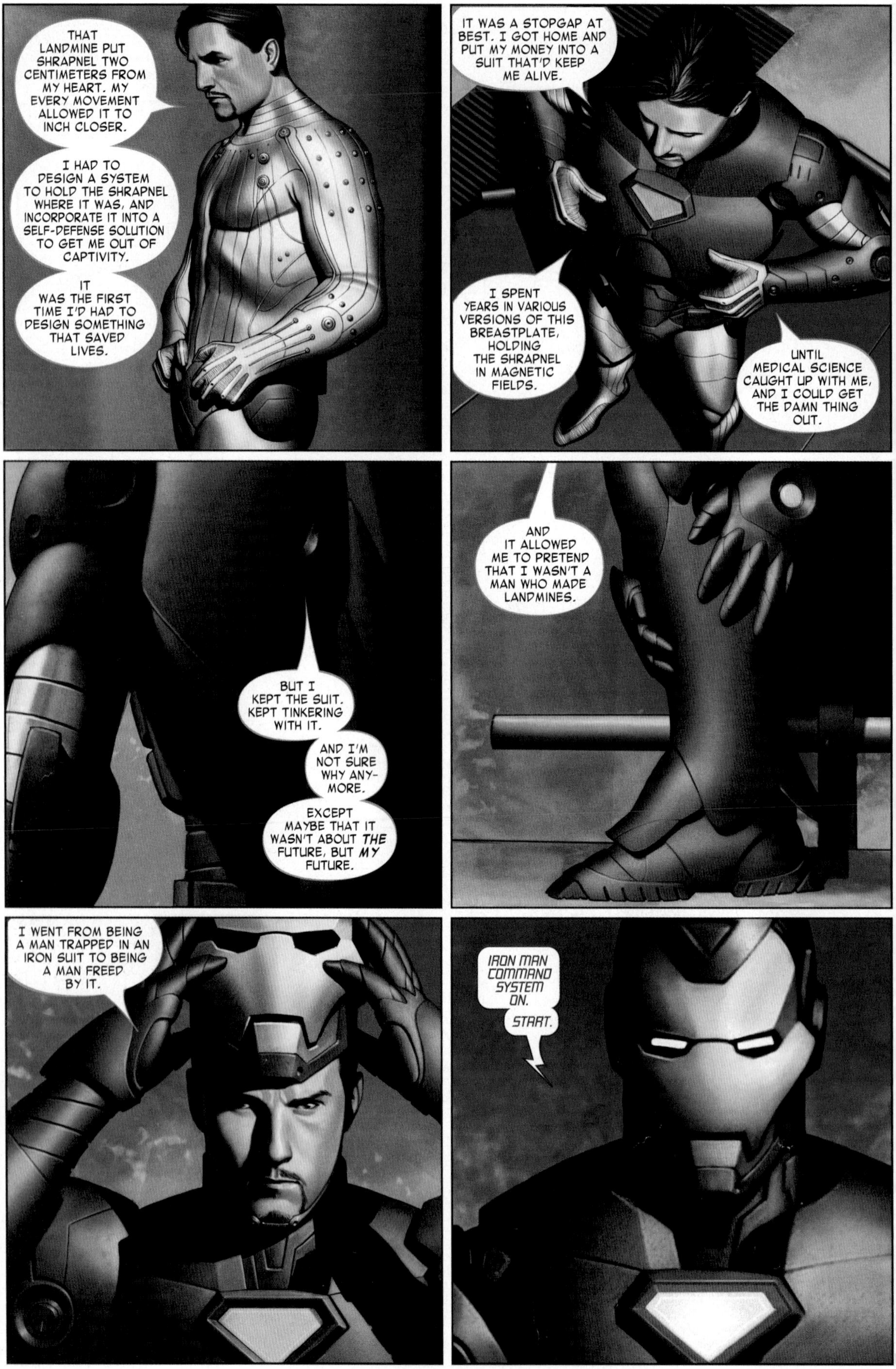
THAT LANDMINE PUT SHRAPNEL TWO CENTIMETERS FROM MY HEART. MY EVERY MOVEMENT ALLOWED IT TO INCH CLOSER.
I HAD TO DESIGN A SYSTEM TO HOLD THE SHRAPNEL WHERE IT WAS, AND INCORPORATE IT INTO A SELF-DEFENSE SOLUTION TO GET ME OUT OF CAPTIVITY.
IT WAS THE FIRST TIME I'D HAD TO DESIGN SOMETHING THAT SAVED LIVES.
IT WAS A STOPGAP AT BEST. I GOT HOME AND PUT MY MONEY INTO A SUIT THAT'D KEEP ME ALIVE.
I SPENT YEARS IN VARIOUS VERSIONS OF THIS BREASTPLATE, HOLDING THE SHRAPNEL IN MAGNETIC FIELDS.
UNTIL MEDICAL SCIENCE CAUGHT UP WITH ME, AND I COULD GET THE DAMN THING OUT.
BUT I KEPT THE SUIT. KEPT TINKERING WITH IT.
AND I'M NOT SURE WHY ANY-MORE.
EXCEPT MAYBE THAT IT WASN'T ABOUT *THE* FUTURE, BUT *MY* FUTURE.
AND IT ALLOWED ME TO PRETEND THAT I WASN'T A MAN WHO MADE LANDMINES.
I WENT FROM BEING A MAN TRAPPED IN AN IRON SUIT TO BEING A MAN FREED BY IT.
IRON MAN COMMAND SYSTEM ON.
START.

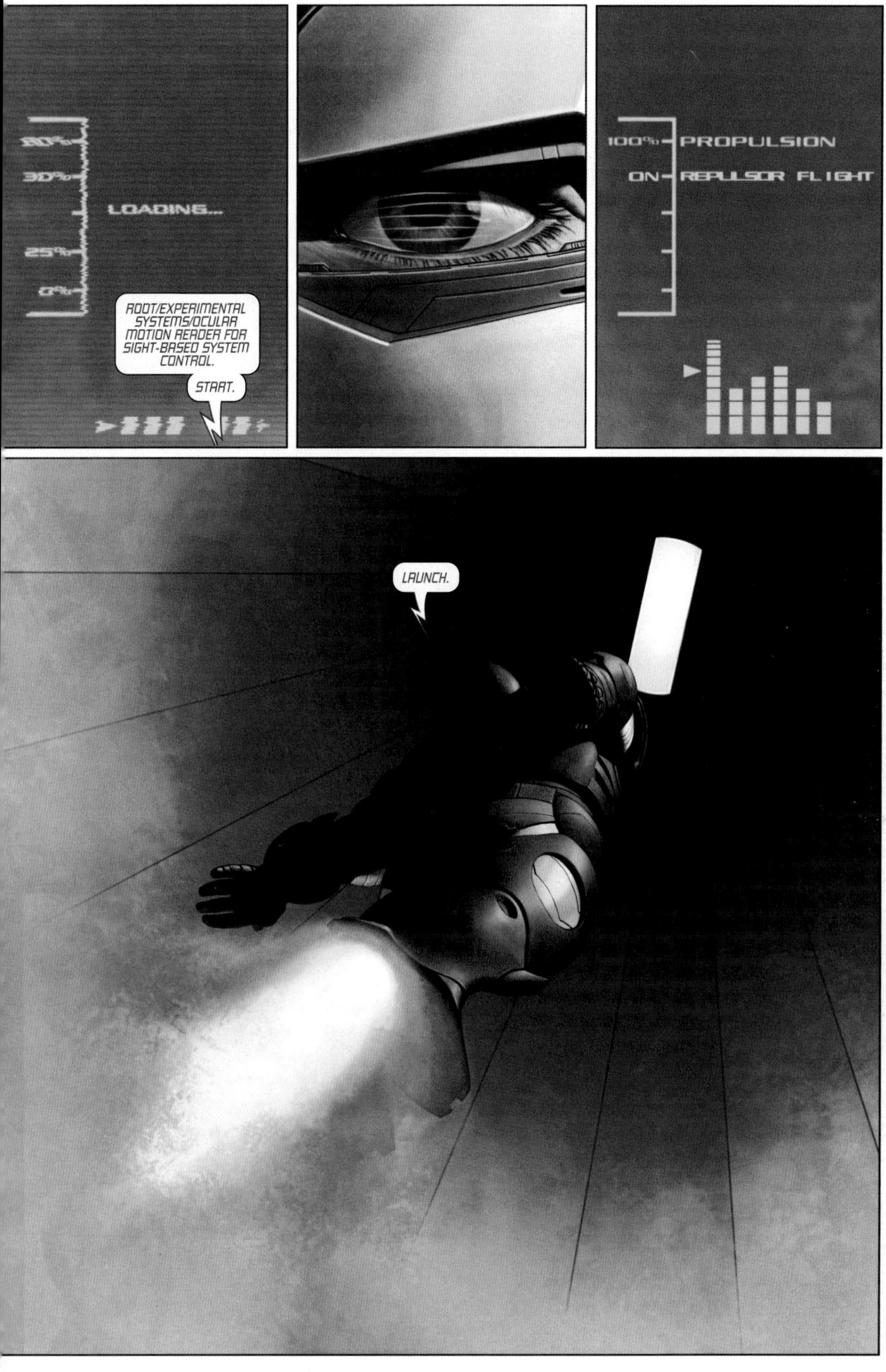
LOADING...
ROOT/EXPERIMENTAL SYSTEMS/OCULAR MOTION READER FOR SIGHT-BASED SYSTEM CONTROL.
START.
100% PROPULSION
ON REPULSOR FLIGHT
LAUNCH.

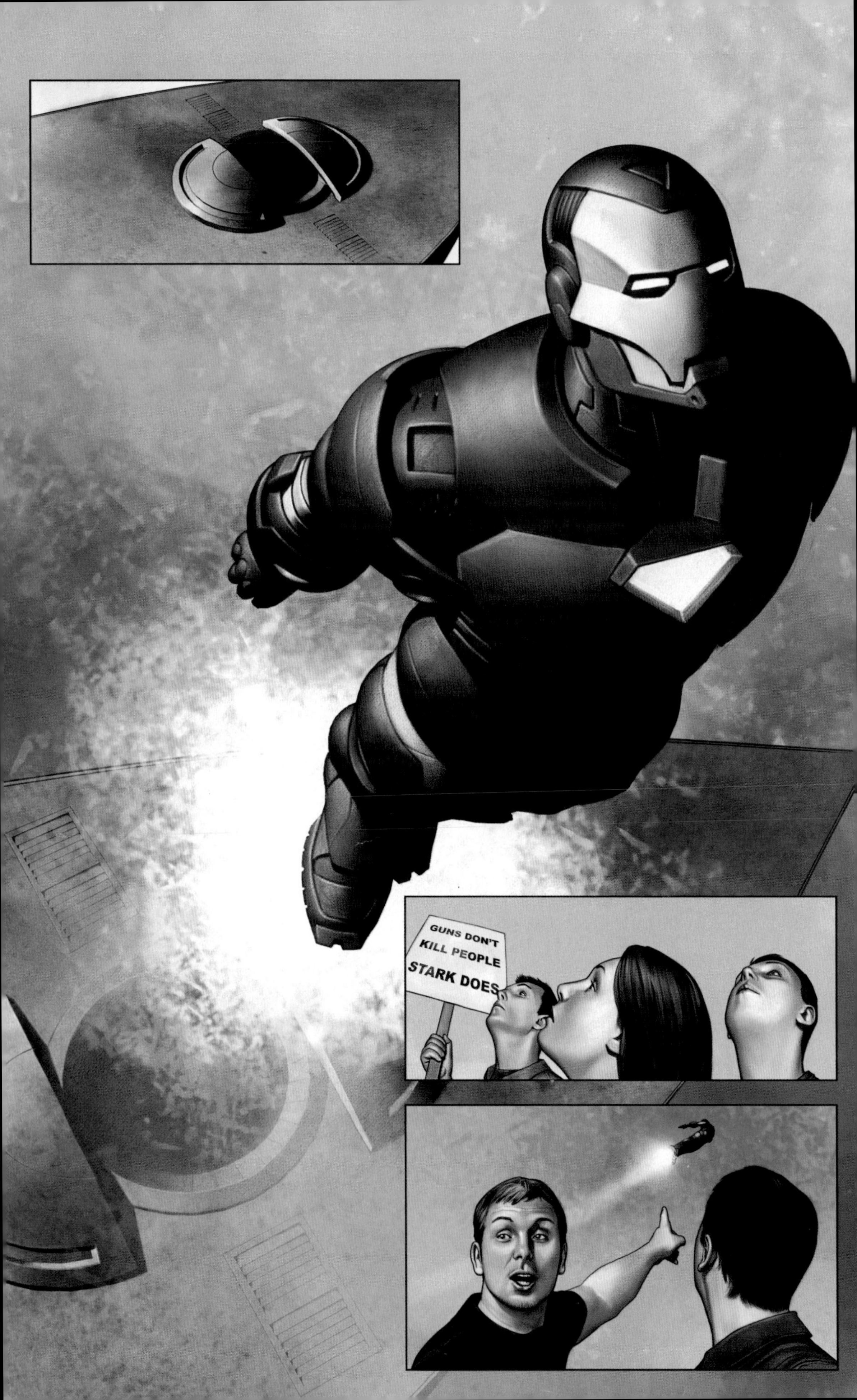
GUNS DON'T
KILL PEOPLE
STARK DOES

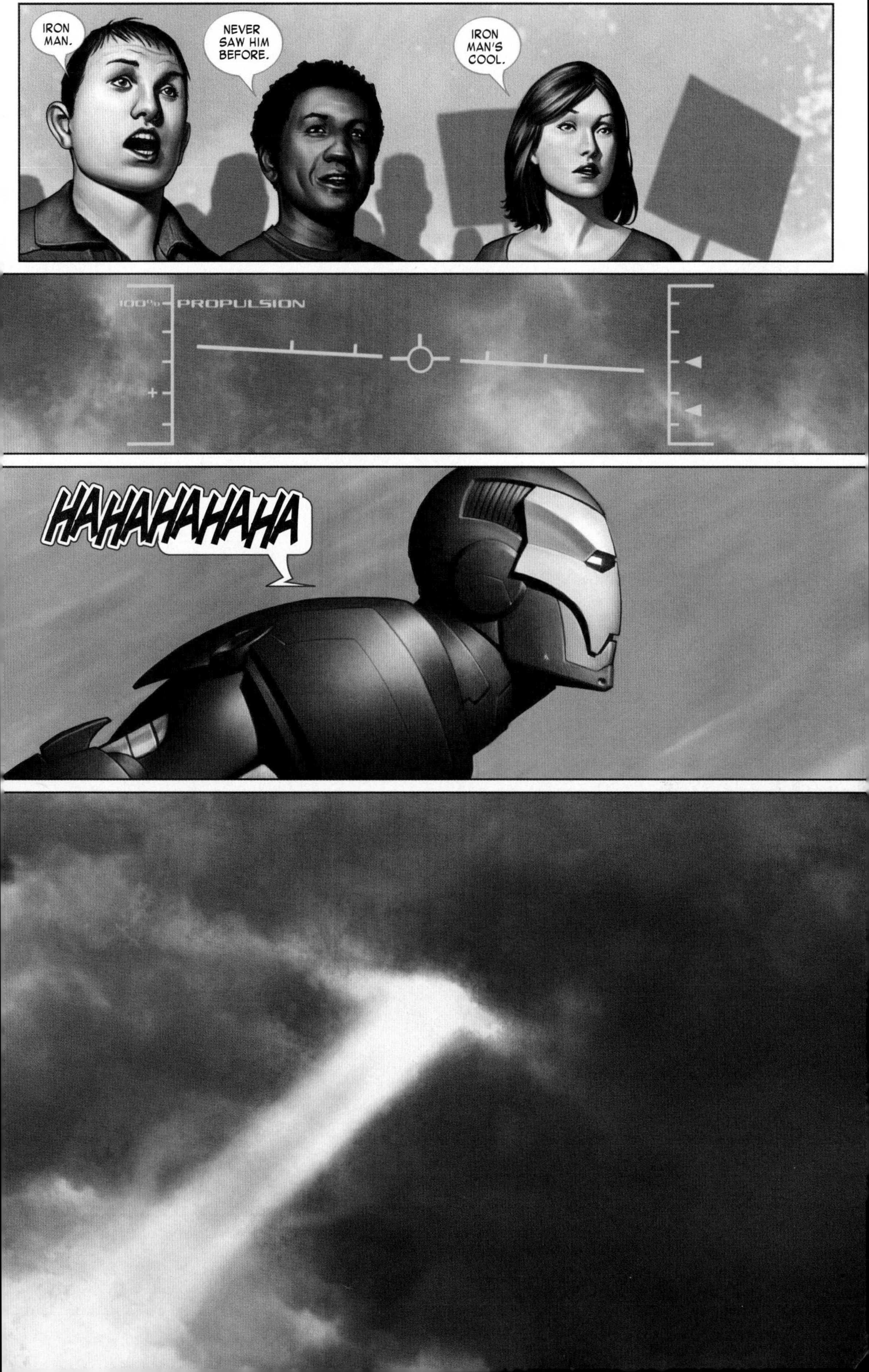
IRON MAN.
NEVER SAW HIM BEFORE.
IRON MAN'S COOL.
100% PROPULSION
HAHAHAHAHA

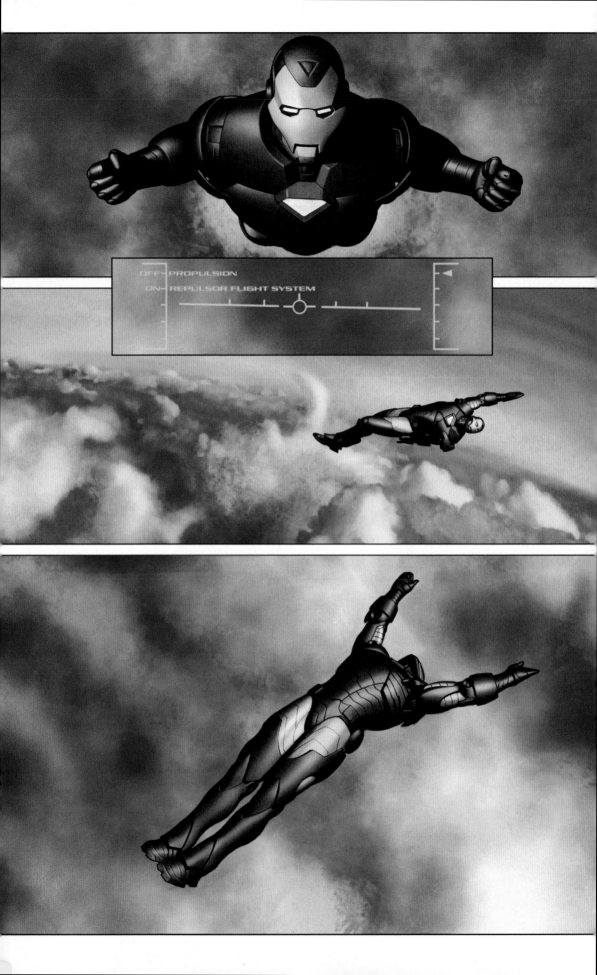

OFF- PROPULSION
ON- REPULSOR FLIGHT SYSTEM

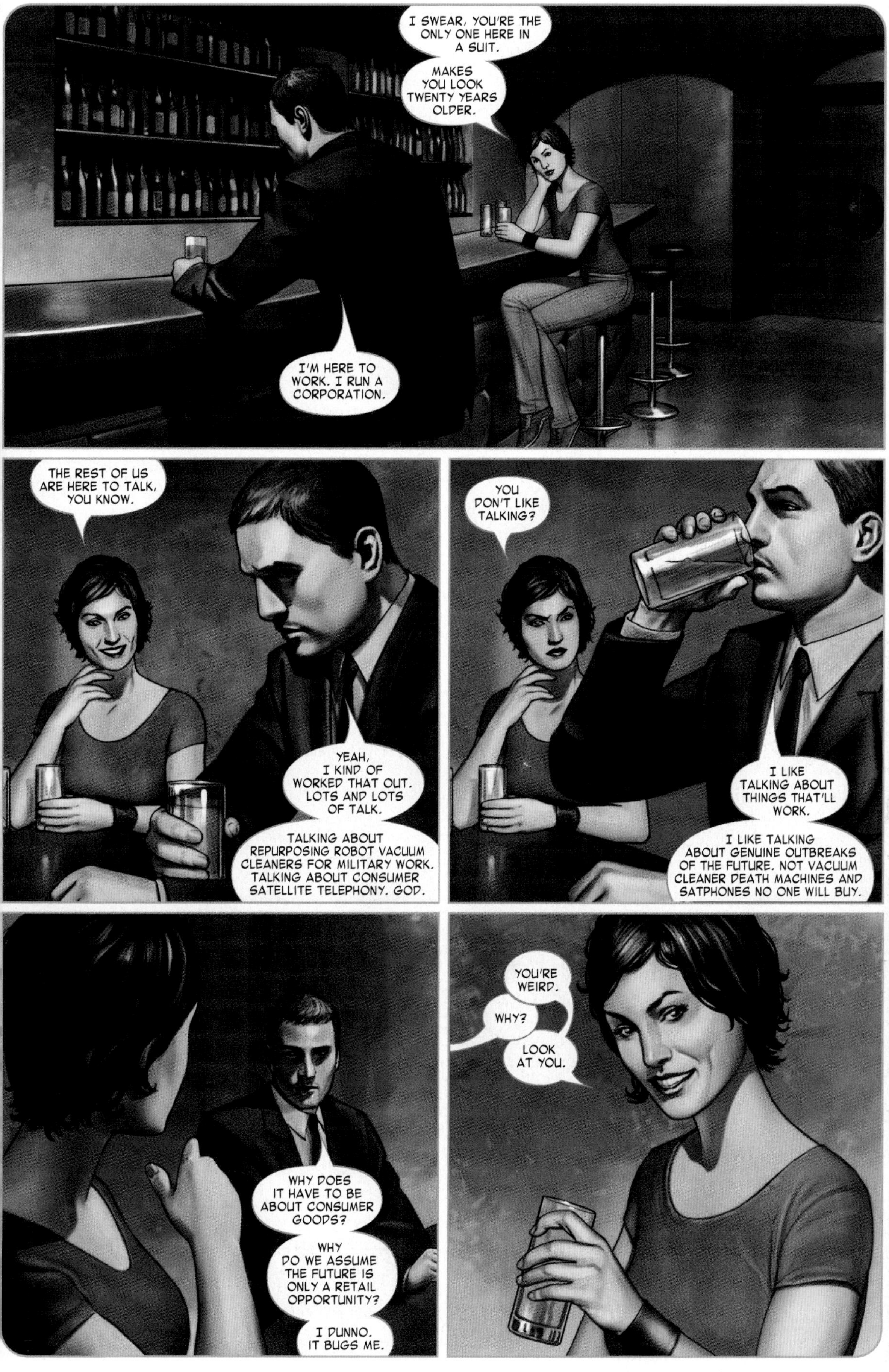
I SWEAR, YOU'RE THE ONLY ONE HERE IN A SUIT.
MAKES YOU LOOK TWENTY YEARS OLDER.
I'M HERE TO WORK. I RUN A CORPORATION.
THE REST OF US ARE HERE TO TALK, YOU KNOW.
YEAH, I KIND OF WORKED THAT OUT. LOTS AND LOTS OF TALK.
TALKING ABOUT REPURPOSING ROBOT VACUUM CLEANERS FOR MILITARY WORK. TALKING ABOUT CONSUMER SATELLITE TELEPHONY. GOD.
YOU DON'T LIKE TALKING?
I LIKE TALKING ABOUT THINGS THAT'LL WORK.
I LIKE TALKING ABOUT GENUINE OUTBREAKS OF THE FUTURE. NOT VACUUM CLEANER DEATH MACHINES AND SATPHONES NO ONE WILL BUY.
WHY DOES IT HAVE TO BE ABOUT CONSUMER GOODS?
WHY DO WE ASSUME THE FUTURE IS ONLY A RETAIL OPPORTUNITY?
I DUNNO. IT BUGS ME.
YOU'RE WEIRD.
WHY?
LOOK AT YOU.

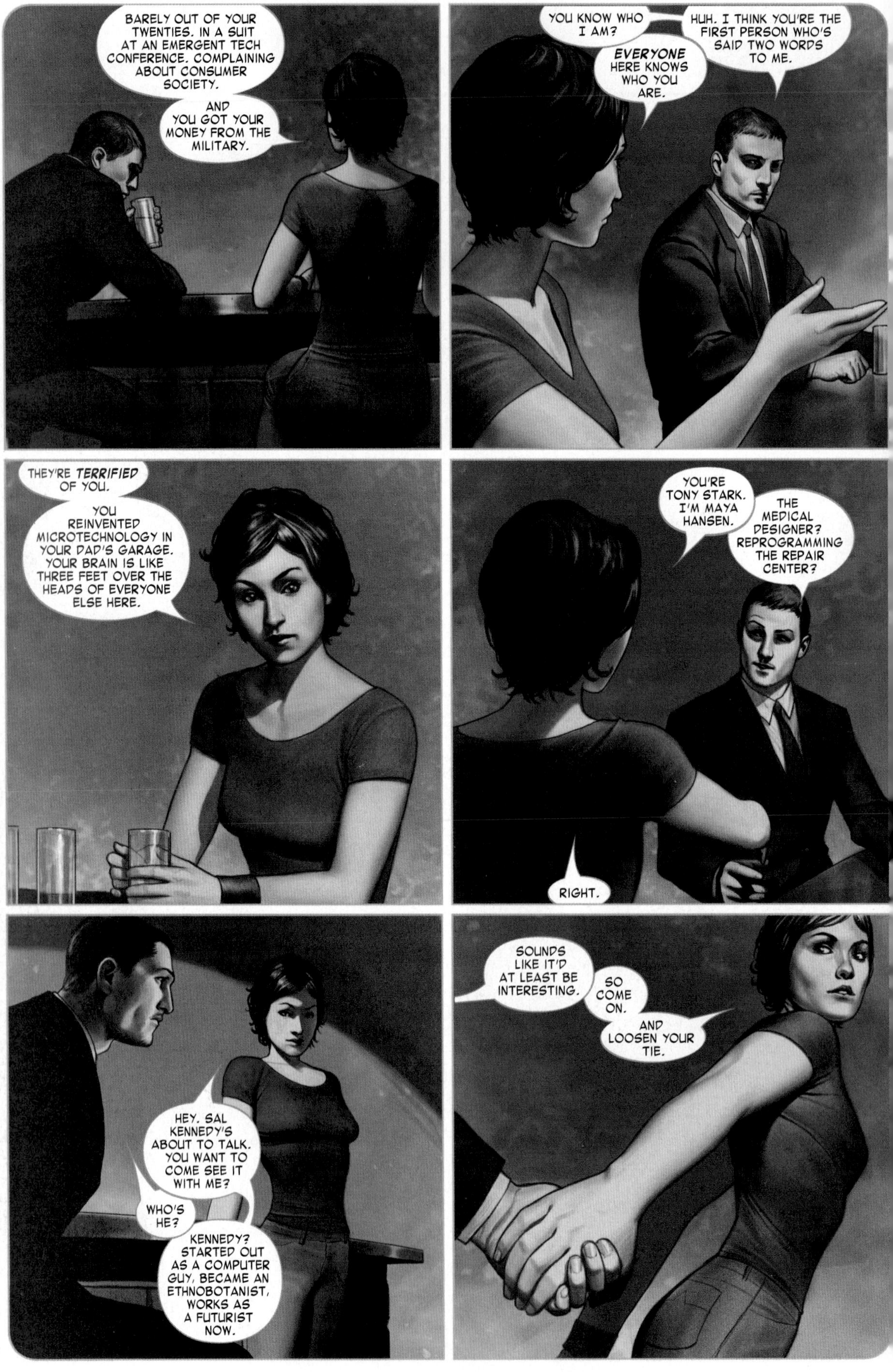
BARELY OUT OF YOUR TWENTIES. IN A SUIT AT AN EMERGENT TECH CONFERENCE. COMPLAINING ABOUT CONSUMER SOCIETY.
AND YOU GOT YOUR MONEY FROM THE MILITARY.
YOU KNOW WHO I AM?
EVERYONE HERE KNOWS WHO YOU ARE.
HUH. I THINK YOU'RE THE FIRST PERSON WHO'S SAID TWO WORDS TO ME.
THEY'RE TERRIFIED OF YOU.
YOU REINVENTED MICROTECHNOLOGY IN YOUR DAD'S GARAGE. YOUR BRAIN IS LIKE THREE FEET OVER THE HEADS OF EVERYONE ELSE HERE.
YOU'RE TONY STARK. I'M MAYA HANSEN.
THE MEDICAL DESIGNER? REPROGRAMMING THE REPAIR CENTER?
RIGHT.
HEY. SAL KENNEDY'S ABOUT TO TALK. YOU WANT TO COME SEE IT WITH ME?
WHO'S HE?
KENNEDY? STARTED OUT AS A COMPUTER GUY, BECAME AN ETHNOBOTANIST, WORKS AS A FUTURIST NOW.
SOUNDS LIKE IT'D AT LEAST BE INTERESTING.
SO COME ON.
AND LOOSEN YOUR TIE.

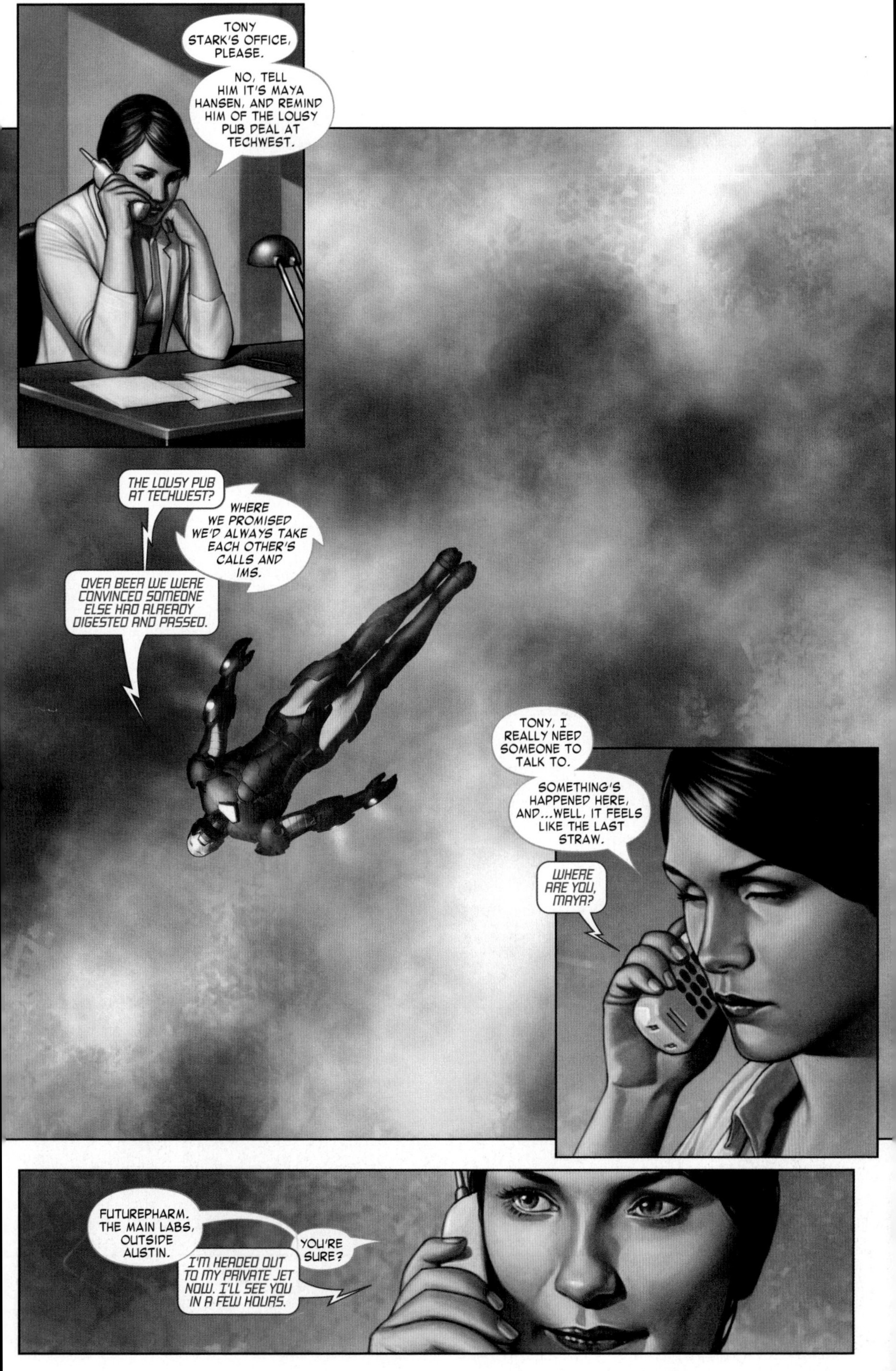
TONY STARK'S OFFICE, PLEASE.
NO, TELL HIM IT'S MAYA HANSEN, AND REMIND HIM OF THE LOUSY PUB DEAL AT TECHWEST.
THE LOUSY PUB AT TECHWEST?
WHERE WE PROMISED WE'D ALWAYS TAKE EACH OTHER'S CALLS AND IMS.
OVER BEER WE WERE CONVINCED SOMEONE ELSE HAD ALREADY DIGESTED AND PASSED.
TONY, I REALLY NEED SOMEONE TO TALK TO.
SOMETHING'S HAPPENED HERE, AND...WELL, IT FEELS LIKE THE LAST STRAW.
WHERE ARE YOU, MAYA?
FUTUREPHARM. THE MAIN LABS, OUTSIDE AUSTIN.
YOU'RE SURE?
I'M HEADED OUT TO MY PRIVATE JET NOW. I'LL SEE YOU IN A FEW HOURS.

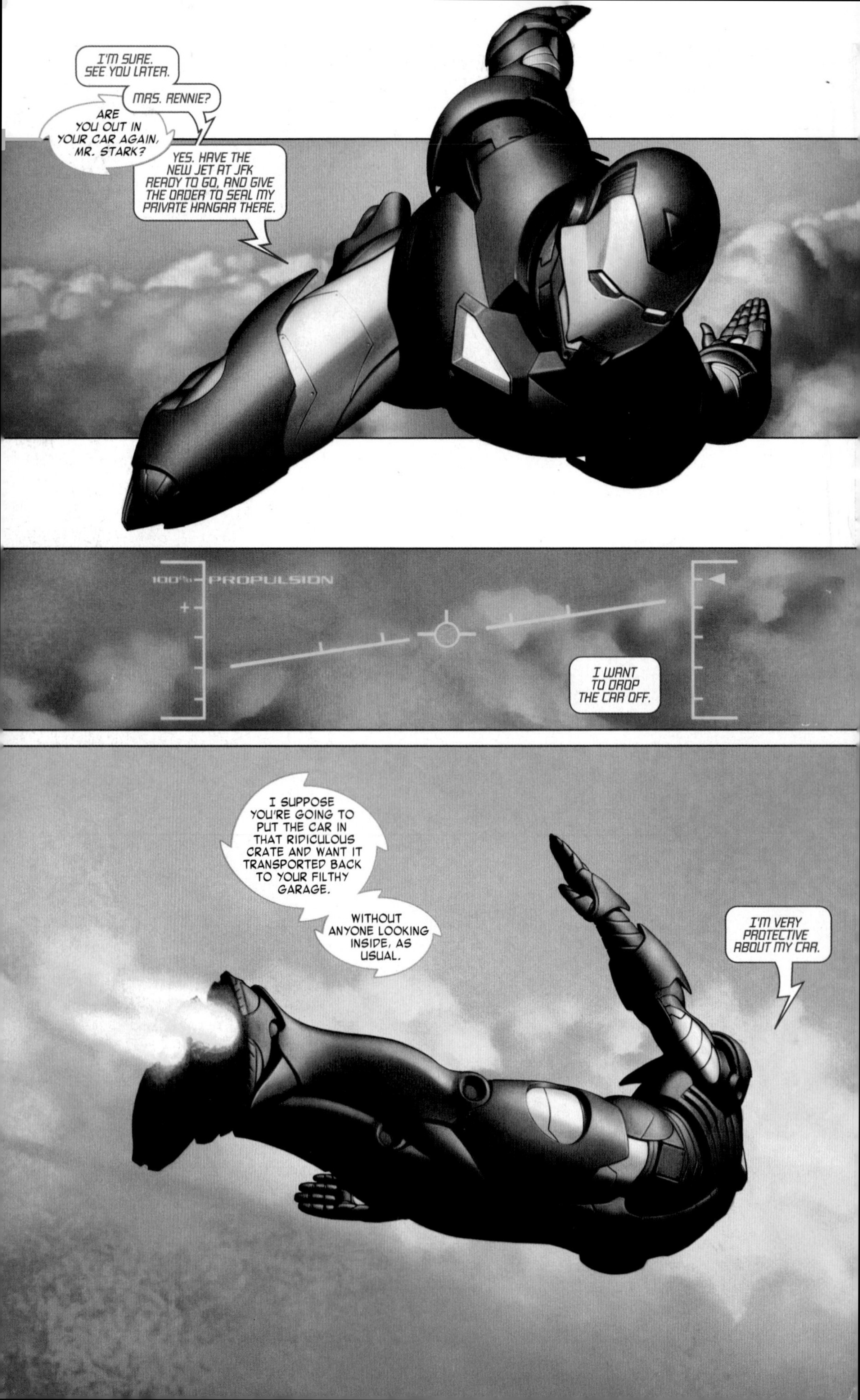
I'M SURE. SEE YOU LATER.
MRS. RENNIE?
ARE YOU OUT IN YOUR CAR AGAIN, MR. STARK?
YES. HAVE THE NEW JET AT JFK READY TO GO, AND GIVE THE ORDER TO SEAL MY PRIVATE HANGAR THERE.
100% PROPULSION
I WANT TO DROP THE CAR OFF.
I SUPPOSE YOU'RE GOING TO PUT THE CAR IN THAT RIDICULOUS CRATE AND WANT IT TRANSPORTED BACK TO YOUR FILTHY GARAGE.
WITHOUT ANYONE LOOKING INSIDE, AS USUAL.
I'M VERY PROTECTIVE ABOUT MY CAR.

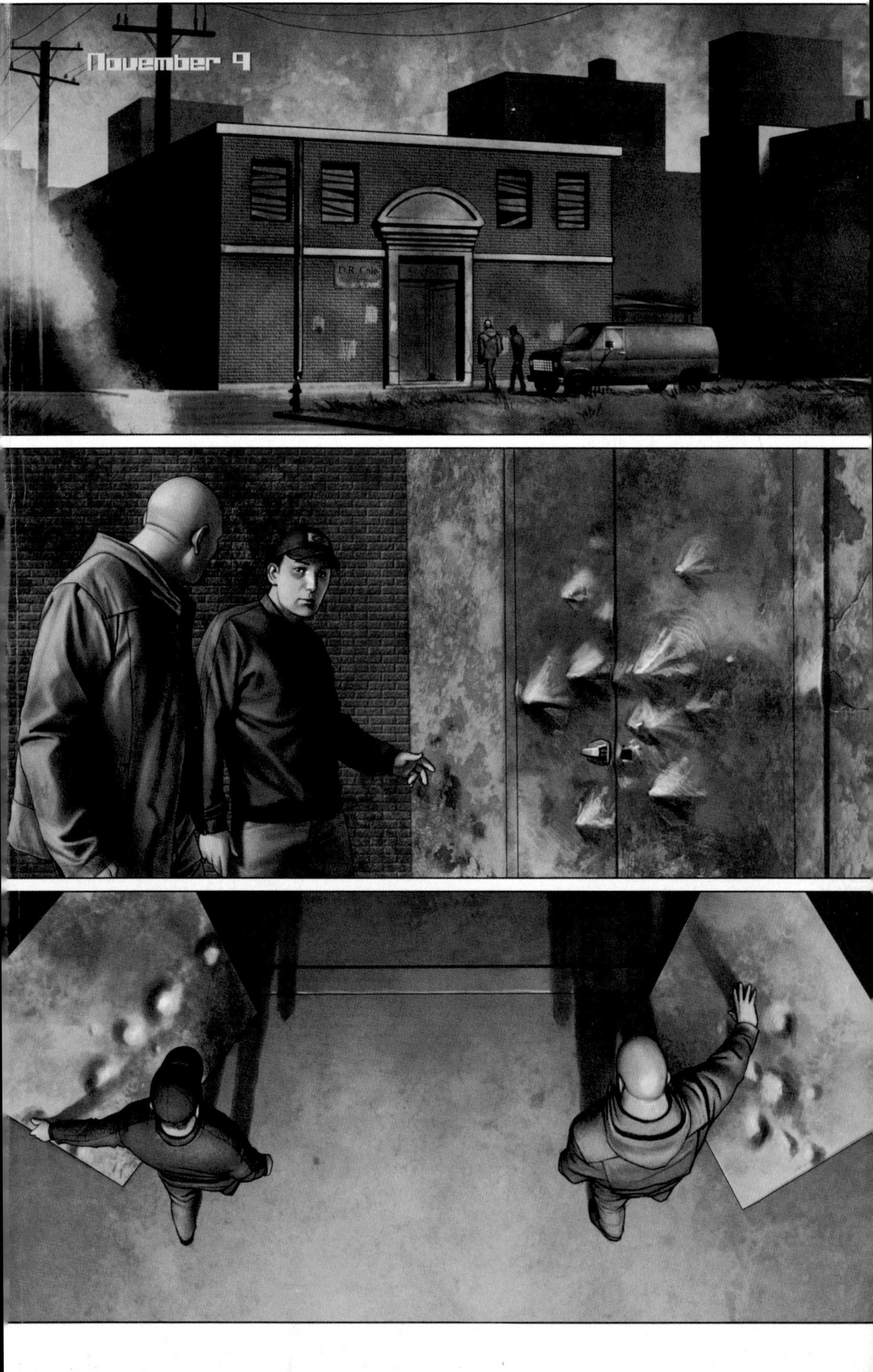
November 9
D.R. Cole

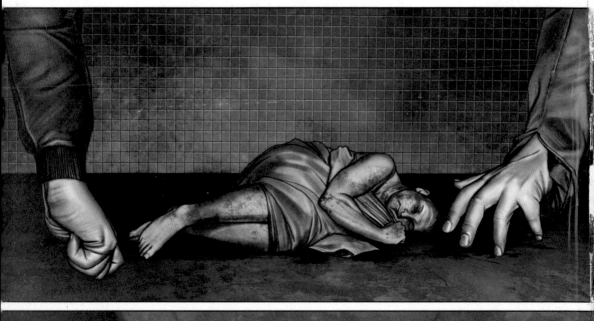

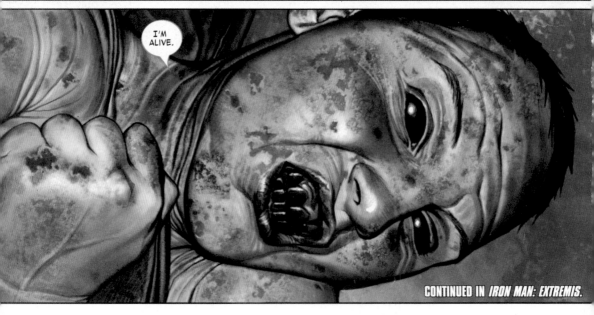

I'M ALIVE.

CONTINUED IN *IRON MAN: EXTREMIS*.